TRUE PREP

HIC LATINE LOQUIMUR

It's a whole new old world.

TRUE PREP

LISA BIRNBACH

with
Chip Kidd

DRAWINGS BY RANDY GLASS

PHOTOGRAPHS BY GEOFF SPEAR

Alfred A. Knopf

2011

New York

Those were the days—apropos of Fifth Avenue—when my mother used to say:
"Society is completely changed nowadays. When I was first married
we knew everyone who kept a carriage."

—Edith Wharton, *A Little Girl's New York*

This Is a Borzoi Book
Published by Alfred A. Knopf

www.aaknopf.com

Library of Congress Cataloging-in-Publication Data
Birnbach, Lisa.
True prep : it's a whole new old world / by Lisa Birnbach and
Chip Kidd.—1st ed.
p. cm.
"This is a Borzoi book."
ISBN 978-0-307-59398-6 hc
ISBN 978-0-375-71201-2 pbk
1. Preppies—Humor. I. Kidd, Chip. II. Title.
PN6231.P69B57 2010
818'.5402—dc22   2010004079

Manufactured in the United States of America
Published September 8, 2010
First Paperback Edition, November 2011

CONTENTS

For Boco, Maisie, and Sam with love
and
for Sandy
and for Shelley

Wake up, Muffy, we're back.

Okay, now where were we?

Oh, yes. It was 1980, and Ronald Reagan was heading to his improbable victory over Jimmy Carter. We wondered whether joining a club before your thirtieth birthday made you into a young fuddy-duddy, we considered the importance of owning a dress watch, and one thing led to another, and before the year was over, our project became *The Official Preppy Handbook*. Yes. That was us. We enjoyed every minute that we still remember, but we seem to have misplaced a number of brain cells in the process.

Though we once maintained that this world has changed little since 1635, when the Boston Latin School was founded, you know we were exaggerating slightly (see p. 63). As our world spins faster and faster and we use up more natural resources, and scientists keep discovering more sugar substitutes, we have to think about how life in the twenty-first century affects our safe and lovely bubble.

Muffy van Winkle, you've napped long enough. It's been thirty years! It doesn't seem possible, does it? Despite changes and crises and the maid quitting, the middle class disappearing, your running out of vodka, your NetJet account being yanked, and the Internet, it's still nice to be prep.

And as we have gotten a bit older and a teensy bit wiser, the world has become much smaller. We are all interconnected, intermarried, inter-everything-ed. The great-looking couple in the matching tweed blazers and wide-wale orange corduroy trousers are speaking . . . Italian. On Melrose Avenue! Whereas once upon a time it seemed unlikely Europeans would be attracted to our aesthetic, now they've adapted it and made it their own. (They're the women with no hips, in case you were wondering.)

Let's begin at the beginning of the year. Here are our resolutions. You'll catch on.

No drinking at lunch.

Call Grandmother once a week.

Get Belgian Shoes resoled (thinnest Cat's Paw rubber).

Sign up for tennis team at the club.

Actually go to team practices.

Have gravy boat reengraved.

Find Animal House *and return to Netflix.*

Send in donation for class gift this year.

And send in write-up for class notes.

Finally use Scully & Scully credit— maybe Pierpont's next wedding?

Drive Mother to cemetery at least once this year.

Order new stationery before supply runs out. (Find die!)

Luggage tags!

Download phone numbers into the thingy.

New Facebook picture?

Work on goals.

Work on topspin.

Get Katharine to do community service somehow.

Clean gutters or get someone to do them.

Repair hinge on broken shutter. Or else!

Finally hire portrait artist for Whimsy. (She's eighty-four in dog years; not much time left.)

1.

PSST! PASS IT ON.

THE TRUE PREP MANIFESTO.

*She regarded Washington Square as the birthplace of Society, knew by heart
all the cousinships of early New York . . . and was determined,
if she married, never to receive a divorced woman.*
—Edith Wharton, *The Custom of the Country*

MANIFESTO.

It's about ease and confidence. It's about fitting in when you do and even when you don't. It's about your endless supply of clothes that always looks the same, no matter what the era or fashion dictates. It's about your ability to tell a story, be the fourth—for tennis or for bridge—or somehow come to the rescue of a social situation. Because you can. Because your parents taught you by example. Maybe you attended an historic prep school. Maybe you didn't. Of course, it's better if you did because then you've been acculturated. You may protest, but you know some literature, know some history, know some sportsmanship, and know that a tie will do when you can't find your belt.

And if by some chance you are entering this world on your own, of your free will, with no one to lead you by the hand, let us guide you. We know the code. We're here to help.

WHO WE ARE NOW.

Formerly WASP. Failing that, white and heterosexual. One day we became curious or bored and wanted to branch out, and before you knew it, we were all mixed up.

Well, that's the way we like it, even if Grandmother did disapprove and didn't go to the wedding. (Did she ever stop talking about the "barefoot and pregnant" bride? Ever?) And now one of our nieces, MacKenzie, is a researcher at the CDC in Atlanta and is engaged to marry the loveliest man . . . Rajeem, a pediatrician who went to Duke. And Kelly is at Smith, and you know what that means. And our son Cal is married to Rachel, and her father, the cantor, married them in a lovely ceremony. Katie, our daughter, is a decorative artist living in Philadelphia with Otis, who is a professor of African American Studies at Swarthmore. And then there's Bailey, our handsome little nephew. Somehow, all he wants to do is ski, meet girls, and drink beer.

Well, that's one out of five.

THE FAMILY.

The prep family, despite its flaws and its mildewed basement, is the institution on which all of our world is based. How we participate in family life is what we learn to think of as "normal." End of science lesson.

Mummy. She is the stealthy head of household, unless she "is away," "has one of her headaches," or is "the chancellor of Germany." Mummy is the centerpiece around which we set our familial tables. If Mummy and Daddy disagree on where Uncle Pinny sits at Thanksgiving, Mummy wins. If Mummy and Daddy disagree on how much to give to the Garden Club, Mummy wins. If Mummy and Daddy disagree on whether or not we are going to Lyford this year, Daddy wins, unless the house is in Mummy's family.

Mummy loves you. Sometimes it is hard to see evidence of that, but deep down, she does. Would she have given you her slightly bent Georg Jensen circle pin if she didn't love you? No. Would she have sent you to her sister's farm for the summer if she didn't? Never mind. She gave birth to you and usually remembers that.

Daddy. Sometimes a buddy, sometimes a distant specter, Daddy is your father. Once upon a time he was also married to Mummy—you have seen their wedding pictures tucked away in the back of the linen closet, next to the dried-out jar of Gordon's silver polish. Whether or not Daddy still lives with you, he is responsible for teaching you some of life's most important lessons. "It's not a Bloody Mary without horseradish." "If you like the girl, always walk on the street side." "We hang to the right."

When it comes down to it, Daddy can do so many things well. He can fox-trot, glue the handle back on the pitcher, center a picture on the wall, turn a million dollars into half a million dollars (just joking), and light a perfect fire on a winter's afternoon. He can climb onto the roof to retrieve a golf ball from the gutters. He can play golf and tennis, sail, ski, and shoot skeet. He can order a steak, rare, in Ital-

ian, German, and French (but he can speak only English). He can button those tiny buttons on the back of Mummy's (or Alicia's, his new special friend) evening dress, though it could take him a long time to find his glasses in order to see those buttons.

When Daddy's been bad, there are always more flowers in the house, and sometimes a delivery from a fancy store for Mummy. But as long as Daddy is living in the same house with you, he is usually fun to have around, unless he won't pick you up from your friend's house at two a.m.

Grandmother. The true power behind the power. Each family has one grandmother to which it defers and one grandmother it traditionally ignores. This depends on how many marbles and cents she has. In order to have a peaceful exis-

tence, it is useful to bend to the powerful grandmother. If she wishes you to go to boarding school, please, by all means go (she intends to pay for it). If she gives you an old fur coat, do wear it (at least when she is around). If she approves of your boyfriend, you can marry him (even if she doesn't know about his tattoo or the night he spent in the pokey in New Hampshire: TMI). Grandmother might even be surprisingly open to your same-sex union. Grandmothers are amazing that way. (Grandmother may have had, once upon a time, a deeply felt long-lost love she dared not introduce to her mummy or daddy: her chemistry partner, Mary.) Have a little faith in Grandma. She will take care of you, especially if she doesn't care too much for your parents.

    Grandfather. Long gone but not for-gotten. Grandfather was "a character." He worked hard, played hard. He once: dated Ava Gardner/was the fraternity president/was in the OSS/was in Cuba with Hemingway/was hit on by Cole Porter/was hit on by Ethel Merman/had a townie girlfriend/shot an elk/recited all of "Hiawatha" while standing on the bar of the Edgartown Yacht Club after closing hours/invented the little thingy on the top of that gadget and made a fortune/spent a summer breaking horses in Montana/wrestled Ted Turner in Buenos Aires/had to jump out of the Barbizon Hotel from a fourth-floor window when the police showed up/ran unopposed for mayor of Norfolk, Connecticut/put a Princeton T-shirt on the statue of Sir Walter Scott in Central Park after his senior thesis passed.

Daddy's New Girlfriend.

If Daddy has been a naughty boy and gotten caught, he has most likely been exiled out of the lukewarm family bosom. But he has received comfort from many other bosoms, some impressive and some embarrassing. The best of his girlfriends—the ones who take you to the theater, buy you drinks, give you their old Chanel bags, and help you get a summer internship at MoMA—are generally too good for him, and thus he sabotaged those relationships with his usual charming duplicity.

Eventually, though, because Daddy doesn't like to be alone or cook, he decides to commit to a new woman. She comes in several styles.

1. Just Like Mummy Only Twenty-three Years Younger. (You can insist, as many daughters do, that Daddy not date any of your friends or anyone younger than you.) How is Margaret an improvement? She bears no grudges towards Daddy. Her family seems familiar. While you cannot imagine falling in love with someone so old, she seems to adore him. But wait! She wants to have a baby with him.

2. The Young Business Tycoon. Her cool prowess (and the fact that she attended Daddy's alma mater) turns him on. She loves him because her contemporaries are young, boring, predictable, jealous. Adding to her allure is the fact that this woman is from a different ethnic background. She's Indian, Filipino, Spanish, Jewish, or Catholic. She's a hard worker (some call her a barracuda behind her back) and talks about her "merger" with Daddy.

3. The Sporty Girlfriend. He met her playing tennis, golf, or whitewater rafting on the Colorado River. She was surrounded by admirers at that yurt dinner in Ketchum. In the worst-case scenario, she is his trainer or yoga instructor. Daddy thinks she's "hot" (eeeww). Daddy thinks he's never looked better. Daddy loves his new active life. Daddy knows that Sporty knows how to administer CPR, can give backrubs, and is willing to practice tantric sex. Sporty likes your house in the country, the dogs, is a 12 handicap, and her best friend just married an old guy, too.

4. The Strumpet. This girlfriend is the most unfortunate choice. Her very obviousness—her too-dyed hair, her obvious surgeries and enhancements, her disgusting PDA with Daddy and calling him by that ridiculous nickname in public—causes everyone to talk behind her back. However, she will bore Daddy quickly, and most of Daddy's loyal friends' wives will refuse to socialize as couples with her. In short, this girlfriend is history.

1.

2.

3.

4.

HENRY: PORTRAIT
OF A SERIAL HUNTER.

We confess to spending hours in the thrall of our wondrous English setter, Henry. What does he think about? Is he happy? Does he dream about us? We are prepared for unrequited love; we were sent to boarding schools, after all. But we would never send Henry away. He is too dear, too affectionate, for us to be without him for more than the two-week annual biking trip to France. Otherwise, where we go, he goes. Constance and Prudence, the twins, came up with this, the phrenological diagram of Henry for their biology class. (Their assignment was the respiratory system, so we're not holding out hopes for an A.) And yes, though we raised gentle vegetarian daughters, our son (Henry) is a confirmed carnivore.

SOME FOUR-LEGGED
PREPS & THE TWO-
LEGGED PREPS
WHO LOVED THEM.

Widgeon, **black Lab**
PRINCE WILLIAM OF ENGLAND
(Eton College)

Petals and Baci, **Italian greyhounds**
SIGOURNEY WEAVER
(Chapin School; Ethel Walker School)

Atticus Finch, **German shepherd**
Boo Radley, **Puggle**
JAKE GYLLENHAAL (Harvard-Westlake)

Garcia, **Australian cattle dog**
OWEN WILSON
(St. Mark's School of Texas, expelled)

Holden, **Labrador retriever**
GWYNETH PALTROW (Spence School)

I WANT

OUT

OF THE VOLVO.

I love woodcock.

LIVING ROOM,

HERE I
COME.

That's Constance whistling. I hope she doesn't go to Lake Forest. I'll miss her.

Oh, to chase a

DEER.

Ready for my scratch.

WHAT COLOR IS MY BANDANA?

Rabbit, run!

LET'S GO TO
THE BOATHOUSE
AND FISH,
FISH,
FISH!

Ready for
my scratch.

PRUDENCE,
I THINK I LOST
YOUR SLIPPER.

Is that a
HEASANT?

Who moved the
squirrel?

ust shook water all
over the mudroom.
Not the first time,
won't be the last.

MARROW
BONES!!

ARKING THE BUSH,
ARKING THE BUSH,
ARKING THE BUSH,
ARKING THE BUSH,
DONE.

TOO TIRED
TO BARK.

Ready
for my
scratch.

SOMEONE'S
making STEAK.

Gorky the
handyman,
you are
mine.

I smell Isabelle, that cute
French bulldog next door.

NOW I'M SLOBBERING

LET'S HUNT SOMETHING
TODAY!

Blue, **Border collie-Jersey collie**
DAVID DUCHOVNY and TÉA LEONI
(Collegiate School and Brearley School, Putney)

Mildred "Millie" Kerr Bush, **Springer spaniel**
(1/12/85–5/19/97) Has own Wikipedia page.
PRESIDENT and MRS. GEORGE H. W. BUSH
BB (Rye Country Day and Ashley Hall)
GHWB (Andover)

Splash, Sunny, and Cappy,
Portuguese water dogs
SEN. EDWARD M. KENNEDY
(Milton Academy)

Fala, **Scottie**
PRESIDENT FRANKLIN DELANO ROOSEVELT
(Groton School)

Harvey, George, and Baby, **Boxers**
HUMPHREY BOGART
(Andover, expelled)

Polar Bear, **a cat**
CLEVELAND AMORY
(Milton Academy)

Shamsky and Monkey, **Pit bulls**
JON STEWART
(Lawrence High School, Lawrenceville,
New Jersey)

Edgar and Bathsheba, **Golden retrievers**
JOHN CHEEVER
(Thayer Academy, expelled, readmitted)

JUST LIKE FAMILY.

We all know family is an accident of birth and luck. For that, we are mostly grateful, even if we don't show it. (You know who you are, Bos.) What's also great about having a family is that you get them without doing any hard work whatsoever.

Such is sadly not the case when choosing employees who will fill in for you when you are busy or otherwise inclined. Don't think of this as a test, think of this as a process.

Your First Hire: The Cleaning Lady.

You might hire someone to help you clean the apartment and do the laundry while you are still sharing your apartment with a roommate from Boulder. You could clean the bathroom and vacuum yourself, but you would rather come home to a clean place, especially after a long day at the office and then an exhausting happy hour. So you—with some sheepishness— hire your first domestic employee, Teresa. You love that she is reliable, and you convince yourself that you could never wield a Swiffer the way Teresa does. You're also helping the economy . . . of Ecuador. Get over your embarrassment, because within ten years you may be adding to your staff.

Your Future Hire? A Baby Nurse.

In some families, this is an amusingly obvious question. The answer to this and other brain teasers is "because." "Because we do." "Because the Hayeses always have a baby nurse." Ultimately, the best reason is "Because Daddy and I will pay for her."

In other families, the very idea sends prospective parents shuddering all the way to the loan officer. Baby nurses are staggeringly expensive. If, however, you are dealing with baby number one, it might be wise to go without hand-printed Christmas cards this year (use Shutterfly) and splurge on this fine addition to your family—at least for a week. If you have an energetic mother, an unemployed unmarried sister, or other children or helpers, a baby nurse might be excessive.

Ask friends who are further along the parent road (NB: We are parents, but we don't believe in "parenting") for their recommendations of nurses, employment agencies, or friends who had good or bad experiences. Obviously, the best thing to do is hire a friend's nurse, as long as you won't be overlapping, but since that rarely works out, you will be asked to supply the attributes you prize most.

What are you looking for? You want someone who is comfortable and experienced with babies, someone with endless patience, who is meticulously clean, cheerful, presentable, and a pleasure to live with. In other words, the very opposite of you.

These women—all seasoned and ready to work—will happily interview for your position. Pretend you are charged with hiring your own aunt. That's who you want to live in the nursery with Clementine and accompany you to the country on weekends. You expect your aunt will respect your privacy. She must sense when you and your partner need time alone, want to go out, or just put up your feet. Your baby nurse will be the baby's caregiver and advocate, but ideally she should help you, too. No law says a baby nurse cannot make her employer an excellent cup of herbal tea in the afternoon, or a lovely cocktail if she is not nursing. There's no statute that says she can't go to Jacadi to return the three almost identical onesies you received from your husband's business associates' assistants. Since all these aunties will tell you they *love* babies, especially your heretofore unborn one, how do you figure it out? You probably don't want a gossip or a constant hummer, someone too lethargic, too religious, or addicted to her soap operas (unless you are open to watching them as well).

You are looking for a woman who will neither patronize you nor scare you. A discreet and mature soul who can discern the cockatoo cries meaning "change me," "hold me," and "feed me." A woman who can hear your angel awaken from across the house, yet becomes magically hard of hearing when you and Duncan raise your voices in anger.

You want a housemate whose voice is musical, whose references are impeccable, whose scarf is silk, whose shoes are a joy. Good luck.

If you're the kind of preppy who is a good financial planner (you must come from the other side of the family), here's a thumbnail overview of what these invaluable helpers cost in New York, Los Angeles, and San Francisco.

According to the Frances Stewart Agency, (212) 439-9222, **Baby nurses in NYC are $235 per twenty-four-hour day, $290 for twins, $340 for triplets (a multiple specialist).**

"The only thing in the world that's cheaper in New York than in L.A. is a baby nurse. Food and rent are much more in New York," says Edie Landau of Nannies Unlimited, "the only child-care employment boutique in Los Angeles": (310) 551-0303.
Los Angeles baby nurses begin at $350 per day, although that is low. Twins will cost a minimum of $450 per day. "The average stay is one month," Landau says. "Celebrities keep them six months or sign an open-ended contract, to keep the nurses until the babies sleep through the night." Celebrities? Oh, yes. "All Hollywood people have their employees sign confidentiality agreements. And if they don't have them already drafted, we do."

San Francisco baby nurses, or "newborn specialists," as they are called, typically work night shifts, seven p.m. to seven a.m. Suzanne Collins of Aunt Ann's In-House Staffing, (415) 749-3650, says for single babies, the price is **$25 an hour, $35 for twins, and RNs get $40 to $45 an hour.** The average length of employment is between twelve and sixteen weeks. The recession hasn't hurt her business. "Parents of newborns? No. They want their sleep." And live-ins? Not in her purview. "Our families choose the night shift. That's the way it is. Some of them also have someone else doing the day shift." When she is looking to place a live-in newborn specialist, she "calls some of the girls in New York."

Meet Your Babysitter.

Your babysitter is more than your child-care provider. She is another member of your family through whose filter your young heir will experience the world. You will probably want a nanny who speaks English, if you wish your children to speak English. Quite a few families hire a nanny or babysitter for whom English is a second language, in order to save a bit for Posey's college tuition.

Should you consider a future career in politics, or any career for which your tax records could be summoned and publicized, you will need to hire a child minder who is an American citizen or a green-card holder. You must pay her "on the books," which means you deduct the taxes from her salary. Quite a few domestic workers would prefer to be paid in cash, or "off the books," so that they don't have to pay income taxes of their own. Whatever decision you make, feel free to blame it on your spouse.

You are aware, of course, that your babysitter is a window into your family, as the other nannies she befriends at nursery school and the playground are windows into *their* families. Through your nanny you know that the Cobbs have one live-in and one live-out nanny, and that they have a separate weekend nanny who comes with them to the Hamptons or Napa. Through your nanny you know that the Brushes are going through a rough patch and Mr. Brush is living downtown, near his office. Through your nanny the Brushes know about your DUI. Once those windows have been opened, it is very difficult to close them. The best you can hope for is a shade pulled down.

Au Pairs.

Perhaps you'd like to hire one of those cute young girls like the Norrises always get, a European or Brazilian *au pair*, an untrained, adorable nineteen to twenty-three-year-old, who—like Starbucks drinks—comes in strange sizes: Hipless, Gazelle, Gisele. (Carter Norris seems fond of them, if you catch our drift.) Good for you to take a chance on a beautiful girl you can't meet until she moves into your house! Good for you to keep your budget in mind, as your au pair is a thrifty way of acquiring childcare. Good for you to trust your husband, Tick, when you go out of town for your occasional Girls' Weekends with Bitsy Norris.

Because she is unskilled, because she goes out frequently after putting your children to bed, and because her new friends will drop by unexpectedly to eat your Cap'N Crunch, call home, and re-paint their nails, you might begin to question your wisdom in agreeing to this au pair situation. But after that shopping trip where she buys the shortest possible garments that qualify as legal skirts in Clayton or Edina, Agethe will help make your center-hall Tudor house one of the more popular destinations in Edina or Clayton.

YOUR PERSONAL TRAINER: A CAUTIONARY TALE.

Interesting how Polk loves seeing his trainer, quotes his trainer, buys his trainer little presents, adds an occasional weekend morning to the trainer's schedule. It's not what you think. Polk's trainer, Matt, is a strapping young male, twenty-six, who didn't make the Olympic slalom team. Polk isn't gay, or even curious. He just has a little midlife man-crush on Matt, his trainer. After a while you want to say, "Polk, you're a fifty-two-year-old lawyer.

Please don't wear leggings to the gym. People are laughing at you." But you don't. Polk seems so . . . um . . . serene. The other day, Matt told him about the new power drink he's been trying. Now Polk wants some, too. You help, and buy bran, flaxseed oil, and frozen blueberries (Hmmm, Polk never liked blueberries before). Polk starts to use the blender every morning (never cleaning up), and the next thing you know, he and Matt are signing up for a half marathon! It's just adorable! You start to notice that Polk is too tired at night to, you know . . . but he looks better and seems more, I don't know . . . youthful? He was definitely more fun when he drank more, but he looks much tighter than Duke or Harry or Crawford.

So you observe what's happening to your husband, and you think, I want my own Matt. You ask around, and Matt finds you Ethan, a stunning black marathon runner from Kenya. You've never seen skin as dark as his. Or muscles so taut. You start training with Ethan twice a week at home. Ethan thinks you should run outside, instead of on your treadmill, so soon you're running together twice a week, plus the twice a week you're doing weight training in your home gym. You feel better, more energized than you ever have. People are noticing. You are noticing. Your upper arms! Now you wear only sleeveless. You understand Michelle Obama, and respect her even more. You've given up diet soda, because Ethan suggested it. You can't remember the last time you drank a mojito. You and Ethan are thinking of opening up a gym in town together.

Now Polk isn't too happy.

The End.

Your Driver.

Formerly known as "the chauffeur," your driver is that extra man you employ who drives the two of you (Polk first) to work. Joe does those errands you cannot do yourself (oh, you *could* do them; you just don't want to) and sometimes fixes things. He keeps the cars in tip-top shape, too. Having a former policeman as your driver is in no way a savings. But Joe makes you feel safe, and by allowing him to call you by your first names or "Mr. and Mrs. B.," you maintain a quasi–social parity with him. As an added bonus, Joe knows some of the guys at traffic court and can help you eliminate some points.

Your Chef.

We used to call her "the cook." But "chef" sounds much nicer, and in truth, she or he has apprenticed at some great restaurants in Europe. We say "chef" as a term of respect. And it lets other people know that it's not just lasagna at our house anymore; it's good. We might have hired a chef to help us eat more healthfully, but you cannot believe his nachos. Or her incredible peach cobblers. Or his homemade gelato. Oh, well.

If the housekeeper is still cooking for you, that's another thing altogether, and you may be eating the same chicken pot pie, meatloaf, and succotash your family has eaten for generations. You like it. Occasionally you will allow the housekeeper to make a treat from her native land, whether it be a kind of wonton, or a kind of lentil thing, or maybe even a fish stew that sounds odd but is actually rather tasty. It's quite nice to serve it to guests, because it's different.

Between all the gourmet stores and epicurious.com, we do not need to feel shame if we don't have a chef, or a cook, or even a cooking housekeeper. People understand.

Your Nutritionist.

Binky hasn't lost all that baby weight. It's only been five years, but she's feeling discouraged and cranky. Or you just discovered that Ace has that awful celiac disease and he is suddenly allergic to gluten. Or Drake's cholesterol is through the roof and he can't find anything to eat without cheese on it. So you hire a nutritionist. You keep a food diary at her behest. You stop drinking for a while. It works. Then you notice you get bored and you start to lie to your food diary. It's almost fun again.

Your nutritionist is a thin woman who loves food. She doesn't eat food, but she loves it, and she helps you to not eat anything you like, too. She costs a lot of money, but if you stop eating food you will lose weight, especially if you subscribe to her special smoothie-delivery service—part detox, part cleanse. If you tried to go on a diet all by yourself, you wouldn't do it. The appointments stunt-double for willpower. So put this woman on your staff for now. In a few years when you make peace with the eight extra pounds, you will find your food diary stuck in the back of a drawer, and it will make you laugh.

Your Child's Tutor.

First you hired Lawrence for Benno because of his problems with math. By the end of the term, Lawrence had helped him eke out a C+. You got your money's worth. Then when that nightmare ended, Lawrence was hanging around one afternoon (why?) when Claire asked him if he understood mitosis. Which he did. Then, seeing Claire and Lawrence studying one day in the library, Gil thought Lawrence could read his college essay since he went to Columbia, and it was better than getting *your* feedback.

If they like your family or your house, or the way you stock your kitchen, some tutors have a way of lingering around your family for years. Hire them with your first child, and they can have a dozen-year sinecure before anyone realizes it. Soon you will have given Lawrence his own key to the beach house, so he can tutor Lila in Spanish all summer long.

This does not include the SAT tutor, whom you are forced to hire because all your children's classmates' parents have hired them (whether or not they fess up). If the grade's average score is 200 points higher than it would organically be, you must not deprive your kids of those points. You can find an SAT tutor through your school, through nationally advertised services or, better yet, through word of mouth.

Remember that these tutors are mind-bendingly expensive. Also remember that SATs alone will not get Benno into college . . . at least not a competitive one.

If you are willing to sink an even larger fortune into the college process, you can find someone who used to work in admissions at a top college who will help your children with their essays and their applications, coach them before each campus visit (just in case), and contact their old friend at Bowdoin on Benno's behalf. It is not foolproof, but it is usually an effective intervention. If Benno isn't going to bother to go to class once he gets in, it might not be worth the fuss and the expense.

ADOPTION.

Thirty years ago adoption was a somewhat unconventional way to enlarge one's family and one's heart. "Adoption" was sometimes one of those whispered words—like "intermarriage" or "lesbian." It was a public acknowledgment that Mummy was barren or that Daddy didn't quite have enough, um, you know, umph.

In the last three decades adoption has become much more common, and it is, in fact, a more conventional way of adding to the family. (Think of surrogacy, sperm donors, egg donors, black-market babies, and eventually, though it's terrifying, cloning.)

Ellie Baxter is a go-getter Vassar graduate. After two years on Wall Street, and a Harvard MBA, she travels the world as a high-tech specialist for Bain & Company. It's hard on relationships (though there was that cute real-estate developer in Amsterdam), but Ellie loves her work, loves to travel, and is basically satisfied with her life. She has more money than she has time to spend. At her twentieth reunion in Poughkeepsie (she came the farthest—from Saigon!) she is struck—though "reminded" might be more apt—by how many of her classmates are living vicariously through their children and the complications of family-work balance. Ellie is elated that she doesn't worry about peanut allergies, sibling rivalry, or finding a babysitter on New Year's Eve. Back on Air France (first-class upgrade), she reconsiders her situation, and by the time she lands in Vietnam, she wonders if it's all been a big mistake.

Being decisive, Ellie contacts adoption agencies in China, begins to house-hunt on the Internet, and within a month is moving to a sweet house in Brookline, twenty minutes' drive from her brother and sister-in-law, ten minutes' walk to a lovely Montessori school, and beginning her new life. She will adopt a Chinese daughter who will be called Freder-icka, a family name. Fredericka's middle name will be Ziang (or River). Ellie will hire a Chinese nanny to support Fredericka's native culture. Ellie Baxter will be a fantastically competent single mom. One day, she might manage a second adoption or even marriage and a blended family. We all know an Ellie Baxter.

Micki and Julian Potter and their daughter, Eloise (known as Skim), have a sweet family life. Try as they might, they can't seem to get pregnant again. In vitro has taken its toll on Micki, and the Potters' relationship has been frayed by the exigencies of scheduled rutting. By the time Skim is seven, even the headmaster of her school thinks it would benefit her and her parents to have a sibling. Julian knows a colleague who adopted an American baby through a lawyer in Dallas, and within ten months, Skim has a baby brother, Cole. We all know a family like the Potters.

Jamie Lee Curtis (Choate '76) has written a charming picture book, *Tell Me Again About the Night I Was Born*, which is a "where did I come from?" story inspired by her own adopted daughter. If you have a friend who is adopting a child, make sure you buy this for him or her. If you have adopted, you already know this book by heart. And you know that you must not treat adoption like a secret. Your child knows the word "adopted" early on, even if he doesn't exactly understand it. You are thrilled to be a mummy or daddy. You chose this particular little person to be in your family. Focus on the positive. This baby from an orphanage—God knows how far away—will now be privileged. She will get to play field hockey and tennis. She will get to learn Mandarin Chinese in the third grade. She will get to play Betsy Ross in the school play. She will develop divine manners, have a wardrobe of argyle socks and cashmere sweaters, and best of all, she will summer.

Notes from an Aging Prepster.

When *The Official Preppy Handbook* came out in 1980, I was twenty-seven. Even by my (admittedly dreadful) prep-school math, I figure that makes me fifty-seven. I have now had as many years on earth as Heinz has varieties of condiments. *Où sont les neiges d'antan?* (Very preppy quote, that.)

Though "preppy" has never exactly been a term of endearment to my ears, in the old days I acquiesced to being of that ilk. The school I attended, Portsmouth Abbey, was run by Benedictine monks, which seemed to put it in a very different time zone from, say, Taft or Andover or Exeter. But "preppy" I admittedly was, for better or worse. I wore corduroy jackets with leather elbow patches. Why buy a new jacket if you can keep the elbows from wearing through, right? One of the cardinal virtues of the prepster was thrift—even if you had a trust fund. Then came Studio 54 and cocaine, and thrift, well, went into recession for a while, so to speak. As the joke of times went: Coke was God's way of telling you you had too much money.

The other day, I found myself subconsciously musing on the term "preppy" while reading the obituary of Louis Auchincloss (Groton), who wrote the ultimate grown-up's book about prepdom, *The Rector of Justin*. Back about the time when *The Official Preppy Handbook* was written, I met the author of the ultimate adolescent's book about that world, John Knowles, author of *A Separate Peace*. He showed no signs of his own preppy past. Is it, in the end, an identity that one grows out of? Does one become, finally, "post-preppy"? Maybe not: I knew George Plimpton right up to the end. He may have been in his seventies when he passed away, but he always looked as though he'd just escaped from Exeter.

About a year ago I found myself addressing the student body of St. Paul's School in New Hampshire. St. Paul's is to preppiedom what the Vatican is to Roman Catholicism: ground zero. I was entranced by the caliber of the students, by their brightness and politesse. Also by their engaging straightforwardness, which bordered on cockiness. In the Q & A with twenty students before my talk, one of them asked me, "What is it you hope to bring away from your experience with us today?" (Translation: "Just what is it you have to offer us, Mr. Buckley?") Actually, a good question. Thus confronted, I wasn't quite sure.

The student there who seemed to me most preppy—by virtue of his clothes and demeanor and attitude—was a very attractive young African American lad of seventeen. We had some chitchat afterwards. I said, "Let's stay in touch." We exchanged e-mail addresses, whereupon I learned that his name was Jordan Buxton-Punch. John Knowles and Louis Auchincloss would be hard-pressed to come up with a better name.

I saw him just the other day, about a year later, when I gave a talk at Yale. He's a freshman now. I wonder if Jordan considers himself a "preppy"? Post-preppy? I wonder if, when he reaches fifty-seven, he'll still think of himself as a product of our once-rarefied world?

— C H R I S T O P H E R   B U C K L E Y
Portsmouth Abbey, Yale

THE VIEW OF OAK BLUFFS.

AFRICAN AMERICAN PREP RESORTS.

Take the Steamship Authority ferry from Woods Hole or Falmouth to Martha's Vineyard and—voilà!—you are in the heart of the black prep experience. Of course, Sag Harbor—on the extreme east end of Long Island—has long been home to the same crowd, too, but islands, which require boats, are inherently preppier. Families and singles, many wearing the preppiest of foul-weather gear, head over to their country houses to spend as much of their summer as they can on the island.

That guy in the Wharton '82 baseball cap? The managing partner of Morgan Stanley. The woman in the Lilly Pulitzer pants and polo shirt? The top producer at Corcoran real-estate brokerage. What about that guy in the seersucker blazer talking quietly on the phone? Oh, he's an undersecretary of state. The kid in the webbed belt and Andover T-shirt? He goes to Andover, silly.

Look at yourself: What are you wearing? An old pair of khaki shorts with that faded ketchup stain on them? Your big brother's frayed button-down shirt? Pull yourself together and go for lunch at Farm Neck Country Golf Club. (As is the Vineyard's wont, it is totally inclusive, open to the public, and nicely maintained.) Take a left at Cornel West and plop yourself near Vernon Jordan.

The majority of tony black resorts trail down the East Coast, from Massachusetts to Florida. Oak Bluffs and Sag Harbor are by far the best-known communities, and draw elite African Americans from all over the country, though neighboring towns have been integrating since the mid-1960s.

Other vacation communities include:
IDLEWILD, MICHIGAN. Known as "Black Eden," it was started by black professionals in 1912 as a haven for families living in Detroit, Chicago, and throughout the Midwest. With 1,300 acres around a lake, it earned its name allegedly because its "men were idle, and its women were wild."

HIGHLAND BEACH, MARYLAND. Founded in 1893 by Charles Douglass, son of the abolitionist Frederick Douglass. He and his wife bought forty acres on the Chesapeake Bay for a summer resort for their family and friends. W. E. B. DuBois, Paul Robeson, and Harriet Tubman lived or visited there. Today it is a year-round community, though it's especially lively as a summer destination for Washingtonians and Baltimoreans, many of whom are descendants of the original settlers.

ARUNDEL ON THE BAY, MARYLAND. Approximately five miles south of Annapolis, Maryland, Arundel on the Bay was started by well-to-do black families who had few summer options. Today its 345 houses have a diverse population. Arundel on the Bay has a private beach, pier, and boat launch, as well as its own fan page on Facebook.

FROM *THE NEW YORK TIMES MAGAZINE*, 2/14/10.

Deborah Solomon:
"[The name] Skip sounds so WASPy."

Henry Louis "Skip" Gates Jr.:
"Hey, you know, I don't think we knew what a WASP was. I didn't realize it until I went to Yale as a student and met 'Chip' and 'Muffy' and—actually, I thought 'Skip' was a black name."

HORSES & CLASSICAL MUSIC.

Where do preppy gays go? They go everywhere and anywhere, because they feel entitled, but even in the usual places (Provincetown [1.], say, or Fire Island Pines) they like to arrive after the season is over (late September) or in a vintage yacht or a spectacular sea plane, and they'd rather stay off the beaten path—in Water Island (2.) rather than the Pines, for instance.

Palm Beach (3.) is a current attraction for gay preppies. South of Sloans Curve, the old "Bar Mitzvah Buildings" on the beach are being bought up by gay prepsters; they love the mid-century yellow-and-white wallpapers and the blue kitchens with blue appliances. On Thursday in Palm Beach there's gay night ("Gentlemen's Night") at the Colony Hotel's Polo bar. Now there are even (sort of) out gay preppies in the infamously exclusive Bath and Tennis Club (B&T).

Middleburg, Virginia (4.) is the mecca of the gay horsey crowd. Preppy gays love riding, teaching dressage, even hunting (if they can afford it).

Washington, D.C. (5.) is gay preppy central—all those well-paying government jobs immune to economic downturns, all those gay preppy colleges (especially Georgetown), and then there's the Hill with all those power-hungry homos who start early as snarky pages.

Yale (6.) is definitely the gayest of the Ivy League universities.

Moving up the map, there's Southampton (7.), so much preppier than Easthampton or Sag Harbor. Go to Flying Point Beach and watch an eastern European prince rubbing suntan oil on his boyfriend's muscled back. If you can, buy a big house and join the Meadow Club. If all you can afford is a pink-and-green outfit, then become a walker for an attractive widow and get her to take you to the Beach Club, where you might find someone to date for the rest of the summer.

All along the Hudson Valley (8.) there are what might be called the "Merchant-Ivory" breed of gay preppies in their Greek Revival country manors and dolled-up Victorian mansions—"preppies" by self-appointment, though they probably don't know what states Andover and Exeter are in. Litchfield County has all those gay couples dying to do a benefit with Anne Bass or Diane von Furstenberg, not because they really care about their charities but because they do want to know those ladies.

Greenwich, Connecticut (9.); all of Vermont (10.) except Burlington; Newport, Rhode Island (11.); Maine (12.) around Blue Hill and Bar Harbor—those are all the Elysian Fields for the good, the gay, and the prepped-out.

In the Midwest there's Mackinac Island in Michigan (13.) (where cars are forbidden and everyone rides around in horse-drawn carriages past huge white summer houses) as well as Grosse Pointe and Bloomfield Hills, home of the automobility. In Chicago (14.) there's the North Shore, especially Lake Forest (pronounced "Farest"). In Cincinnati (15.) there's Indian Hill, and in Cleveland (16.) there's Shaker Heights.

On the West Coast there's Sonoma County (17.), of course, which is close to San Francisco (18.), but the epicenter is Montecito (19.), where well-to-do gays and straights mix freely (fund-raisers for the Santa Barbara Museum of Art are at the very cross-section of the two worlds, where they show up in nearly equal proportions).

Of course, anywhere in Kansas (20.) where there's a Princeton alumni event, or in New Mexico (21.) where the opera crowd mixes with the painters, you can find gay preppies. Remember, no matter where you are, look for the horsey set or join the subscribers to the symphony and you'll find gay preppies within five minutes.

Horses and classical music—those are the two big magnets for the gay elite.

—EDMUND WHITE
Cranbrook, University of Michigan

Gay and Lesbian Prep America: A Map.

For some men, the term Preppy is practically synonymous with Sissy. Ronald Reagan on George H. W. Bush: "A Yalie, a preppy, a sissy." As with preps, naturally there are areas of gay concentration where they can comfortably huddle with sympathetic peers. When the two groups intersect you have, well, David Hyde Pierce. Here's a look at the gay prep landscape, where at any time one can feel free to wear his pastel-colored cashmere sweater tied around his neck as a scarf. With pride.

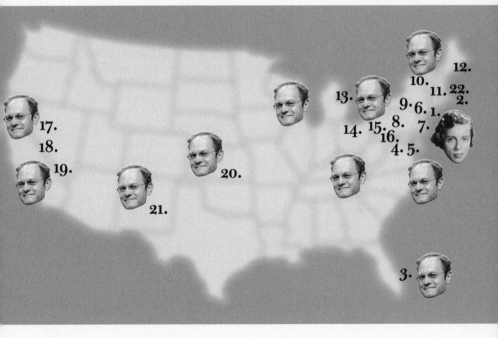

PREP LESBIANS: REDUNDANT?

Think about it: androgynous haircuts, sensible shoes, plaid, a love of golf matched only by a disdain for sex in general. What could be preppier? From Nancy Kulp (representing Northampton, Massachusetts, 22.) to Jodie Foster to that woman who left her husband for Martina Navratilova, prep lesbians (dare we say "presbians"?) have been with us long before Gertrude Stein ever started writing those strange little poems. Whether they're grooming the horses, fixing the station wagon, organizing some sort of angry protest, or just helping you improve your tennis swing, it's more than likely there's a presbian in your life. Hey, someone has to run things.

THE TRVE

B.O. V.W. C.R. E.W.

PANTHEON.

J.T.   V.T.   S.C.   A.C.

THE TRUE PREP PANTHEON.

As you pass through the grosgrain pillars of our Pantheon, we expect you will be inspired by the legacy of those who came before you. They may have achieved prominence in the arts or in industry. They may be philanthropists or authors. Wastrels or world beaters. They may have left the world a better place than when they first found it. They may have left the world a worse place but scattered fun nicknames around. ("Brownie, you're doing a heck of a job.") Some of them are historic figures; others have yet to enter their primes. And yet they've all earned entrance into this exclusive club through some form of preppiness. They didn't all start out that way, but they have added dash and spirit to their personal and thus our collective histories. And, oh, yes. Many of them are interconnected.

Jonathan Adler (b. August 11, 1966) From his bio: "1979: Begs parents to buy him a wheel and a kiln . . . 1980–1984 spends entire adolescence in basement . . . throwing pots. 1984–88 Allegedly studies semiotics and art history at Brown but actually spends all his time at RISD throwing pots. 1989 . . . Evil professor advises him to bag pottery and try a career in law . . . 2003 . . . Develops raging obsession with waspy country-club style . . . Concerned Jewish mother schedules an . . . intervention."

Josephine Patterson Albright (December 2, 1913–January 15, 1996) Although she was born into the powerful Medill journalism family in Illinois (Northwestern's journalism school is called Medill), Josephine and her older sister, Alicia, were raised as socialites. Her father, Joseph Medill Patterson, founded the New York *Daily News* and cofounded the *Chicago Tribune*. His sister, Eleanor Medill Patterson, was the publisher of *The Washington Times-Herald*. Mr. Patterson forbade his daughters to go into the family business but approved of Josephine getting her pilot's license. At sixteen, Josephine did just that, and she was the youngest pilot to fly the mail route between Chicago and Saint Louis. Josephine attended the Foxcroft School in Virginia, and during her debut at eighteen, she and her sister decided to fly to India to shoot tigers. They left Chicago without telling their mother. When Josephine killed her first tiger, Alicia became annoyed and told Josephine not to come on the next hunt. As her obituary in *The New York Times* described it, "So Josephine went on the next hunt carrying only a book. She was sitting in a tree reading when a leopard bounded up behind her. Josephine threw the book and hit the leopard in the nose. Alicia finished it off." After this whirlwind adventure, Josephine defied her father and began writing for his rival newspaper, *The Chicago Daily News*, where she did hard-core crime reporting (think Roz Russell in *His Girl Friday*). She met lawyer Jay Frederick Reeve then, and once married, she opened a pig and dairy farm that became a major success. After divorcing Reeve, Patterson began raising stallions in Wyoming. She married painter Ivan Albright in 1946 in Montana. Together they traveled widely and had four children. From 1949 to 1952 Mrs. Albright wrote a column for *Newsday* (the Long Island, New York, newspaper founded and run by her sister, Alicia). After Alicia's death, Josephine established the Alicia Patterson Foundation, which awards fellowships of six months to a year to journalists.

Tina Barney (b. October 27, 1945) Photographer of the inner sanctums of prepdom. A graduate of The Spence School, she began taking arresting, outsize color photographs of America's blue bloods (her family and friends) that caught their rituals in such places as Locust Valley, Rhode Island, or Sun Valley. Family function and dysfunction close-up. She also photographs the blue bloods of Europe. Her work is collected in many museums, including MoMA in New York and the Museum of Fine Arts in Boston.

Leonard Bernstein (August 25, 1918–October 14, 1990) This Massachusetts native, who at fifteen changed his name from Louis to Leonard, studied the piano, despite his father's discouragement. After Boston Latin School he studied music at Harvard. In 1943 Bernstein, then the assistant conductor of the New York Philharmonic, became an overnight star when he took over at the last minute for conductor Bruno Walter, who had fallen ill. Besides conducting, composing classical music, hosting the "Young Peoples' Concerts" from 1958 to 1972 (the longest-running program ever devoted to classical music on television), and composing the scores of *West Side Story, On the Town,* and *Candide,* Bernstein was also famous for hosting a cocktail party in 1970 for the Black Panthers, which was in many ways the first instance of political correctness. Tom Wolfe (see Tom Wolfe, p. 39) wrote about it in *Radical Chic & Mau-Mauing the Flak Catchers.* Bernstein left his wife, Felicia, in 1976 in order to live with a male lover, though he returned to take care of her when she was ill. Bernstein was a Jew, a genius, a bisexual, a provocateur, and a preppy.

Stephen Birmingham (b. May 28, 1932) This Hartford native and Williams College graduate started his career writing advertising copy for a New York department store before plunging into commercial nonfiction. A lifelong interest in the privileged classes resulted in more than thirty books, road maps to America's various elites: *Our Crowd, Real Lace, Certain People: America's Black Elite, The Grandes Dames, California Rich,* and *The Wrong Kind of Money* among them.

Cory Anthony Booker (b. April 27, 1969) The mayor of Newark, New Jersey, since 2006 is the son of a couple of early African American IBM executives. Booker played football (he made all-American) for a largely white high school in New Jersey and, at Stanford University, continued to play varsity football, this time making the All-Pacific Ten Academic Team. He spent five years in Palo Alto, getting his master's in sociology, went to Oxford on a Rhodes

Scholarship, and then to Yale, where he earned his law degree in 1997. In his first term he lowered crime and created more affordable housing, and has been the focus of an unusual amount of attention: He was the subject of a multipart documentary on the Sundance Channel, and got into a faux feud with Conan O'Brien (see Conan O'Brien, p. 31).

Sandra Keith Boynton (b. April 3, 1953) When she was two, Sandra's parents became Quakers, and Boynton spent her youth at Germantown Friends, a Quaker school in suburban Philadelphia. Her father taught English and was the head of the upper school there. At Yale, where she was in the second coed class, Boynton ended up marrying a fellow Eli, and they had four distinguished offspring together. Meanwhile, there were the greeting cards. Preppies may not know a Monet from a Manet, but they certainly know their Recycled Paper Greetings by Boynton. This artist is responsible for the cards with whimsical animals that have jollied away our fear of growing old. She has sold well over 200 million of them.

Benjamin Crowninshield Bradlee (b. August 26, 1921) If for no other reason than he owns Grey Gardens . . . really, we love the crusading former editor of *The Washington Post* Ben Bradlee. Another descendant of early Americans, Bradlee is a born patrician whose family tree included the creator of *Vanity Fair* magazine, an ambassador to England, and an all-American football player. He graduated from St. Mark's School, and at Harvard played football all four years, was tapped for the final club AD, and majored in classical Greek—a major that is prep because it is as far as one can get away from being practical. During World War Two, Bradlee served on a naval destroyer in the Pacific. In 1946 he began his career at a New Hampshire newspaper, moving to *The Washington Post* in 1948. He went to Paris in 1951 to work in the press office of the American embassy, and then at the USIE (forerunner of the USIA), disseminating American propaganda and working with the Voice of America. Bradlee joined *Newsweek* in 1953, first in Paris and then in Washington, where his crowd included Senator and Mrs. John F. Kennedy. As Washington bureau chief of *Newsweek*, he helped steer the sale of the magazine to his friends the Grahams, who owned the *Post*. In 1968, Bradlee was named executive editor of the *Post*, and he took on the Nixon White House, allowing the ad hoc investigative team of Bob Woodward and Carl Bernstein to dig deep into the Watergate scandal. Bradlee was portrayed by Yankee actor Jason Robards Jr.—perfect casting—in the movie, *All the President's Men*.

Kingman Brewster Jr. (June 17, 1919– November 8, 1988) This direct descendant of *Mayflower* ticket holder William Brewster, a Plymouth Colony pilgrim, was raised in New England. After graduating from the Belmont Hill School, he went to Yale. Brewster achieved campus-wide fame—or notoriety—by turning down Skull and Bones.

Chairman of the *Yale Daily News*, as a student he had been opposed to America entering World War Two, but he changed his mind after the bombing of Pearl Harbor, when he enlisted as a naval pilot. He entered Harvard Law School after the war, and was an editor of the *Law Review*. Brewster went to Europe to work on the Marshall Plan, and returned to join academia, first as a professor at MIT, and then at Harvard Law School. He is best known, however, as president of Yale, from 1963 to 1977, the years of long hair, Vietnam protest, and the sexual revolution. During and thanks to Brewster's tenure, Yale went coed, demoted ROTC from an academic program, hired the Rev. William Sloane Coffin (Yale alum, Skull and Bonesman, and CIA operative) as its chaplain, and supported him as he became an ardent anti-war activist. From 1977 to 1981, Brewster served his country as Presi-

dent Carter's ambassador to the Court of St. James.

Thomas John Brokaw (b. February 6, 1940) While Brokaw has professed to be an "anti-preppy," the longtime anchor and managing editor of the *Nightly News* on NBC (1982– 2004) is included here for his boyishness as a newsman, making him prep whether he likes it or not. The eldest of three sons born in Webster, South Dakota, Brokaw attended public schools and went to the University of Iowa. He dropped out, claiming he "majored in beer and coeds" (so prep it hurts), then went to the University of South Dakota, from which he graduated. He also received honorary degrees from such prep institutions as the College of William & Mary, Dartmouth, Duke, and the University of Pennsylvania. Brokaw and his wife sent their three daughters to private schools. He is a confirmed outdoorsman, and consequently has aged perfectly.

Christopher Taylor Buckley (b. December 24, 1952) This journalist, humorist, and novelist is the trophy son of all-time Pantheonist William F. Buckley Jr. (see William F. Buckley Jr., p. 40) and his wife, Pat, known to their boy as "Mum and Pup." A product of Portsmouth Abbey and a Bonesman like his old man, Chris parted with the legacy in the twenty-first century when he began to misbehave in the public eye: He endorsed Barack Obama (see Barack Obama, p. 31) for president in 2008, thus having to resign from the board of the *National Review*, the magazine his father founded in 1955. Buckley wrote one of our favorite novels, *Thank You for Smoking*.

Tory Robinson Burch (b. June 15, 1966) Daughter of suburban Philadelphia. A graduate of Agnes Irwin School and the University of Pennsylvania, she knows her way around classic American sportswear. Her signature ballet pump, the Reva, and blouses and dresses are sold in boutiques in East Hampton, Greenwich, Palm Beach, San Francisco, Los Angeles, Atlanta, Chicago, Dallas, Houston, and Bellevue, Washington.

George Walker Bush (b. July 6, 1946) The oldest child of George H. W. and Barbara Bush attended the family schools of Andover and Yale. Though just an average student, he was tapped, like the previous Bushes, into Skull and Bones. After college, "Dubya" dabbled in a few careers. He would have preferred to have been named baseball commissioner (no objections here). Instead, he became the forty-third President of the United States. Typical quote: "I was raised in the West. The west of Texas. It's pretty close to California. In more ways than Washington, D.C., is close to California."

Mary Stevenson Cassatt (May 22, 1844–June 14, 1926) From a good Pennsylvania family, young Mary became serious about painting as a teenager. Cassatt was able to study at the Pennsylvania Academy of the Fine Arts in Philadelphia as long as she didn't expect to pursue this work professionally. Unlike men, women were not permitted to draw from live models, and Cassatt got her mother to agree to spend time in Europe as her chaperone while she studied and copied masterpieces. Eventually, taken  under the wing of Edgar Degas, Cassatt made her life as a painter, as an expatriate, and as an unmarried woman. She is considered the greatest female Impressionist.

Stockard Channing (b. February 13, 1944) Named Susan Antonia Williams Stockard at birth, this native New Yorker lived on the Upper East Side and attended Chapin before heading off to Madeira in Virginia. She hated her name (see Sigourney Weaver, p. 38), and while attending Radcliffe married a fellow named Walter Channing when she was nineteen—and became Stockard Channing. (Though they were divorced within four years, the name stuck.) With some good reviews for small projects, Channing was finally noticed in a big way when she played tough teenager Betty Rizzo in the movie musical *Grease* in 1978; she was thirty-four. Channing won awards for her

work as Ouisa, the mummy, in both the Broadway production and film of *Six Degrees of Separation*. She won an Emmy for her work on *The West Wing*. She has been married and divorced four times, and when not working, Channing lives with her boyfriend in Maine.

Cornelius Crane "Chevy" Chase (b. October 8, 1943) A fourteenth-generation New Yorker, listed in the Social Register, Chase has ancestors who arrived on the *Mayflower*, played a role in the American Revolution, and were early mayors. He attended the Stockbridge School, graduated from Riverdale Country School, and went to Bard, where he dated Blythe Danner (see Gwyneth Paltrow, p. 32) and played in a band with "Bardians" Donald Fagen and Walter Becker of Steely Dan. From the *National Lampoon Radio Hour* alongside John Belushi, Gilda Radner, and Bill Murray, it was an easy segue to *Saturday Night Live*, where Chase delivered his signature line, "I'm Chevy Chase, and you're not." Long, lean, and cute, he was a leading preppy crush of the late 70s and 80s.

Julia Carolyn McWilliams Child (August 15, 1912–August 13, 2004) Formidable, both in height (6'2") and in accomplishment, the Pasadena native graduated from Katherine Branson and then went on to Smith, earning her BA in 1934. After doing copywriting for a high-end furniture store, she worked for the OSS during World War Two, where she was posted in China and Sri Lanka (née Ceylon) and helped create a shark repellent to keep them from bumping into and detonating Allied bombs. She married Paul Child in 1946 and, on moving to France, learned how to cook. The rest of her story is available on DVD as *Julie and Julia* (see Meryl Streep, p. 36).

Stephen Tyrone Colbert (b. May 13, 1964) The youngest of the eleven Colbert children of South Carolina, and the only one who insists on the French pronunciation of their surname, Stephen Colbert was neither class clown nor misfit. He graduated from Charleston's Episcopal Porter-Gaud School, then went on to Hampden-Sydney College (the preppiest college in the United States—see p. 72), whence he transferred to Northwestern for his last two years, ultimately ending up within the Second City hemisphere. Eventually joining *The Daily Show*, he is the spin-off supremo, winning awards for truthiness and the American way.

Anderson Hays Cooper (b. June 3, 1967) Former child model for Calvin Klein and Ralph Lauren, Cooper is best known for being a broadcast journalist for CNN. The son of socialites Gloria Vanderbilt Cooper and Wyatt Emory Cooper, Anderson graduated from the Dalton School and Yale University. Following in many distinguished and shadowy Yale footsteps, he spent a couple of summers interning at the Central Intelligence Agency but decided against a career as a spy in favor of being the original host of ABC TV's *The Mole*.

Charlotte Curtis (December 19, 1928–April 16, 1987) Born in Chicago to a surgeon and the first woman diplomat who held field posts in Haiti, Panama, and Switzerland, Curtis graduated from the Columbus (Ohio) School for Girls and then Vassar. She arrived at *The New York Times* in 1961. By 1965 she was the editor of the Family/Style section, winning fans for her witty reporting. It was she who quoted Leonard Bernstein at his "radical chic" fundraiser for the Black Panthers as saying, "I dig absolutely." (See Leonard Bernstein, p. 23. See Tom Wolfe, p. 39.) Always ladylike in appearance, even in the very male newsroom, Curtis wore French perfume and high heels, and her hair was always impeccably done. In 1974 she was promoted to editor of the op-ed page, making her the first woman on the editorial masthead. She maintained that position for eight years. A collection of her articles, *The Rich and Other Atrocities*, was published in 1976.

Edward Bridge "Ted" Danson III (b. December 29, 1947) Kent School, Stanford—

Carnegie Mellon, BFA. With great savoir faire, Ted Danson has become the ultimate prep multitasker: at publication he was appearing on two HBO comedies simultaneously: *Curb Your Enthusiasm* and *Bored to Death*. Natch, it was his finesse in playing ladies' man and alcoholic barkeep Sam Malone in *Cheers* that puts him in the Pantheon. Why? Because it was set in the heart of Yankeedom, Boston.

Bruce MacLeish Dern (b. June 4, 1936) When you watch actor Bruce Dern in the movies or on *Big Love*, does it occur to you that you are watching a Choate and Penn graduate, the grandson of a former governor of Utah, a nephew of American poet Archibald MacLeish, the godson of Adlai Stevenson (see Adlai Stevenson, p. 40) and Eleanor Roosevelt (who used to babysit for young Bruce)? Didn't think so. Furthermore, Dern played Tom Buchanan in *The Great Gatsby*, starring Robert Redford as Jay Gatsby, Mia Farrow as Daisy Buchanan, and Sam Waterston (see Sam Waterston, p. 38) as Nick Carraway.

Thomas Cowperthwait Eakins (July 25, 1844–June 25, 1916) Born in Philadelphia before the Civil War, Thomas Eakins was the son of a "master calligrapher." He went to Central High School, the best public school in that city, where his talent for drawing was noted. Next it was the Pennsylvania Academy of the Fine Arts (see Mary Cassatt, p. 25); there his interest in the human body almost made him consider a career as a surgeon. Eakins studied anatomy at Jefferson Medical College for a year, and then went to Paris to study with the Orientalist painter Jean-Léon Gérôme at l'École des Beaux Arts. Eakins was also happy to paint from nude models, which wasn't yet done in the United States. Upon returning to Philadelphia, Eakins became a teacher at the Pennsylvania Academy of the Fine Arts, where he had only recently studied. Passionate about precision and locomotion, he made his first sale with a picture of a sculler whose shoulder muscles' strain was evident. Rowing was an early theme, and he encouraged his students to look at the human body—even sending them to observe medical dissections. Instead of drawing from wax molds, he preferred the use of photographs, like those of Eadweard Muybridge, who broke down movements into each and every motion. Probably Eakins's best-known painting, *The Gross Clinic*, was considered, in fact, gross for its time (1875). Eakins became appreciated, sadly, after his death.

Fantastic Mr. Fox (b. 1970) Although the son of a single father, British writer Roald Dahl, Mr. Fox ("Foxy" to his missus) has certainly earned his place here. He was born in England but has lived around the world, thanks to George Allen & Unwin Ltd., Alfred A. Knopf, Rizzoli, Viking, Puffin, Collins, Dorling Kindersley, Bantam—and  that's just in the English language. We admire Fox for his reliance on wearing corduroy suits—even at leisure—his laissez-faire attitude towards his newspaper job, and making his naughty streak (stealing chickens and cider) work for him and his family. Director Wes Anderson (né Wesley Mortimer Wales Anderson, St. John's School, Houston) certainly understood Fox's preppiness; allowing George Clooney to voice him with his devil-may-care mammal voice was inspired.

Jane Fonda (née Lady Jayne Seymour Fonda) (b. December 21, 1937) Greenwich Academy, Emma Willard School, Vassar College. The fact that the "Barbarella"–"Hanoi Jane"–"Workout Jane" daughter of Henry Fonda and former wife of media magnate Ted Turner (see Ted Turner, p. 37) is an honest prep should surprise no one. Fonda has the finest elocution of any American actress, not to mention perfect posture. Her activism makes her a black-sheep preppy, her activity keeps her young.

Jodie Foster (b. November 19, 1962) One of the few actors around who can and does dub herself whenever one of her films is distributed in a French-speaking country, Jodie Foster was born Alicia Christian Foster in Los Angeles. By the time she was three, she was appearing in commercials (she was a "Coppertone baby"), and soon she was starring in Disney productions. None of this sounds like a typical prep biography, and it is not. Yet Foster applied herself academically, becoming the valedictorian of her class at the Lycée Français in Los Angeles, and then went on to Yale. Today she is an Oscar-winning actress who wears either jeans or Armani.

Alan Stuart Franken (b. May 21, 1951) The junior senator from Minnesota, Franken attended the Blake School in Minneapolis, where he was a varsity wrestler. More important, he began a long partnership with classmate Tom Davis, with whom he wrote comedy. He graduated from Harvard cum laude with a degree in political science. As the professional writing team of Franken and Davis, the two young men moved to New York, where they were staff writers for the new *Saturday Night Live* (a postgraduate program of Harvard College). Initially they shared a weekly salary of $350. Franken went on to perform in the show, and earned three Emmy awards for his work. He also named his daughter Thomasin, in tribute to his professional partner. He was a Shorenstein Fellow at the Kennedy School of Government at Harvard in 2003. Moving on to writing books and hosting the flagship show on Air America Radio, Franken has been a staunch progressive who's supported and visited the troops in Kosovo, Afghanistan, and Iraq. You might think he was admitted to the Pantheon only for his unwavering choice of traditional tortoise-shell glasses; in fact, it was his understated restraint as he waited through the endless recounts of his 2008 election vote that wins our admiration.

Theodor Seuss Geisel (March 2, 1904–September 24, 1991) Our beloved Dr. Seuss attended public school in Massachusetts and, according to one of his biographers, "Ted grew to respect the academic discipline he discovered at Dartmouth—not enough to pursue it, but to appreciate those who did." This explains why Seuss is a stalwart member of the

Pantheon. Punished for throwing a party with coeds, Geisel was demoted from the editor-in-chief position of the college humor magazine, the *Jack-O-Lantern*, so he began to use his mother's maiden name as his byline. After college, Seuss told his dad that he'd won a fellowship to Oxford. His father was so proud, he announced the news to the local paper. Alas, Ted had misled his father, and had not been admitted to Oxford. Mr. Geisel was so embarrassed, he scraped together money to send his son there anyway. Again, this is a Pantheon-worthy move. Dr. Seuss began doodling at Oxford, where he met his wife. Does it matter that he never got his degree?

Vartan Gregorian (b. April 8, 1934) Though born in Iran, Gregorian represents the prep American dream as a solid member of the prepescenti. After schooling in the Middle East, Gregorian matriculated as a freshman at Stanford when he was twenty-two years old. He earned his degree and his Ph.D. there with honors in history, and moved on as a professor. Within short order, he became a chaired professor at the University of Pennsylvania, the provost there, but then, having been overlooked as the next president of Penn, he moved on to the presidency of the New York Public Library. A social powerhouse in Manhattan, in eight years Gregorian raised a gazillion dollars (Hello, Brooke Astor!) and returned to academia as the sixteenth president of Brown. During his tenure the university climbed up the social ladder of the Ivy League, with titled Europeans and the very rich suddenly choosing to go there. A Presidential Medal of Freedom holder, Gregorian is now the president of the Carnegie Corporation. He has more than sixty honorary degrees. So far.

A. R. (Pete) Gurney (b. November 1, 1930) Albert Ramsdell Gurney Jr. is *our* leading playwright. Even the untalented among us who wish to act can find a partner with whom to spend an evening performing *Love Letters* in front of an audience (the script allows the players to read from it). Having lived the life (St. Paul's School, Williams College, Yale School of Drama), Gurney has exposed the uncomfortably unemotional private natures of Yankee preps and dramatized our unrequited love, our feelings of being discovered as frauds, and our sexual and professional ambiguities.

W. Averell Harriman (November 15, 1891–July 26, 1986) The son of Union Pacific Railroad chief E. H. Harriman, Averell was raised in New York City. After Groton and Yale (Skull and Bones), he established a banking business with his brother, Roland—Brown Brothers Harriman & Co. is still in operation today. In 1936, Harriman, a passionate skier, established the Sun Valley resort in Idaho as a way to increase revenues for the Union Pacific Railroad. During World War Two, Harriman served as FDR's envoy to Europe before becoming Ambassador to the Soviet Union. He became President Truman's Commerce Secretary, then was the head of the Marshall Plan. Harriman was Governor of New York from 1954 to 1958, when Nelson Rockefeller (see Nelson Rockefeller, p. 33) defeated him. He ran unsuccessfully for the Democratic nomination for President, losing to Adlai Stevenson (see Adlai Stevenson, p. 40). As the prototypical elder statesman, he was appointed to major positions by presidents Kennedy and Johnson. He was nicknamed "the Crocodile" by Bobby Kennedy for his snap. Married three times, he is buried in Arden, New York.

Buck Henry (b. December 9, 1930) Born Buck Henry Zuckerman in New York City. A graduate of Choate and Dartmouth, with a glorious career as writer, director, producer, and actor, he wrote the screenplay for *Catch-22* and co-wrote the Oscar-winning screenplay of *The Graduate*, enough reason to be included here.

Thomas Pearsall Field Hoving (January 15, 1931–December 10, 2009) was the son of the longtime head of Tiffany & Company, Walter Hoving, and his wife. A top-drawer upbringing sent Thomas to Hotchkiss and Princeton, where he earned his BA, MFA, and Ph.D. Hoving went straight to the Metropolitan Museum, first as an assistant curator of The Cloisters, the museum's off-site medieval collection. After a year as Mayor Lindsay's Parks Commissioner (see John Vliet Lindsay, p. 40), Hoving became the Executive Director of the Met in 1967, a position he kept for ten years. Under Hoving's showmanship, the grand museum's "circulation" increased, as he expanded the physical plant and made the museum swing with the times. Afterwards, he wrote, appeared on TV, and consulted.

John F. Kennedy Jr. (November 25,1960–July 16,1999) Forever known as John-John, he was the true scion of President Kennedy's Camelot. Born at Georgetown Hospital, John-John attended Collegiate and graduated from Andover, Brown, and the NYU School of Law. Like many of us, he had to take the New York bar exam multiple times before he passed it. Famously nice and insanely handsome (perpetual holder of *People* magazine's "Sexiest Man" title), John-John died at age thirty-eight while piloting his own plane to Martha's Vineyard. Our collective hearts are still broken.

Alfred Abraham Knopf (September 12, 1892–August 11, 1984) A native New Yorker, Knopf went to Columbia University, where he tasted elitism as a member of the Peithologian Society, a literary club.  After graduation in 1912, young Knopf visited the British author John Galsworthy, and decided to try a job in publishing. He started Alfred A. Knopf in 1915, at first focusing on European writers, including E. M. Forster, Somerset Maugham, Joseph Conrad, and D. H. Lawrence, and then such American writers as John Updike (see John Updike, p. 37), Theodore Dreiser, Conrad Aiken, and Willa Cather. In 1960 Knopf sold his company to Random House. In 2010, Alfred A. Knopf published *True Prep* (though he didn't know it).

Nancy Jane Kulp (August 28, 1921–February 3, 1991) While not a graduate of a tony boarding school, nor of a private college, Nancy Kulp earns her way into the Pantheon the hard way: through work. That plus a dazzling lockjaw as Miss Jane Hathaway on *The Beverly Hillbillies*, where her character was an uptight, class-conscious spinster who worked in banking (see p. 201). Kulp was married to a man for ten years but later in life announced that "birds of a feather flock together." One can even hear her say it in her inimitable way.

Iris Cordelia Love (b. August 1, 1933) Her most important discovery was the Temple of Aphrodite in Knidos, Turkey, in the summer of 1969. Described as a kind of madcap heiress-archaeologist (you know the type), she grew up in Manhattan, attended The Brearley School, went on to Madeira, and graduated from Smith College. After her great find, this descendant of the Guggenheim fortune turned more of her attention to her beloved dachshunds. She has raised champions who've won the Westminster Dog Show, and keeps dozens of dachshunds on her property in Vermont. A lifelong party girl, Love was for years the companion of gossipeuse Liz Smith. According to one article, Love's criteria for choosing friends are twofold: that her dogs must like you, and that you like to drink. Welcome, Iris Love.

Yo-Yo Ma (b. October 7, 1955) The beloved cellist moved with his family from Paris to New York as a child. While in the 2nd grade, he performed at the White House, for President Kennedy. After high school and Juilliard, Ma, already a world-renowned musician, attended Columbia University before transferring to Harvard. He graduated from Harvard in 1976 and won an honorary doctorate from the same in 1991. It's not because of his schools, his experience playing for heads of state or on *Sesame Street*, *The West Wing*, etc. that puts Ma in the Pantheon. It's because he once left his rare cello, a 1733 Domenico Montagnana, insured for $2.5 million, in the back of a New York City taxicab.

Rachel Lowe Lambert Lloyd Mellon (b. August 9, 1910) Known forever as "Bunny," Mrs. Mellon was the daughter of the president of the Gillette Safety Razor Company, Gerard Lambert, who went on to co-found Warner-Lambert  (of Listerine fame), which is now part of the Pfizer Pharmaceutical empire (Viagra). (The only mention of Viagra in *True Prep*.) After her first marriage to Stacy Lloyd, she was married to Paul Mellon, son and heir of Andrew Mellon and grandson of the founder of Mellon Bank. *That* Mellon. As a close friend of Mrs. John F. Kennedy, Bunny, known for her elegant taste (a member of the International Best Dressed List), was asked to help out with the decoration and art for the White House and, as a noted gardener, was asked to redesign the Rose Garden, which she did. Between 2005 and 2008, Mrs. Mellon donated generously to the presidential campaign of adulterer John Edwards.

James Ingram Merrill (March 3, 1926–February 6, 1995) The American poet grew up in New York City as the only child of Helen Ingram and Charles Merrill of Merrill Lynch. *That* Merrill. He learned German and French from his governess, before his by-then-divorced parents sent him away to Lawrenceville. He went to Amherst (his father's alma mater) afterwards, though he had to interrupt his college education when he was drafted by the army in 1944. He returned, and graduated in 1947, and by then he'd had an affair with his (male) professor, who privately published Merrill's first book of poems, *The Black Swan*. That volume is considered one of the rarest souvenirs of modern publishing. In 1951, Alfred A. Knopf (see Alfred A. Knopf, p. 29) published *First Poems* in a numbered edition that is also considered a rarity. With a significant inheritance, Merrill established a foundation, often subsidizing other writers anonymously. He and his longtime partner,

David Jackson, lived part of the year in Greece and part in Connecticut, and eventually added Key West, Florida, to their annual itinerary. As a poet, Merrill had the pleasure of being recognized in his lifetime, winning the Pulitzer, Bollingen, National Book Critics Circle, and Bobbitt National prizes, and the National Book Award twice.

Robert Morris Morgenthau (b. July 31, 1919) If family is destiny, Bob Morgenthau was destined to serve. His father, Henry Morgenthau Jr., was secretary of the Treasury for Franklin Roosevelt. He raised the money for the New Deal. His grandfather Henry Morgenthau Sr. was U.S. ambassador to the Ottoman Empire (!) during World War One. Young Morgenthau was raised in Manhattan and graduated from the New Lincoln School, Deerfield Academy, and Amherst College. During World War Two he enlisted in the navy, fighting for four and a half years in both the Pacific and the Mediterranean, mostly on destroyers. After the war, Morgenthau went to Yale Law School and then to the corporate firm of Patterson, Belknap, and Webb, and was made partner. President Kennedy asked him to be the U.S. Attorney for the Southern District of New York, a prestigious and high-visibility appointment. Although Morgenthau ran unsuccessfully as the 1962 Democratic nominee for governor of New York (see Nelson A. Rockefeller, p. 33), he served as U.S. Attorney throughout the Kennedy and Johnson presidencies. Yet as a political creature, Morgenthau was pushed to leave his post by various men in the Nixon administration. In 1974, Morgenthau was elected the District Attorney of New York. He served eight consecutive terms, an unprecedented record. Among the jewels in his prosecutorial crown: Mark David Chapman (John Lennon's killer); the Tyco crooks; Bernie Goetz, the subway vigilante; and Robert Chambers, the "Preppy Killer" (see p. 145); Morgenthau retired from the DA's office at the end of December 2009. As of January 2010, at age ninety, he had joined the law firm Wachtell, Lipton, Rosen & Katz.

Frederic Ogden Nash (August 19, 1902–May 19, 1971) Despite all the right skills and entrée, Ogden Nash never graduated from college. He did graduate from St. George's, the boys' boarding school in Rhode Island, and he did matriculate at Harvard, but he only lasted through his freshman year. Among other jobs, he taught at St. George's for a bit and wrote advertising copy for streetcars before he ended up working at Doubleday. A natural-born rhymer, Nash was famous for his comic verse:

> *I think that I shall never see*
> *A billboard lovely as a tree.*
> *Indeed, unless the billboards fall*
> *I'll never see a tree at all.*

He published many casual light poems and became a longtime contributor to *The New Yorker.* He cowrote the book for *One Touch of Venus,* the Kurt Weill musical, with S. J. Perelman. The Rye, New York, native was transplanted to Baltimore, a city he loved devoutly. Though he lacked a college degree, Nash spent much time on American college campuses, giving talks and classes.

Barack Hussein Obama (b. August 4, 1961) The 44th President of the United States and Nobel Laureate was born in Hawaii. After a few years in Indonesia, Obama attended Punahou School, America's largest private school (enrollment over 3,750) from K through 12th grades, went to Occidental College for two years, then transferred to Columbia University, from which he graduated. Obama is a possessor of many "firsts," including first black president of the *Harvard Law Review,* meaning he was the top-ranked student in his class there. Creator of the "Beer Summit" in the White House garden in 2009, he has not yet managed to quit smoking.

Michelle LaVaughn Robinson Obama (b. January 17, 1964) Model wife, Mom-in-Chief, First Lady of the United States, Michelle Obama is admired for her style, her cool, and

her intelligence. At 5'11", she has arms that look sculpted out of onyx and, for covering up, often chooses cardigans from J.Crew. A graduate of Princeton University (cum laude) and Harvard Law School, Michelle Robinson was an associate at the Chicago law firm Sidley Austin, where she was  asked to mentor a summer associate named Obama. The Obamas still cherish their "date nights."

Conan Christopher O'Brien (b. April 18, 1963) Class valedictorian at Brookline High School, Harvard University student, and president of the Harvard Lampoon for two years, O'Brien picked up the preppy-sounding nickname "Coco" when he became a cause célèbre in the January 2010 NBC late-night coup. His hairdo is lamentably unprep, but (and this is a compliment) his sense of humor is downright sophomoric.

Frederick Law Olmsted (April 26, 1822–August 28, 1903) Where would prepdom be without America's premier landscape architect? Combining two prep professions into his genius, Frederick Law Olmsted designed all or part of so many campuses and parks where we have whiled away the hours and years . . . Multiple thank-you notes would never suffice. He gave us Central Park, Phillips Academy (Andover, his alma mater), Berwick Academy, Groton School, Lawrenceville School, Noble and Greenough School, Pomfret School, and St. Albans School, as well as many of our college and university campuses: Berkeley, Bryn Mawr, Colgate, Cornell, Denison, Miami University (Ohio), Mount Holyoke, Smith, Stanford, Trinity (Hartford), Rochester, Washington University, Wellesley, and Yale are among his 355 commissions. Hospitals, parks, parkways, historic neighborhoods—indeed, even the landscaping around the U.S. Capitol was created by Olmsted, clearly an overachiever.

Gwyneth Kate Paltrow (b. September 27, 1972) This Spence School graduate, known as "Gwynnie," was first famous for dating Brad Pitt, then Ben Affleck, and is now married to preppy English rock god Chris Martin of Coldplay. Daughter of prep actress Blythe Danner (George School, Bard College; see Chevy Chase, p. 25) and TV producer Bruce Paltrow (*St. Elsewhere, Homicide*), she was raised between the best zip codes in New York City and Los Angeles. As the title character of the feature film *Emma,* Paltrow needed no extra coaching for archery, horseback riding, piano playing, singing, or her peerless English accent. This Academy award–winning preppy (*Shakespeare in Love*) is now a blogger.

Sister Parish (July 15, 1910–September 8, 1994). Dorothy May Kinnicutt got her nickname for being the only girl in a gaggle of five children. Her father, Gustav Hermann Kinnicutt, had gone to Harvard and was in finance. She was born in Far Hills, New Jersey, but her parents had an apartment on the Quai d'Orsay in Paris and a house in Dark Harbor, Maine. She attended Chapin and Foxcroft, made her debut at nineteen, married an investment banker by the name of Parish, and opened up her decorating business in 1933. Eventually, her eye brought her loads of important clients, including such names as Astor, Vanderbilt, Whitney, Paley, Mellon, Getty, Engelhard, Annenberg, Rockefeller, and Mrs. John F. Kennedy, when she moved to the White House. Albert Hadley became her partner in 1962. Today, two nice ladies in Bedford, New York—one Sister's granddaughter—run her company and have a cute Web site.

David Hyde Pierce (b. April 3, 1959) is well-spoken enough to be the believably persnickety sitcom psychiatrist Dr. Niles Crane, a preppy and a Yalie (see p. 201). A native of Saratoga Springs, New York, Hyde Pierce arrived in New Haven thinking he would be a classical pianist. There, he discovered he loved the theater, and he performed in everything from Gilbert & Sullivan to Beckett. He is married to TV writer and director Brian Hargrove, and

has won four Emmys for his work on *Frasier,* and a Tony for best leading actor in a musical for *Curtains.*

Fairfield Porter (June 10, 1907–September 18, 1975) This representational painter who was influenced by Vuillard, Bonnard, and de Kooning grew up in Winnetka, Illinois, majored in art at Harvard, and stayed on the East Coast to live the life of an artist. He studied with Thomas Hart

Benton at the Art Students League. Celebrated for his beautiful landscapes, depictions of nice people in the suburbs, and self-portraits, he was also a respected art critic at *The Nation* and at *ARTnews,* when it was the art world journal of record. He wrote a series of books about artists, including one on Thomas Eakins (see Thomas Eakins, p. 26), not because he was a fan but because it was assigned. In 1949 he and his family moved to the prep resort of Southampton, New York, but they spent summers at the house built by Porter's father on Great Spruce Head Island, off the coast of Maine. He and his wife were married for forty-three years and had five children together, though Porter had a brief affair with poet James Schuyler, who then lived with the family for almost a decade. Porter was also a friend of Frank O'Hara, John Ashbery, Jane Freilicher, and Larry Rivers. From photographs we can tell Porter often painted on easels set outside, in cotton Bermuda shorts or khaki pants.

John Silas Reed (October 17, 1887–October 19, 1920) From an affluent background in Portland, Oregon, Reed, known as Jack, and his brother were tended carefully by their parents; even their little playmates were selected from among Portland's social elite families. After several years at private Portland Academy, Jack was sent to Morristown Academy in New Jersey to prepare for his college entrance exams. After a couple of tries, he got into Harvard, where he was a member of the swimming and cheerleading teams, a member of the drama club and the Harvard Lampoon, the president of the Harvard Glee Club, and wrote a play that was produced by the Hasty Pudding Club. After his graduation in 1920, Jack moved to New York to live  "la vie bohème" as a journalist and a muckraker. Soon he was politicized, and Reed became a respected war correspondent, following Pancho Villa in Mexico, meeting Lenin and Trotsky in Russia, and being arrested several times for sedition in the United States. He is buried in the Kremlin. Best of all, he was portrayed by Warren Beatty in his epic film *Reds*.

Christopher D'Olier Reeve (September 25, 1952–October 10, 2004) Descended on both sides from early-American patriots, including *Mayflower* passenger William Bradford and Governors Dudley, Winthrop, and others, Christopher Reeve earned his world renown as the gorgeous young Juilliard-trained unknown who was cast in 1978 to portray Superman/Clark Kent in *Superman: The Movie*. A graduate of Cornell University, Reeve was a natural athlete who sailed, skied, rode, and flew. As an actor, he felt he came into his own only in the 1990s after the public forgot him as Superman. His career was cut short by an equestrian accident in Culpepper, Virginia, over Memorial Day weekend 1995, which left him paralyzed below the neck. Reeve's commanding wisdom, drive, and verve enabled him to become one of the world's leading activists for stem cell research. He led the Christopher and Dana Reeve Foundation until he died in October of 2004. He is truly missed, as is his radiant and dynamic wife, Dana.

Nelson Aldrich Rockefeller (July 8, 1908–January 26, 1979) The first ever "Rockefeller Republican," since the term was coined for him, Nelson Rockefeller, grandson of Standard Oil empire founder John D. Rockefeller, was a moderate Republican from New York. Born in Bar Harbor, Maine, he attended the progressive Lincoln School in Manhattan, then went to Dartmouth, where he was in Casque and Gauntlet, Big Green's club for campus leaders. After graduation Rockefeller followed in his father's footsteps at Chase bank, at Rockefeller Center, and as a trustee of the Museum of Modern Art. As New York's forty-ninth governor (see W. Averell Harriman, p. 28), Rockefeller won four four-year terms, though he retired in his fifteenth year of service. In that time Rockefeller expanded the state university system from twenty-nine to seventy-two campuses, helped create 22,000 miles of highway, founded the Urban Development Corporation to build more lower-income housing, coalesced all public transportation and bridge authorities into the N.Y. Metropolitan Transit Authority, and made a statewide commitment to the arts. In 1974, Gerald Ford appointed Rockefeller the forty-first Vice President of the United States, following the resignation of President Richard Nixon. "Rocky," as he was known, was always considered a socially liberal member of the GOP. Because he died suddenly while working with a young female assistant, Rockefeller achieved a kind of immortality that most men could not dream about until the invention of the Internet.

Paul Mayer Rudnick (b. December 29, 1957) Gay preppy writer with food issues. First produced play *Poor Little Lambs*, a drama about the Whiffenpoofs at Yale, his alma mater. *Addams Family Values, In and Out, Sister Act* (under the pseudonym Joseph Howard), and *I Hate Hamlet* are some of his other works. He eats candy. Only.

Aline Bernstein Louchheim Saarinen (March 25, 1914–July 13, 1972) If Aline Saarinen had been born in the latter part of the twentieth century, she would have become one of the most famous women journalists in the United States. Though the media world was more quiet, more tasteful, more prep during her lifetime, she left a remarkable legacy just the same. Born to well-to-do Jewish parents in Manhattan, she graduated from the Fieldston School and then was Phi Beta Kappa at Vassar. She returned to New York and married, entered graduate school at the Institute of Fine Arts of

NYU, and had two sons by the time she had her master's degree in architectural history. She joined the staff of *ARTnews*, becoming its managing editor for four years. Divorced with two young boys, Louchheim  won awards for her critical writing, and was sent to Michigan to interview prominent architect Eero Saarinen (designer, eventually, of the Saint Louis Gateway Arch, the Black Rock building in New York, Dulles Airport, the kinetic TWA headquarters at Kennedy Airport, as well as many familiar pieces of furniture) for *The New York Times*. They instantly fell in love, and within a year Saarinen divorced his wife and married Aline Louchheim, who became her husband's staunchest advocate. She continued to work, winning a Guggenheim fellowship, and published a bestselling book. When Eero died, suddenly, Aline Saarinen reinvented herself as a television journalist, entering this field at the age of fifty in 1964. Beginning with documentaries about the arts, she moved into harder news, becoming the third female correspondent at NBC News. At her death at fifty-eight, she was the Paris Bureau Chief of NBC News, the first woman to have been entrusted with an overseas bureau.

Erich Wolf Segal (June 16, 1937–January 17, 2010) That Segal was the son of a Brooklyn rabbi is beside the point. After Midwood High School (Woody Allen's alma mater), he went to Harvard, where he was the Latin salutatorian and the Class Poet. Segal earned his master's and Ph.D. from Harvard as well, in comparative literature. Rabbi Segal's son is not anointed here because of all that learning, nor for writing the kicky screenplay for the Beatles' animated feature *Yellow Submarine*. Segal earns his spot the old-fashioned way, for using the term "preppy" as a declarative in his novel, then movie blockbuster, *Love Story*.

Brooke Christa Camille Shields (b. May 31, 1965) is not admitted to the Pantheon for her remarkable physical beauty, nor for her academic pedigree of Dwight-Englewood School and Princeton '87. No, she is included because her handsome grandfather Frank Shields was once a tennis star. We regret to mention it here, but Ms. Shields risked being expunged from the Pantheon for her long-term public friendship with Michael Jackson, her marital annulment from Andre Agassi, and her public brouhahas with Tom Cruise, but her solid marriage to comedy writer-producer Chris Henchy, providing two daughters with preppy names (Rowan and Grier), keeps her within the fold.

Stephen Joshua Sondheim (b. March 22, 1930) An only child, Sondheim grew up on Manhattan's Central Park West and attended the Ethical Culture School. After his parents' divorce, he went to the George School in Bucks County, where he became friendly with Jimmy Hammerstein, the son of musical theater great Oscar Hammerstein Jr. Hammerstein père recognized talent and drive in young Sondheim and became a sort of surrogate father to him, as well as a teacher and a boss. After high school Sondheim went to Williams College, and won a prize enabling him to study with composer Milton Babbitt at Princeton. A meeting with Arthur Laurents led to introductions to both Leonard Bernstein (see Leonard Bernstein, p. 23) and Jerome Robbins. In 1957, Sondheim wrote the lyrics to his first Broadway production: *West Side Story*. Two years later he wrote the lyrics to another Laurents show, *Gypsy*. For *A Funny Thing Happened on the Way to the Forum*, Sondheim composed as well as wrote the lyrics; it played for more than three years on Broadway and won a Tony Award for Best Musical. His show *Company*, which he produced, wrote, and composed, won Tonys for Best Musical, Best Lyrics, and Best Score. Always a favorite of the critics, Sondheim's name suggests complicated compositions, devilishly clever lyrics, and an often discernible aura of darkness hovering above the stage. Other works include *Follies*, *A Little Night Music*, *Sweeney Todd*, *Sunday in the Park with George* (for which Sondheim received a Pulitzer Prize), *Into the Woods*, and *Assassins*.

Sondheim's songs are usually too intense for medleys, though "Send in the Clowns" has been sung in Las Vegas showrooms. Not that any of us have been to any of them.

Kate Spade (b. December 24, 1962) was born Katherine Noel Brosnahan in Kansas City, Missouri. After her all-girls' Catholic school and the University of Kansas and Arizona State, Katy, as she was known, moved to New York to work in the world of fashion magazines. As Katy Brosnahan she was an editor at *Mademoiselle* magazine. With her boyfriend, Andy Spade, Brosnahan began Kate Spade, a handbag company with a lot of optimism and fabric swatches. They married in 1994, and the Kate Spade company, a successful purveyor of clothing, accessories, and paper goods, is now owned by Liz Claiborne. That optimism and an appreciation for her retro aesthetic earn her a spot in the Pantheon.

Gertrude Stein (February 3, 1874–July 27, 1946) Coiner of eternal phrases ("There is no there there"; "America is my country, but Paris is my hometown"; "You are all a lost generation"). Born in Vienna, Stein moved to Oakland, California, with her family. After her parents died she was sent to live with relatives in Baltimore. Stein attended Radcliffe College, class of 1897, and then studied at Johns Hopkins Medical School but left after two years. Well known for her salons as well as her alternative lifestyle, Stein lived an enviable life, surrounded by art, the avant-garde, and her mustachioed companion, Alice B. Toklas. She died in France.

Frank Philip Stella (b. May 12, 1936) After an education at Phillips Andover and Princeton University, Frank Stella, influenced by such diverse artists as Caravaggio and Jasper Johns, became a highly regarded abstract painter. Best known for his flat striped and shaped canvases, at thirty-three he was the youngest artist ever to have a retrospective at New York's Museum of

Modern Art. Stella's work is collected around the world, in museums, galleries, and private collections. As a prolific printmaker, he has made thousands of prints for those with humbler budgets. (And students can decorate their dorm rooms with his posters.)

Martha Helen Kostyra Stewart (b. August 3, 1941) The second of the six Kostyra kids of Nutley, New Jersey, Martha went to Barnard College. This alone would not be Pantheonworthy. She met Andy Stewart while attending Barnard, modeling part-time, and even working as a live-in housekeeper, and they soon married. Stewart was a student at Yale Law School at the time, so his bride moved up to New Haven for a year. She returned to Manhattan to finish her degree and graduated from Barnard in 1963. Still not Pantheon material. Within two years, the Stewarts had their (only) child, daughter Alexis. With modeling no longer an option, Martha decided to give stockbrokerage a whirl. She did well at that, quickly demonstrating her talent for making money. She started her catering business, Uncatered Affair, with a friend from Westport, Connecticut. *That* was prep. The partnership unraveled over issues of control, and now Martha was the manager of a gourmet food business in her town. Her meticulousness won her fans, and one of them signed her up to write a cookbook. *Entertaining* was a smash. More books, and soon products, followed. Out went Andy, though his last name persisted. A brand was born! Stewart has been on a gajillion TV shows, demonstrating her skills in the kitchen, the smokehouse, the abattoir, the garden, and the gift-wrap room. She has become ubiquitous, and when she took her big public fall, she reemerged undaunted and unashamed. She makes workaholics look like slackers. Come to think of it, that's not preppy at all.

John Whitney Stillman (b. January 25, 1952) Whit Stillman is the only writer-director to date who has sensed the drama within a single deb season and known what it was: cinematic gold. Revel in the preppiness of his 1990 film *Met-*

ropolitan: "You don't have to read a book to have an opinion"; "I've always planned to be a failure anyway, that's why I plan to marry an extremely wealthy woman." Stillman has lived in Europe the last dozen or so years. He may no longer even be an auteur, for all we know.

William Oliver Stone (b. September 15, 1946) Possibly the best-known preppy who is a conspiracy theorist, screenwriter, and director, Oliver Stone grew up in New York City. After attending Trinity School (when it was all male, natch), he went on to the Hill School and then to Yale. Alas for Mummy and Daddy Stone (by now divorced), Oliver dropped out of Yale . . . twice. He was inspired by his own drug use when he wrote the screenplays for *Scarface* and *Midnight Express*. No stranger to controversy, Stone's film *JFK* promoted the theories of the obsessed Jim Garrison, the New Orleans DA who believed there was a cover-up. A Vietnam vet, Stone made three movies (as writer-director) set during that war, including his masterpiece, *Platoon*. He wrote and directed *Wall Street* and its sequel, *Wall Street 2: Money Never Sleeps*.

Mary Louise "Meryl" Streep (b. June 22, 1949) is not only our greatest actress; she is *our* greatest actress as well. Raised in Bernardsville, New Jersey, in the heart of horse country, Streep went to Vassar, though she spent a semester at Dartmouth when it was still a men's college. Afterwards, while studying at the Yale School of Drama, she was a standout. Streep, married since 1978 to the same husband (a modern show-business anomaly), has been nominated for more Academy Awards, Golden Globes, Tonys, etc., than anyone else in the industry. She is famous for her meticulous rendering of accents, dialects, and knife skills (see Julia Child, p. 25). However, we welcome her here for appearing to resist the ineffable lure of the plastic surgeon's knife.

Newton Booth Tarkington (July 29, 1869–May 19, 1946) Named for his uncle, California governor Newton Booth, Tarkington was a prolific author of many important American works, some of which have been transformed into classic American movies, such as *The Magnificent Ambersons* and *Alice Adams* (see Katharine Hepburn, p. 40), and others that were not, such as the series about Penrod, a mischievous teenager. After graduating from Exeter, the Hoosier went to Purdue University and after sophomore year transferred to Princeton, where he was  voted the most popular student in the class of 1893. Somehow, though, despite this award and his presidency of the drama club (now the Triangle Club), as well as his membership in the Ivy Club, the prestigious eating club, Tarkington never graduated from Princeton. He did receive two honorary degrees from Princeton, a record he still holds. Having donated the money to build a men's dorm at Purdue, Tarkington Hall, NBT also got an honorary degree from Purdue. He won two Pulitzer Prizes for literature, and ran and served one term in the Indiana House of Representatives. He was a Republican.

James Vernon Taylor (b. March 12, 1948) made his worldwide debut at Massachusetts General Hospital in Boston, as his father was a doctor on staff. In 1953, after the Taylor family had relocated to North Carolina for Dr. Taylor's practice, they began spending their summers on Martha's Vineyard, where "Jamie" Taylor began writing and performing. After a few years at Milton Academy, Taylor returned home to public high school and then signed himself in to McLean Hospital, the noted psychiatric institution affiliated with Mass General and Harvard Medical School. Years lost to depression and serious drug addiction never diminished Taylor's beautiful singing, writing, and performing. Marriage to Carly Simon (Riverdale Country School, Sarah Lawrence) produced a new generation of singer-songwriters, Ben and Sally Taylor. Finally, like many daddies who've been married several times, Taylor became the father of twin boys, Henry and Rufus, at age fifty-three.

Uma Karuna Thurman (b. April 29, 1970) is one of the principal movers within the cadre of bohemian preppies. To know of Uma is to be aware that her father, Robert Thurman, is the Columbia University professor and Buddhist monk who married a former model once married to Timothy Leary. Uma attended the boarding school Northfield Mount Hermon as well as the Professional Children's School in NYC. Instead of graduating from either of them, she was cast in the movie *Dangerous Liaisons*, naked. Uma, what a wild girl you are.

Andrew Previn Tobias (b. April 20, 1947) Youthful-looking author and financial columnist Andy Tobias attended the Horace Mann School when it was still all-male and therefore way more prep. Afterwards he went to Harvard, where he was a president of the Harvard Student Agencies, which among other entrepreneurial ventures publishes the *Let's Go!* travel series that is beloved by the Eurail pass set. By the time he was attending Harvard Business School, he was also contributing articles to *New York* magazine, among others. Tobias has written thirteen books, including *Fire and Ice* and *The Best Little Boy in the World*, which was a fictionalized account of his life growing up gay. It was first released under the pen name of John Reid (don't see John Reed, p. 32) in 1973. It was reissued under his own name and expanded in 1998. Tobias has been the treasurer of the Democratic National Committee since 1999.

Robert Edward "Ted" Turner, III (b. November 19, 1938) The son of privilege, Ted was born in Cincinnati, but his family decamped for Savannah when he was nine. A graduate of McCallie School, he went on to Brown where he studied Classics. His dad, a billboard entrepreneur, reacted to this news by writing his son that he "almost puked." No problem. Ted was expelled when a girl was found in his dorm room. Besides giving the world CNN and all the various Turner cable networks, Turner is outspoken in the extreme. His 590,823-acre ranch in New Mexico is the largest parcel of land in private hands in the United States, and his estancia in Patagonia is 93,900 acres (he owns eleven other ranches). A talented sailor (America's Cup winner) and a philanthropist, he is referred to by his third wife, Jane Fonda (see Jane Fonda, p. 27) as "my favorite ex-husband."

John Hoyer Updike (March 18, 1932–January 27, 2009) Born and raised in Shillington, Pennsylvania, the area and topography he would use as the settings for his major *Rabbit* novels, John Updike was co-valedictorian of Shillington High School. He won a full scholarship to Harvard, where he was president of the Harvard Lampoon and graduated cum laude with a degree in English, and a Radcliffe  wife. At this point Updike dreamt of becoming an artist, and he won a fellowship to study at the Ruskin School of Art at Oxford. He also sold his first short story to *The New Yorker.* In 1955 he was offered a column there, and soon he was able to move to Massachusetts while supporting his family as a writer. This began his long, distinguished, prolific, and rich life as a writer of fiction, poetry, essays, and art criticism, as well as his long association with *The New Yorker*. For all his industry, his reputation and sheer artistry, he remained humble, seeing himself as a chronicler of the "Protestant middle class." He wrote about sex frequently, lustily, as if still a young man. Updike married twice and had four children. He also won the Pulitzer Prize twice, for *Rabbit Is Rich* and *Rabbit at Rest*. In later years, Updike would interrupt his writing day for another passion: twice weekly golf games at Myopia Hunt Club.

Eugene Luther Gore Vidal Jr. (b. October 3, 1925) As the only child of colorful parents, Gore Vidal had a lot to live up to. His father, West Point's first aeronautics instructor, was said to have been Amelia Earhart's great love. The elder Vidal was an all-American quarterback who helped found what became Eastern

Airlines, Northeast Airlines, and TWA. Gore's mother was an actress and socialite who had had a long on-and-off affair with Clark Gable, and who became, through remarriage, distantly related to Jacqueline Bouvier Kennedy. Vidal attended Sidwell Friends School and St. Albans in Washington, D.C., before going off to Exeter. He served with the army during World War Two, and had his first book published at nineteen. Although he is said to have had affairs with women—including Anaïs Nin, and he was once engaged to Joanne Woodward—Vidal has been a public homosexual, and had a fifty-three-year relationship with the late Howard Austen. Vidal has always enjoyed feuds with other intellectuals, including Norman Mailer, but most especially with William F. Buckley Jr. (see William F. Buckley Jr., p. 40), with whom, as co–political commentators for ABC News in 1968, he came to blows.

Vera Ellen Wang (b. June 27, 1949) A stylish Chapin and Sarah Lawrence graduate, Wang grew up in a large apartment on Park Avenue. She began a promising journey as a competitive figure skater but chose to pursue her education instead. After a career in the fashion department of *Vogue*, Wang started her wedding-dress business when she could not find a gown she liked for her own wedding. Now that it's a diversified multimillion-dollar business, brides from Weston, Massachusetts, to Ross, California, depend on her designs, as do smart women dressing up.

Samuel Atkinson Waterston (b. November 15, 1940) On his mother's side, a *Mayflower* descendant, and on his father's, a first-generation American, as his father was born in Scotland. Sam attended the Brooks School in North Andover, Massachusetts, where his father taught, then graduated from Groton. A scholarship student at Yale, he spent his junior year at the Sorbonne. Waterston began his acting career onstage, then moved to film, where, among other roles, he was Nick Carraway in the 1974 production of *The Great Gatsby* (see Bruce Dern, p. 26). Waterston has acted in every it-

eration of *Law & Order*; consequently, he will be in reruns for eternity. He is the eighth cousin four times removed from forty-third president George W. Bush (see George W. Bush, p. 25).

Sigourney Weaver (b. October 8, 1949) was named Susan Alexandra Weaver, but took the name Sigourney after a character in *The Great Gatsby* (see F. Scott Fitzgerald, p. 40) when she felt she was just one of too many Susans (see Stockard Channing,  p. 25) in her classes at the Chapin School and the Ethel Walker School. A graduate of Stanford University and the Yale School of Drama, Weaver comes from parents who also used different names from those they were given. Her mother, Elizabeth, an English actress who was in Hitchcock's *The 39 Steps*, was named Desirée Mary Lucy, and her father, Sylvester, who was chairman of NBC until 1956 and campaigned unsuccessfully for pay TV, was known as Pat. Tall and statuesque, Weaver often portrays patrician women on the big screen.

Edith Wharton (January 24, 1862–August 11, 1937) Born Edith Newbold Jones, the niece of the "keeping up with the Joneses" Jones. To the manor born, young Edith, her two brothers, and her parents lived between New York City; Newport, Rhode Island; and Europe. Like most young girls from her set, she was "educated at home." Although the fact that she published scandalously honest fiction about her world in the closed societies of New York, Newport, and Europe—showing ambition, wit, and intellectual curiosity—would deem her to be unprep, her fearlessness and devotion to detail enable us to forever understand how the upper classes lived, from the end of the nineteenth century to the mid-twentieth century. Wharton won a Pulitzer Prize for *The Age of Innocence* in 1921, the first woman to ever win that award. Wharton died at her home in France in 1937. Serious fans can visit her house in the Berkshires, The Mount.

James Abbott McNeill Whistler (July 11, 1834–July 17, 1903) Born in Lowell, Massachusetts, Whistler attended West Point before going to Europe to become an artist. He studied in France but spent most of his adult life in London. A very social bohemian, he earned hugely negative reaction from critic John Ruskin, who said he "never expected to hear a coxcomb ask two hundred guineas for flinging a pot of paint in the public's face." Whistler sued Ruskin for libel. He won a Pyrrhic victory, netting only one farthing. Whistler was bankrupted by his suit. The artist had a long-standing feud with Oscar Wilde as well. He published a book in 1890 called *The Gentle Art of Making Enemies*. His best-known painting is *Arrangement in Black and Grey: the Artist's Mother*.

Richard Treat Williams (b. December 1, 1951) Named for ancestor Richard Treat, an early settler in Connecticut, Williams grew up in Rowayton, in Fairfield County, and went to the Kent School, all the way in Litchfield County. He studied acting at Franklin & Marshall College in Pennsylvania. Williams was discovered by director Miloš Forman, who cast young Treat as Berger in his great movie musical *Hair*. Like many preppy actors, Williams has performed in *Love Letters* (see A. R. Gurney, p. 28).

Robin McLaurin Williams (b. July 21, 1952) is the only child of Laurie and Robert Williams, a senior car executive in suburban Bloomfield Hills, Michigan. After he attended rather straightlaced Detroit Country Day School, his family moved to looser Marin County, north of San Francisco, which changed his outlook forever. Williams went to Claremont McKenna College in southern California and was accepted to the competitive graduate acting program at Juilliard, run by imposing actor John Houseman. There, rooming with Chris Reeve (see Christopher Reeve, p. 33), Robin developed his "Mork" character. If you look carefully enough, within his portrayal of Mr. Keating in *Dead Poets Society*, there lurks the inner Detroit Country Day stu-

dent. Williams is the best known William F. Buckley impersonator in the world (see William F. Buckley Jr., p. 40).

Thomas Kennerly Wolfe Jr. (b. March 2, 1931) Born in Richmond, Virginia, Tom Wolfe graduated from Washington and Lee University and earned his Ph.D. in American Studies at Yale. He began his career as a journalist, first in Springfield, Massachuetts, then at *The Washington Post* and the *New York Herald Tribune*, which spawned *New York* magazine. Thanks to his incredibly colorful, dialogue-as-sound-effect style, Wolfe was considered more or less to be the first and the principal practitioner of the "new journalism" (see Leonard Bernstein, p. 23). He has subsequently written essays about it and his role in shaping it. Wolfe moved into book-length reporting, including *The Electric Kool-Aid Acid Test*, about Ken Kesey and his "band of merry pranksters," and *The Right Stuff*, about the *Apollo* 7 space launch and the very soul of the space program, which won the National Book Award. Wolfe has turned to fiction in more recent years. His reportage often reads like fiction, and his fiction includes dense reportage (see Master Reading List, p. 180).

Frank Lloyd Wright (June 8, 1867–April 9, 1959) Born in rural Wisconsin, Wright decided as a young boy that he wanted to be an architect. A high-school dropout, he went to work in the engineering department of the University of Wisconsin, where he also attended classes for a  while. At twenty he moved to Chicago, where he became a draftsman and assistant in the flourishing world of high-profile American architecture. Wright vowed to become the greatest architect of all time, and got a head start by working as the chief draftsman of influential architect Louis Sullivan. By 1893, Wright had established his own practice, and he married Catherine Tobin. With a loan from his former boss, Louis Sullivan, the two moved to Oak

Park (now a historic neighborhood, in fact, due to all the houses Wright designed there). His office and staff were downstairs, his growing family of six children lived above. He was considered a pioneer of the Prairie School, which favored low unpainted buildings, natural materials, and many windows and skylights to enhance their natural settings. In 1919 Wright walked out on his family and moved to Berlin with his lover, an intellectual and early feminist who left her family as well. The scandal made it impossible for Wright to get commissions in this country. The couple lived in Europe for a few years, while monographs of his work were published there. They returned to Spring Green, Wisconsin, where his mother's family owned land, and there he established Taliesin, his first academy for aspiring architects. While it was being finished, an employee set the compound on fire, killing several people. Wright rebuilt Taliesin, married two more times, and also built Taliesin West, in Arizona, when the Wisconsin weather proved too harsh. He insisted that all applicants design and build their own shelters, know how to prepare a fine dinner, and, in their own formal clothes, be able to entertain guests. In this way, they would also learn how to comport themselves with future clients. Wright died before the Guggenheim Museum, his final work, opened. The AIA declared him to be the finest American architect of the twentieth century. Of the 1,141 buildings he designed, 532 were completed, 409 of which still stand. More than one-third of them are considered national landmarks.

Louis Auchincloss
1917–2010.

Louis Stanton Auchincloss, who died on January 26, 2010, occupied a special place in the private-school universe. His novel *The Rector of Justin* (1964), based on the life of Groton's Endicott Peabody, is to the American prep school what *Tom Brown's School Days* is to the British public school—the defining text, our best fictional account of the schools of the Anglo ascendancy and the values they embraced.

In many ways Auchincloss himself personified the man these schools hoped to turn out: navy officer, devoted husband and father, East Side society fixture, civic leader (president of the Museum of the City of New York, etc.), white-shoe lawyer (specializing, of course, in trusts and estates)—the life, in short, he was brought up to live. But what hadn't been expected was the range and productivity of his literary life—more than sixty books of fiction and nonfiction—or the sharp, often satirical eye he would cast on the rector's students.

The right address or a lucky inheritance gets no dispensation in an Auchincloss novel. He was interested not only in what people make of their circumstances, but also what they make of themselves. Readers were enticed by the trappings of his privileged world—the Park Avenue apartments, the clubs—but then found themselves in a novel of moral inquiry. How should we live? What are our responsibilities to one another?

In a literary culture that prizes the outsider, even the outlaw, Auchincloss was the consummate insider. The corporate boards, the law firms, the parties that make up his fictional world are drawn with a knowing intimacy. But he doesn't celebrate them; he sees them for what they are, with all their human failings. He was part of the establishment but was never taken in by it, both insider and critic, a literary misfit in a tailored suit. Auchincloss went to Wall Street every working day, but he took the subway. For years a sight familiar to commuters with folded tabloids on the Lexington Avenue line was Auchincloss with his patrician nose in a book—Flaubert, often, in the original French. What would the rector have made of that?

    —JOSEPH KANON (BA, Harvard; MA, Trinity College, Cambridge) was Louis Auchincloss's editor and publisher at Houghton Mifflin

WE DON'T TALK ABOUT IT.

IF YOU KNOW WHAT WE'RE TALKING ABOUT.

The only way not to think about money is to have a great deal of it.
—Edith Wharton, *The House of Mirth*

It is not for lack of funds

that preppies hew strongly to the concept of thrift, though it can be. Remember that the original preppies are descended from Pilgrims: we are sturdy, nature-loving puritans who enjoy the tradition of passing our used garments and silver down the ancestral line. We prefer modest discretion to the outward manifestations of wealth that are the signs of the new hordes. We are also cheap.

Is it better to inherit your money or make it on your own? Depends on the original source. If your money comes from something fundamental, like steel or oil, then your money is clean and pure. Or look at it this way: The dirtier a worker gets unearthing this substance—with the exception of coal—the cleaner the fortune of the well, mine, or quarry owner. If your money comes from other people's money, it is still honorable, as long as you don't own a pawnshop. Let's review: steel, oil, gold. And land. That requires getting dirty, too.

If your money came many generations ago from something a little iffy, such as bootlegged hooch or sanitation services, guns, or pork sausages, you can still be very well off, but you are sensitive when people whisper about the source of your money.

If your money is new (also a relative term, meaning that your daddy earned it, or that it is spent or expressed as if it's new, i.e., too many new cars in the driveway, too many plaques with your name on them at your alma mater, local hospital, library, and the museum), people might presume your money is newer than it is.

If, on the other hand, your money has just always quietly been there . . . if it is a fact of your family's life . . . if you take regular vacations but stay in rooms, not suites . . . if you have a family retainer who has always been with your grandmother and then with your mother . . . if somehow your checking account is never quite empty, never overflowing with funds, then your inheritance is dull enough that it won't cause conversation or jealousy. We can then say it is old enough. The media are responsible for distorting the truth about us. We've all seen the misleading movies and TV shows (see p. 202). Those people with the faux lockjaws emerging from a stretch limousine are not preppies; they are actors. We do not engage stretch limousines. We spend our money in more covert ways: education, a country or beach house (peeling paint and the aroma of off-season mildew are entirely acceptable), and travel.

As you get acclimated, you will understand our logic.

PRIORITIES.

PRIVATE EDUCATION.

Worth it. Worth every penny. You don't have to spend your entire precollegiate life in private school, and in fact, after the first three suspensions or "misunderstandings," you may not have that choice. But preppies believe in the opportunities afforded by a competitive, historic, and tradition-filled school that cannot be found elsewhere. Here is the guarantee that you will be surrounded by other preps. Here is the comfort of knowing that the Field House was paid for in part by Great-grandfather's little oil business when you are late again for curfew. Here is the security of seeing Mummy's maiden name on the wall of the Great Hall. Here is your path to future successes and prosperity. Here is the feeder school to the Ivy League. Here is a great crest you can wear on your pinkie or on your sweatpants. Here is a provenance you can use your entire life (as your children will eventually do themselves), that gives you that certain patina of knowingness. Must we go on?

If compromises need to be made, make sure your parents live in a town or city with remarkable public schools. This may mean a Chicago or Boston suburb. Move. If there is no appealing day school in your neighborhood, apply to boarding school. Take advantage of the generous financial-aid grants offered. Otherwise, living remotely from the East Coast in a college or university town is the closest thing you have to a guarantee of Eastern Liberal Arts College placement.

SECOND HOME.

A second house isn't a trophy. It is a guarantee ensuring you are at ease in the ultimate playground of prepdom, Nature herself. Depending on where your place is, you will learn skills indigenous to your community: sailing, tennis, golf, skiing, snowboarding, antiquing, gardening, biking, bartending, snowshoeing, swimming, hiking, squash, surfing, Nordic skiing, tailgating, soccer, touch football, softball, golf-cart polo, sunbathing, drinking at bonfires—these are all useful talents to cultivate in your youth. We especially value any recreation that uses specific equipment; tennis is more prep than a spin class because it requires you to own a tennis racquet. Equipment is important, because like your dogs, it stays in the back of the car or in the mudroom. It is important because it makes you a desirable guest for weekends at other people's houses.

This second house can be bought, or you can live on a compound with your parents or grandparents. There is always the chance, especially if you are an only child, that you will inherit the property or lose it to taxes. Let your elders know how much you love their summer place; how you feel so much more alive there than you do in your city railroad flat with illegal cable that you rent with a roommate who pays you off the books. If you have siblings who move far away, say, to Colorado or Portland, Oregon, you also have a good chance of inheriting the old pile, since you love the region more than your brother does. It is never too early to start working this angle. We recommend you bring it up at Grandparents' Day at nursery school.

There is practically no such thing as a too-shabby beach house. If the paint peels, if the furniture is scraped, if the fridge is old, if the bathrooms predate "spa bathrooms," so much the better. (Remember: Old is preppier than new.) You can always throw sheets over the couches, add a nautical print or some framed photographs . . . It looks exactly like it always did, only now you've personalized it. The shells used to hold candy and keys; you found them yourself!

Although preppies favor bright colors, you might see that the interiors of your second house are beigey and colorless. That is because your upholstery fabrics and wallpapers are old and sun-bleached. Excellent! Do not rush to redecorate. This is authentic prep. You couldn't buy properly aged furnishings as beautifully made as the old odds and ends that come with the house.

Unless the house or its land is substantial enough, do not name your house. However, if it comes with a name, by all means order letterpress stationery with that name on it, and use it for your many correspondences.

You can keep an old car there, the one you would never take on the highway, the one that somehow remains sandy, with years and years of beach permit stickers on the rear left window that block visibility. It will always have an errant flip-flop in the back, a golf umbrella, and a golf ball or two, perhaps a dead tennis ball.

TRAVEL.

We travel, and we're rather good at it. Some of us travel from a very early age, even if it's just back and forth from Princeton to Newport. We may travel to see relatives, to take a semester away, or to go to rehab. We go to Europe because it's there, and there is so very much to learn from Europeans.

In Europe, we learn how to kiss people on both cheeks, how to do math when we convert the dollar to the euro, and how to make ourselves understood in adverse conditions. We get to practice the little bits of foreign languages we've retained from school and to see that Italian men can carry off the sweater-around-their-shoulders look easily. While we do not encourage smoking, when in Budapest and all that.

PREP TRAVEL COMMANDMENTS.

1. Thou shalt not fly first class.

2. Thou shalt use thy frequent-flier miles whenever possible.

3. Thou mayest fly business class if thy destination is more than five hours away.

4. On board, the wine will not be fine; therefore, drinkest beer or spirits.

5. *Naturellement*, thou never wearest shorts, sweatpants, or flip-flops on an airplane, and thou shalt attempt not to sit next to a miscreant in such garments.

6. If thou takest a sleeping pill, thou must try not to snore, Pookie.

7. Thou must not complain about jet lag.

8. Thou must take loads of photographs.

9. Thou art encouraged to rent cars in strange places and get into colorful misunderstandings with local drivers.

10. If there is a Harry's Bar at thy destination, thou should eat there. (Try the carpaccio and the cannelloni.)

11. Exotic locations are to be encouraged.

12. Thou must tryest not to lose thy passport, but, indeed, it could happen and will provide dinner-table fodder for many happy years to come.

13. Although thou art traveling in order to "broaden thy horizons" and meet different kinds of people, thou will prefer looking up friends of friends who are also traveling.

14. Thou shalt tryest the tonic water in other lands, as it tastes different from thy domestic tonic water.

15. Thou willst always have (had) a wonderful time.

Our private economic code is again useful when on the road. We do not waste money on first-class travel. Unless McKinsey or Aunt Toot is footing the bill, we fly coach. (On the other hand, it would be rude to turn down a no-expense upgrade.) It is consistent with everything we've been talking about. Why spend a fortune on first-class air travel? On the other hand, we have been known to splurge on luxury hotels. Wouldn't it be better to apply those savings to a wonderful room in a wonderful hotel? (Or at the very least, a small room facing a wall in a wonderful hotel?)

If you cannot stay at the wonderful hotel with the famous bar, you must at least drink at the famous bar. Lunch is also lovely there. During holiday, we always drink at lunch, and of course, we "walk it off." Lunchtime drinking is not an obligation, but, well, yes it is. You're on vacation, the ultimate in prep experiences!

We try to squeeze some work or school time in between vacations if we can.

Luggage: You do not need to invest in designer luggage. What you carry should be made by a manufacturer of suitcases, not, say, a fashion runway designer. (Do you think Diane von Furstenberg or Nicole Miller or even the current Burberry spends any time whatsoever personally designing the luggage line that bears its logo?) What you carry should be sturdy, no uglier than all the other black nylon bags on wheels, and be properly marked as yours. Rather than spell out your name in duct tape, a colorful luggage tag should suffice. If you spend year after year vacationing at the same wonderful resort and your luggage generally has an easy shelf life, you might consider looking into

the canvas and leather-trimmed pieces made by T. Anthony.

They may not last a whole lifetime, but they are **TPFW** (too prep for words). They are expensive but can be imprinted with your initials for free.

T. ANTHONY.

Until the 1940s in the United States, if you went on a trip (no Disney or Las Vegas then!), you bought luggage at department stores. There was some ready-made, but most likely, you ordered it bespoke. In the era before populist air travel, the well-heeled flew, sailed, or took trains with piles and piles of suitcases, hard-sided hat boxes, and matching pieces of all shapes and uses.

That's why they invented porters.

We've all seen pictures of elegant old trunks, fitted to the exact dimensions of Fred Astaire's shoes or Bette Davis's gowns, or Grandmother Putnam's golf clubs. Think of the visuals for *On the Twentieth Century.*

In 1946, Anthony T. Froitzheim, a former luggage salesman at Saks Fifth Avenue and a cosmetic-case designer for Elizabeth Arden, opened his own shop in New York, called T. Anthony (it was just after World War Two, and German names weren't commercial), way uptown in the East 60s, a residential neighborhood. He made hard-sided, classically simple leather luggage, and hard-sided canvas and leather "packing cases," as they prefer to call them. (They also sell Dopp kits, jewelry boxes, wallets, photo albums, backgammon and chess boards, and more.)

That very luggage is still available today. T. Anthony occupies just one store, now at 445 Park Avenue. But it has a loyal following around the world, through mail order and now the Interthingy.

The first canvas was black with tan leather trim. It was followed by bright blue, then red with black leather trim, which was created for. Marilyn Monroe. Now T. Anthony offers black canvas with white leather trim. Très moderne.

Michael Root, the grandson of Mr. Froitzheim, has been the president of T. Anthony since 1998. He assures us that though very much a "niche" business, T. Anthony has no plans to "pack it in." Still offering great service, on-the-spot engraving (embossing initials for no charge, either in gold or without color), and discretion, T. Anthony has customers who want to "fill in their luggage collections" or start anew. Yes, there is nylon, and yes, there are wheels, but for old-school preppies, there's nothing like a set of matching packing cases from T. Anthony.

And yes, you can FedEx them to the ski slopes or fill them with your Vilbrequin and ship them to Anguilla.

PREP ATTITUDES TOWARDS CASH.

Although the first ATM (automated teller machine) was installed in America in 1969, preppies are still often a little short of cash. Is it too much trouble to find an ATM machine? (Note: Calling it an "ATM machine" is redundant, but we do it anyway.) Have we forgotten our password? Damn it, did we forget our card somewhere last night? Did you just leave money for the cleaning lady? These are all viable reasons that may explain why we are undersupplied. Perpetually. You might want to do some work to come up with new excuses of your very own.

It's not having money that matters, it's being near money that matters. You don't need a private jet, but it is lovely to have friends who do. This doesn't mean you should solicit friends on the basis of who has what—you're not setting up your sophomore-year dormitory suite, after all. Nor do you choose friends based on who has the biggest house—unless you want to count Candy Spelling or Ira Rennert as a close friend.

Preppy math.

1. It costs $82.50 to buy a ticket to a James Taylor concert on the tenth of next month at the Fox Theatre in Saint Louis. If you wait until the night of the concert, you might find a scalper who will sell you a ticket for $100 or more. You are hoping that since it is last-minute, you'll be able to persuade the seller that in a free market, the ticket has now declined in value, and offer him 20 percent less than the printed price. Right or wrong?
Wrong. You are hoping when you arrive at the theater, you will bump into Lulee and her sister—no, the older one—who will give you their extra ticket and buy you a beer during intermission.

2. Which costs less: two Big Macs for the price of one with a coupon at McDonald's or three grams of caviar from the gourmet store?
Too easy. You've been eating the caviar during the caviar promotion at Marche Artisan Foods (1000 Main Street, East Nashville, Tennessee 37206) as you circle around with your shopping cart to buy a single French baguette. Total price for the Big Macs: $3.19. Price for the baguette: $2.50. The osetra? Priceless.

3. You have a $30 credit at Under the Palm Tree (4823 West 119th Street, Overland Park, Kansas 66209). You want to redeem it. What do you use it for?
A. A gift for Aunt Bunny's sixty-fifth birthday—that cute pink webbed belt with the golden turtle buckle. It goes with everything she has, and costs $45—on sale from $78.
B. A teeny Lilly Pulitzer bathing suit for your newborn stepsister, Allegra. Irresistible at $40.
C. A pair of pink, aqua, and lime-green Capri pants that look like everything else in your closet. $120.
The answer is C. You can't buy Aunt Bunny a present that was on sale. Allegra doesn't need a stupid bathing suit, and besides, she might outgrow it before she can wear it . . . and she'll never know the difference. The Capris? You love!!! You'll wear them forever! Now they only cost $90 with your credit, so they are a steal.

4. Your friend Win mentions that he and some friends from work will be watching the Masters Tournament at his house, and you are welcome to stop by. As you are heading over, you receive a text from Win that he underestimated the size of the group, and could you please bring more alcohol? You are right near the Stop & Shop. Do you buy: two six-packs of Stella Artois ($16) or a bottle of The Glenrothes single-malt scotch ($49)?
You buy both.

47

Cheapness of All Kinds.

You have just inherited a six-story prewar building in a gentrifying neighborhood of Los Angeles from an aunt you never quite knew. Real-estate brokers are already hovering nearby before you even take possession of it. This is the kind of windfall that people dream about. What do you do with your new fortune? You put it in the bank, and as it grows slowly, you continue to pry off postage stamps that have been unmarked by the postal service, reuse manila envelopes from your lawyer's office, save paper clips that come in the mail, and use your child's rollover minutes on the phone. Why change now?

When Jacqueline Kennedy Onassis (Miss Porter's School, 1947) died in 1994, leaving an estate of approximately $200 million, her children culled through her things and sold many pieces at auction at Sotheby's in New York City. Items ranged from one of her late husband's desks to the common woven baskets used by florists to give arrangements a countrified look. She saved them, and they did indeed sell. So before you throw out your useless detritus, think first: Will you one day become famous enough for your children to make money from your junk? Will you marry the future President? Will *you* be President one day? As they say on commercials for the New York State Lottery, "You never know."

Cheapness begins at home, but it is portable, as is generosity, its virtuous twin. It is rare that a preppy considers himself cheap to begin with. He sees himself as evenhanded and appropriate, though to be fair, with all the sailing and cocktails and tennis and ski weekends, do you actually think Trip sits down to calculate how many dinners or drinks or tickets or

tabs he paid compared to any of his friends? Of course not! He is too busy enjoying life to be an accountant. And if you point it out to him, he'll feel sheepish and pay for drinks or dinner or the movies next time you go out, and then who knows? You can be frugal and generous at the same time. The lesson here? Give your friends the shirts off your backs, but wear them out first.

Frugal Do's and a Frugal Don't.

Do keep repairing old appliances to try to extend their lives. Don't store them on your front porch or driveway. Invest in great-fitting, well-made shoes. (Italian-made shoes are nice.) Your feet will thank you. Keep resoling them. Subscribe to a concert, opera, or ballet series. Buy season tickets to basketball. Pairs of tickets you can't use make great no-occasion gifts. Some nonprofit institutions accept them as tax-deductible donations. Buy very cheap plane tickets to Europe on discounted Web sites. Stay at your friend's grand villa for three weeks. Oh, make it four. Buy him a house gift and pay for dinner a couple of times. Let him win one tennis match every now and then. Complain about the heat.

Have your trustee dump an allowance in your checking account every month. If you can't get your newsstand or barber to accept a check for cash, walk seven blocks out of your way (or drive, if necessary) to the ATM of your bank, so you are not charged that extra $1.95 to $3 withdrawal fee. Leave the office a little early to take the off-peak commuter train. (Even though you live in one of the ten most affluent zip codes in the United States.)

Wherefore the second home?

The preppiest Hampton? Mark Hampton, though he was a Hoosier decorator who was raised on a farm. These days if you want to live surrounded by the combination of good zoning and familiar neighbors, look elsewhere. Perhaps look for a town with a general store instead of one with its own branch of Dior. Or Tiffany. Or Gucci. Preppies are decisive in their wanting to live amongst other preppies but are ambivalent about money, so they prefer to settle someplace undervalued and less glamorous than the Hamptons.

However, if you like, consider "Pine Coast" the preppiest of all the Hamptons. ("Pine Coast" could be on Long Island, but it could also be in Delaware, North or South Carolina, Georgia, Colorado, Idaho, Wyoming, California, or Washington State. "Pine Coast" could be somewhere along the Croisette in the South of France, in Dorset, England, or near Porto Ercole in Italy. If "Pine Coast" is in Europe, call it something else, like "Le Cadeau.") This is where the family home has been deeded to you in the will, and therefore, it is a great place to summer. Even if it's near the epicenter of the P. Diddy, Paris Hilton, Lizzie Grubman re-

sort, those people can be shut out for more low-key neighbors and pastimes. There are still plenty of restricted clubs to join, plenty of tennis courts that insist on tennis whites, and beautiful large families that colonize compounds of their very own.

These Hamptonites don't go to store openings or to restaurants or to movie premieres. They eat at home or at their friends' houses. They enjoy a simple cookout. In fact, their lives are so circumscribed by their inherited community, you might say these preppies are practically invisible. You might see one or two on the train or on the bus, but in transit they wear protective coloration. Once they arrive at their destination, they disappear until the next commute.

GATED COMMUNITIES.

If you think these are preppy, you are wrong. Aside from Tuxedo Park and a few others from another time, to us gated properties suggest assisted living, retirement communities, condo clusters with shared pools and recreational centers, or Sun City. If we live somewhere that is actually exclusive, its barriers are virtual, its constituency self-selecting. If your Pine

Coastal house is already stone-walled and gated, so be it, but to put in an electric gate seems a bit *de trop,* doesn't it? We don't think the average burglar population has a keen appreciation for old glass vases, warped wooden tennis racquets, or Deerfield yearbooks.

MOUNTAINS, LAKES, OR BEACHES?

Preppies love everything about water: swimming in it, surfing in it, skiing in it, drinking it, bathing in it, throwing the dogs in it, rowing in it, sailing in it, splashing a little in their scotch, showering, especially in an outdoor shower near the pool or behind the house.

Lake types are incredibly partisan to lakes. They love their private docks; they love rowing to their boathouses for barbecues in the summer, or swimming to the floating raft; and they're surprisingly game when it comes to the water snakes or—in the Adirondacks—the bears and blackflies; in winter they love skating on the black ice. While you can, of course, have your own swimming pool built on your mountain-adjacent property, or bike to the lake, or join a swimming club, it is preppier to live near a beach. Nothing says summer like saltwater-perfumed air. How else are you going to get sand into the crevices of your thick summer paperback? And after all, hydrangeas don't flourish near chlorine.

Pools, Lakes, or Oceans?

Lakes are preppier than pools. Real lakes are made by nature. Real lakes, as noted, have yucky lake bottoms, occasionally with leeches and snapping turtles. Some lakes never warm up during the summer, because they are surrounded by tall, dark pines. If you want the real, unequivocal answer, oceans are preppier. Because they are natural and uncontrollable, and offer very short seasons in which to swim. You can do your best, but you can't swim laps like a self-improvement nut. Oceans have waves, jellyfish, beach glass, fish. They are influenced by jetties, the moon, and the club's beach committee.

The 41 Preppiest Places to Have a Summer House.

The Adirondacks
Annapolis
Aspen
Block Island
Cap d'Antibes
Chatham
Corfu
Dark Harbor
Deer Isle
Deer Valley
Fishers Island
Harbor Point
Hilton Head
Hyannis
Hydra
Jackson Hole
Jupiter Island
Lake Geneva
Lake Tahoe
Lenox
Locust Valley
Mabou Mines
Martha's Vineyard
Millbrook
Montauk
Nantucket
Newport
Northeast Harbor
Oxfordshire
Oyster Bay
Point of Pines
Porto Ercole
Saint-Rémy
Santa Barbara
Santa Cruz
Southampton
Spetses
Suburbs of Siena
Sun Valley
Todi
⟵ Watch Hill

Because We Are Givers.

The charity circuit is the perfect excuse for getting dressed up and, like Lily Bart, putting on one's best face. For preppies, there are several important events in the annual calendar, and otherwise, one doesn't have to don black tie (unless a friend is being honored by a nonprofit you never supported and you are obligated to attend).

The actual beneficiaries of the charity events may not be of any significance to the guests; the party's history and the party's constituents are what matter. If the event sponsors medical research, the fewer reminders of sick people the better, though it may be what Uncle Harry died of. If it supports inner-city charities, however, the guests love to feel empathetic and are moved by being thanked for their good work by some of the organization's offspring. If the party benefits an organization in the arts or the environment, so much the better, as there is nothing sad, poor, sick, or "needy" to confront.

If you haven't guessed, the point is to again (or still) be with the Morses, who you would see anyway, if you didn't go to these big parties. Your husband doesn't mind the circuit because he can hang with Sheldon or Dickie from the Exchange. He might even be able to get a fourth for the weekend or a piece of business. They get points for attending these events and therefore won't have to accompany their wives to the Whites for the reading from Pauline's book on fifteenth-century calligraphy in Persia.

The real giving, of course, happens not through ticket sales, silent auctions, loud auctions, raffles, journal ads, or anything that occurs at a party, though benefits these days can raise sums in the seven figures. It is a dignified tradition among those who have much to give back. Starting at the turn of the twentieth century, families of means established foundations that have nurtured all kinds of advances in scientific, medical, and cultural causes—even land use. The nicest and preppiest of the foundations do their work in relative quiet.

THE PARTICULARS.

BOSTON

February
• Boys & Girls Clubs of Boston annual dinner
April
• Art in Bloom gala, Boston Museum of Fine Arts
• Vincent Club annual spring luncheon
May
• Emerald Necklace Party in the Park (like the "Hat luncheon" in New York, it celebrates Frederick Law Olmsted's "only intact linear park")

• Newton Wellesley Hospital gala
• Wellesley Hills Junior Women's Club annual Kitchen Tour
June
• The One Hundred Dinner, Massachusetts General Hospital Cancer Center
August
• Dana Farber Cancer Center Pan Mass Challenge (huge bike-a-thon from west of Boston to Provincetown)

September
- Brigham and Women's Hospital In Party

November
- Kenneth B. Schwartz Cancer Center dinner ("usually gets 1,000 people")

December
- Beth Israel Deaconess Medical Center dinner
- Boston Symphony Orchestra

CHARLESTON
Two seasons: February through mid-June; September-December.

February
- Charleston Ballet Theatre Oscar Gala
- Dee Norton Lowcountry Children's Center Chart a Course for Children event
- La Dolce Vita annual auction benefiting the Spoleto Festival USA Orchestra

September-October
- Fall Tours of Homes and Gardens benefiting the Preservation Society of Charleston (their foremost annual fund-raising event)

October
- American College of the Building Arts Red Party
- Historic Charleston Foundation

CHICAGO

April
- Joffrey Ballet of Chicago (it moved there from New York in 1995) annual gala
- Museum of Contemporary Art performance gala

September
- Chicago Botanic Garden Harvest Ball
- Women's Programs at Northwestern Medical Center: The Evergreen Horse Show
- After School Matters annual gala, featuring teenagers who have benefited from after-school programs; very dear to Mayor and Mrs. Daley
- Rush–Presbyterian–St. Luke's Medical Center fashion show

October
- The Primo Center for Women and Children Red Hot Gala

NEW YORK

January
- Winter Antiques Show Opening Night Party

February
- Young Fellows Ball at the Frick Museum
- Museum of the City of New York Director's Council Winter Ball

March
- Associates Committee of the Society of Memorial Sloan-Kettering Cancer Center Annual Bunny Hop
- Private School Fundraisers

April
- Spring Gala, the New York City Ballet

May
- The Frederick Law Olmstead in Central Park Luncheon—"The Hat Lunch" held at the Conservancy Garden (big hats prevail; attendance is 85 percent female)
- The Frick Museum May Dance ("Free with membership, so the perfect preppy party.")
- Memorial Sloan Kettering Spring Ball

June
- New York Botanical Garden Ball
- Museum of Modern Art Party in the Garden

September
- New Yorkers for Children Gala
- Metropolitan Opera Opening Night Gala

November
- Opening night of the New York City Ballet
- Opening night of American Ballet Theater

December
- New York Botanical Garden Winter Wonderland Ball ("Junior event. Husbands complain bitterly about the trip up and back.")

PALM BEACH
Season: February-May, except for the Coconuts New Year's Eve dance at the Flagler Museum.

February
- The Flagler Museum's Whitehall Society—Dancing After Dark. Younger Event in Palm Beach ("a relative term here")

March
- Boys & Girls Clubs of Palm Beach County—Barefoot on the Beach
- Young Friends of the Historical Society of Palm Beach—Evening on Antique Row

April
- The Garden Club Small Flower Show

May
- The Preservation Foundation of Palm Beach's May Garden Party

PHILADELPHIA

January
- The Academy of Music Anniversary Concert and Ball, Philadelphia Orchestra

March
- The Philadelphia Flower Show

May/June
- The Bryn Mawr Hospital's Devon Horse Show and Country Fair

June
- Zoobilee, Philadelphia Zoo

November
- Philadelphia Museum of Art Craft Show, Philadelphia Museum of Art
- Your child's prep-school benefits

SAN FRANCISCO

January
- The Benefactor Dinner, San Francisco Ballet ("You need to be a 'great Benefactor' in order to sit in the City Hall Rotunda for the pre-dinner. Don't go if you can only afford the side courts.")

April
- Director's Circle Dinner, SFMoMA
- Zoo-fest, SF Zoo

August
- Speaker Nancy Pelosi's annual dinner for the Speaker's Cabinet is $30,000 a couple; held at Ann Getty's house
- Save the Lake benefit luncheon in Tahoe; fashion show by Oscar de la Renta

September
- Patrons' Dinner, San Francisco Symphony Opening Night Gala—sit in the patrons' tents.
- Opera Ball, San Francisco Opera—season opening, sit in patrons' tents

October
- Hardly Strictly Bluegrass Festival—founded and fully funded by billionaire banker Warren Hellman, so it is not a fund-raiser; open to the public; gets about 750,000 people; must have VIP friends and family passes
- Enterprise, a youth job-training center's annual fall antiques show ("Buy the top ticket, which gets you in a couple of hours before the climbers. A biggie.")

November
- San Francisco Free Clinic—the Luncheon ("especially important for Nancy Pelosi to come by your table to say hi")
- Golden Gate National Park
- Your children's independent school's dinner auction

Crazy, Hairy Money.

The fellows known as Larry and Sergey (pictured) started Google while graduate students at Stanford; its original address was google@stanford.edu. A mathematician and computer scientist, Larry had an idea (for which he recruited his friend Sergey) to combine all Web pages into one digital library that was based on numbers of views per page and algorithms, and even in its simplest closest-to-English *I Can Read*–level explanation, the basic history of the formulas that made the company is somewhat unintelligible to the art and English majors behind *True Prep*.

This much we know. The company was founded on September 7, 1998. By August 19, 2004, the date of the company's initial public offering, 900 millionaires were born, some worth multimillions on paper. The stock opened at $85 a share, closed at $100 that day, and has slid between $283 and $630 per share in 2010.

Silicon Valley has long been familiar with the haphazardly or geeky rich. (Indeed, they are indigenous to the region, with Apple, Google, Yahoo!, eBay, etc., all local petri dishes.) What makes these millionaires different from the garden variety of American millionaires (bankers, CEOs, musicians, ne'er-do-wells) is that you cannot look at them and know they have money.

Most pictures of Larry and Sergey are of men in T-shirts and baggy jeans. Most pictures of Bill Gates, Paul Allen, Steve Ballmer, Steve Jobs, Jeff Bezos, Larry Ellison, and their ilk are of guys in open-necked sports shirts and jeans (or black turtlenecks, in Jobs's instance). If their images weren't so well disseminated, you might think they were still beer-drinking, animation-loving, *Avatar*-obsessed fraternity boys. They all have jets and backpacks. They wear Tevas. They drive expensive hybrids with incredible stereo systems. When there are wives, they are mostly fresh-faced. Some, like the inventor of Facebook, Mark Zuckerberg (see the Timeline, p. 235), graduated from Exeter. (He launched Facebook as a kind of techy prank for his friends at Harvard. True.) Mostly, though, this cohort (one of their words) is not preppy, but they do resemble preppies in a significant way.

According to *The New York Times*, the motivation to go to work in the high-tech world isn't filthy lucre. " 'It isn't considered "Googley" to check the stock price,' said an engineer, using the Google jargon for what is acceptable in the company's culture. 'As a result, there is a bold insistence, at least on the surface, that the stock price does not matter,' said the engineer, who did not want to be named because it is considered unseemly to discuss the price."

If you would like to know if you are in the presence of engineery wealth, we suggest you take your mountain bike to northern California. While in Palo Alto or Sausalito, Woodside or San Rafael, check out the locals who wear baggy shorts or trousers and unfortunate shoes. If they are pale, eureka!

There's money,

Once upon a time, nice people did not speak of money. Daddy went to an office. No one really had a clue what he did there. He sold things. He bought things. He built things. He traded things. He went out to lunch. The three times we met his secretary, Rosemary, she was very nice to us and let us use the stapler and copy machine as much as we liked.

Was there a lot of money? Who knew? There was enough. We went on vacations. There was always some staff working in the house. Still, we were often cautioned to save our allowance and not spend it all on some dumb thing, like ice cream from the truck on the way home from school.

Did we have a driver? No. A plane? No! Who ever heard of a thing like that? Did Mummy have a stylist, a nutritionist, and a personal shopper? No, she did not. She had her own style, and she went to the hairdresser pretty frequently and got a new mink stole every few years, but no one talked about it. Life was pleasant and private. Nannies did not come on vacation with the family, since the point was spending time as a family. Personal trainers and even SAT tutors weren't in evidence then . . . Since they weren't invented, no one needed them yet.

Then Ronald Reagan became president while *Dynasty*, *Dallas*, and *Falcon Crest* were hits on TV. Everyone adored John Forsythe as the limousine-taking, tuxedo-wearing, mansion-dwelling oil tycoon Blake Carrington. Rich was fun! It didn't help things that this was the exact moment that Donald Trump announced himself with his brass and crystal and marble structures all T'd out till kingdom come.

What happened? Suddenly it wasn't enough to drink vodka; you had to drink Ketel One or Stoli. You couldn't drink champagne; it had to be Cristal. Brand names were used in polite company. And smart people like you joined in because you wanted to fall in step. Your car wasn't in the shop; your Mercedes was getting fixed. You didn't wear shoes; you wore Manolos. *Sex and the City* made it safe to be a profligate clotheshorse, and worse, a label slave. (In the show, women—whom we were supposed to believe had accomplishments and careers of importance—could weep with joy for certain designer handbags. Whole plots revolved around expensive accessories.) That certainly didn't help. You wanted everyone to know you were flying out of Teterboro, so they knew you had a G5 of

then there's big money.

your very own (or a fractional ownership, but still . . .). And houses! Whoa! Was it in Greenwich that *The New York Times* said, without a Dumpster parked in front of your house, you felt like a have-not? No extensive renovations for you? No screening room, sauna, or chapel in your McMansion? Well, certainly a room for the masseuse who comes weekly. America had known its share of giant estates and white elephants. Asheville, Hearst Castle, Mar-a-Lago, Pocantico—all from a more gracious if still ostentatious time. But now there are aerial views of houses that resemble full campuses and resorts. For a family of three! Sixteen thousand square feet of indoor space. An extra garage for the extra cars that are never driven. Full-sized basketball courts. Indoor and outdoor pools. Upstairs kitchens, so no one has to go downstairs if they want a snack.

In a word, it was gross.

Currently, during the extended, um, "market correction," people with money have tried to tone down their materialism. Mrs. Richard Fuld, wife of the Lehman Brothers rascal, shopped over Christmas

2009 with plain brown shopping bags so people wouldn't see her expensive brands. Others, more sensible, have begun to "shop in their closets," take "staycations," and are even depilating at home for the first time.

But if you are not suffering with the markets, follow the lead of Bill and Melinda Gates, or the Tisch family, and start your own foundation. Being philanthropic is the 2010s' answer to Dumpsters on the front lawn and enormous gourmet kitchens.

Buy some land and quietly donate it to your local land trust or the national parks. Or endow a sixth-grade class in the "I Have a Dream" project, and pay for tutors for underprivileged kids until they graduate from high school. Or give money to The Mount, Edith Wharton's Berkshire home, which could use your donations.

Whatever you do, whatever you decide, please don't announce that you want to "give back in the time I have left." That's a cliché.

And don't hire Rod Stewart, Michael Bolton, Elton John, or Céline Dion to entertain at your sixtieth birthday. It's been done.

The Building at School with
Grandmother's Name on It.

It appears that the first naming opportunity in North America occurred on May 14, 1607, when English settlers organized themselves as the residents of the Jamestown Settlement Colony, in what became Virginia. King James I put the James in Jamestown, as well as in the James River.

Since then, practically anything can be named: a museum, a library, a hospital, a college, a road, a field house, a museum wing, a dormitory, a lounge, a seat at the symphony, an endowed chair, or, at Brown University, for the sum of $100,000, "name a lane in the new swimming pool." Add $700,000 to your gift and you can name the lecture hall in Rhode Island Hall after whomever or whatever you like.

Yale University, née Yale College, got its name from one Elihu Yale, in 1718. According to the university's official history, Mr. Yale, a Welshman, had "donated the proceeds from the sale of nine bales of goods together with 417 books and a portrait of King George I." His sons probably had no trouble gaining admission into the school in New Haven.

Harvard University's main library, the Harry Elkins Widener Memorial Library, was given to the university by his mummy, Eleanor Elkins Widener, in her son's memory. Harry, who graduated in 1907, died on the *Titanic*. Before his voyage, he would talk about his plan to donate his own books to Harvard when the university built a bigger, better library than the one in the basement in Gore Hall that was used during his tenure there. Widener opened in 1915, with more than fifty miles of shelves. It has been expanded, modernized, renovated, and improved several times since then, and is still the flagship library of all Harvard.

Payne Whitney, after whom the Payne Whitney Psychiatric Clinic and the Yale University gym are named, was in fact Mr. William

Payne Whitney, a Groton and Yale graduate (and a Bonesman). It is said he inherited almost $65 million from his uncle alone (about $600+ million today). In 1923 he donated $12 million to the New York Public Library (the equivalent of $153,336,568.05 in 2010 dollars), and at his death in 1927, $20 million to New York Hospital ($244,010,169.49 in 2010), specifically for its psychiatric facility, which grew to be one of the most important in this country. There was a great deal of interest in why Mr. Whitney would associate his name in perpetuity to a "mental hospital," the same institution which inspired books recommended in our Master Reading List (see p. 180, *The Group* and *My First Cousin Once Removed*).

Philanthropist and statesman Andrew W. Mellon wanted to help establish a major art museum in Washington, which he thought our capital needed. In 1930 and 1931, Mellon bought twenty-one paintings from Leningrad's Hermitage Museum, including works by Rembrandt, Raphael, and van Eyck for more than $6.6 million (or $87,184,378.88 today). He was prepared to donate his collection to what he hoped would become the National Gallery. President Franklin D. Roosevelt advised his Congress to accept the gift, and so it did on March 24, 1937, as part of the Smithsonian Institution. Mellon commissioned John Russell Pope to design the building along the Mall near Capitol Hill. Andrew Mellon died less than three months after construction began. John Pope died less than twenty-four hours later. When the National Gallery was dedicated in 1941, Mellon's son Paul (see Bunny Mellon, p. 30) gave the building and his family's exceptional art collection to the United States.

Not all donations are preppy. In 1718, Mr. Yale might have been rewarded without asking for the college to bear his name. (And it goes without saying that Eli is a nickname for

Yalies.) But these days modesty has left the building (along with Elvis).

When Stephen A. Schwarzman, a Yale graduate, pledged $100 million to the New York Public Library in 2008, negotiations on signage were extensive. New York City has had two major libraries since the nineteenth century. In 1849, the Astor Library was opened as a reference library with a $400,000 bequest ($11,111,111 today) from John Jacob Astor, who was, at his death the year before, "the wealthiest man in America." It was located on Astor Place, in downtown Manhattan. The Lenox Library was given to New York by James Lenox in the space that became the Frick Mansion on East 71st Street. It was filled with rare books, including the first Gutenberg Bible on this continent. By 1886, former governor Samuel J. Tilden had donated $2.4 million ($57 million currently) to establish a library and reading room for the city.

In 1895, the powers-that-be agreed to combine the Astor and Lenox collections with the Tilden money to form the New York Public Library. Its location on Fifth Avenue between 40th and 42nd streets, where it has presided ever since, was then a reservoir. Its cornerstone was laid in 1902. The library was dedicated by President Taft in May of 1911, and the very next day, when it was finally opened to the public, between 30,000 and 50,000 visitors arrived (in 2010 population, that would be between 30,000 and 50,000 people).

Now the Main Library—with all of its history and Beaux-Arts splendor—is part of the Stephen A. Schwarzman Building.

3.

THAT'S WHERE MY BROTHER WENT.

SCHOOLS.

*Life is the only real counselor; wisdom unfiltered through personal experience
does not become a part of the moral tissue.*
—Edith Wharton, *Sanctuary*

Fewer than one percent

of the secondary-school population board, where they live with their friends and their English teachers, their choral directors and their soccer coaches. In fact, the number is closer to two-tenths of 1 percent. There are approximately 17 million high-school students in the United States, and 35,000 of them are enrolled in college preparatory boarding schools.

We admit we got a leg up, maybe two legs up, when we were sent by our parents to prep school. But for the record, it is not just the lifelong ability to be able to say, "While I was at Farmington" or "At Brooks, we . . ." or "The art collection was better at Andover than it was at . . ."

It is, when all is said and done, an excellent place to grow. To be surrounded by the most curious, ambitious, and creative young minds. To be encouraged by dedicated teachers, who are as inspired as they are inspiring.

Not to mention that graduation from one of these elite schools helps pave the way towards an elite college or university for you. You really can't beat that. Especially at today's prices (no matter when today is).

You are not a prisoner of your history. We hate to dispute all-time prep great F. Scott Fitzgerald, who said, "There are no second acts in American lives," but he never got to live through the TMZ era. If Tom DeLay can compete on *Dancing with the Stars*, if Mario Lopez can interview the president, then you can have a second or even a third act. You can reinvent yourself at any point along your travels.

You can decide you want to be a preppy now, right this moment (see Manifesto, p. 3). Or you can be one of the few who attend private school and don't become affected by its long reach. You can have that great education but deny your privileged past.

For a while.

Then one day, it will come out. It might be the quote from Cotton Mather you didn't know you remembered. Or the way your cuffs hang just so. Or that while wearing a wrist full of leather thong bracelets, and even with a tiny tattoo on your wrist (naughty!), you'll be able to tie a reef knot with your eyes closed.

It'll come out in a trickle at first, but within no time at all, it could become a flood. And by the time you have children yourself, you will be hoping that favoritism to legacies is still the modus operandi at your alma mater.

Thirty years ago, some boarding schools resembled prisons. Now prisons are aiming to emulate boarding schools. You had a strict dress code, had to spend most every weekend on campus, and if you left, it was only because one of your parents picked you up. Your room had to pass daily inspection. You could go downstairs to the common room of your dorm to watch *Miami Vice* with the other girls or boys, but, of course, no dorms were coed, and most schools were not coed.

Thirty years ago, daily chapel was compulsory, and there was an Episcopalian perfume to the campus (unless you were at Portsmouth Abbey or Canterbury). Everyone chose to buy the school ring senior year, and wore them with pride.

Thirty years ago, students who required medication for their asthma or diabetes would go to the infirmary on an as-needed basis. Today the line for those on daily meds is so long that students are put on a schedule.

Thirty years ago, *The Catcher in the Rye* was everyone's bible. Today it's *A Heartbreaking Work of Staggering Genius* (see p. 180), although reading books for pleasure has become a rare pleasure among teenagers.

Today each campus has expanded and been beautified. You can find a fabulous new science center (LEED-approved), a museum and/or an art gallery, several ice rinks, new squash courts, a new dining hall featuring a vegan meal plan, and the Ethernet wired through and through.

Unlike day schools, boarding schools are more realistic in the homework department. They ensure each student's schedule allows for a healthy dose of sports and arts. Homework is organized to take no more than two to three hours (one free period per day plus the two-hour study hall) so that students are finished before Jon Stewart's opening salvo. Of course, TV is viewable in students' rooms via computer, as well as in the lounges.

Most reputable boarding schools are now coed. Couples can sometimes form, especially in the winter, when people want to be cozy. Dress codes are relaxed—many schools have none whatsoever, except for a scheduled formal dinner. Chapel is now of the nonsectarian, secular-humanist variety, unless the school is Quaker, in which case, *plus ça change*. Students are allowed to travel home most weekends, except for the rare "closed weekend," which could mean exams, proms, or the drug education program. Most schools have opened their ranks to day students . . . local kids who have cars and know how to drive them to the liquor store.

Mandarin Chinese has replaced German as the hardest language to learn, and it has replaced French as the most popular language to study.

And thanks to cell phones, you are no longer isolated in the woods. In fact, while at boarding school, many students still are able to ask their parents to do everything for them, just as they did at home, including waking them up.

Admissions Advice.

Nothing is more fraught than putting one's very young children (whether they are of the easygoing or the entitled variety) at the mercy of strangers who will decide their lives' fates for them. That is enough of a reason for parents to be at their neurotic worst when the admissions process must be faced. Personal rejection is humiliating enough; to think that your genes are being rejected (an evolutionary slap in the face) is beyond. People have relocated for less.

At True Prep Central Command we approached a seasoned admissions director (no names please, not of the director, certainly, nor of the institution) who offered a few words of advice:

• Do apply online. No points will be taken away for penmanship or lack thereof.
• Remember that all the children going forward into this maw are "gifted" in one sense or another. Avoid using that word.
• Flatter the school. It's only human.
• Attempt to offer a balanced view of the applicant. (He's not perfect at everything. Her only imperfection is not her perfectionism.)
• Try not to micromanage your child's behavior during the observation session. The admissions personnel are watching the children interact to see how emotionally and socially ready your preschoolers are.
• And most important, if you can possibly avoid it, do not tell your three-, four-, or five-year-olds that "we are all applying" to private school. Try to relax; they pick up on all your stress. Pretend that you are going to a new place with a new room with new children and grown-ups who like to play and talk with children.

All the foregoing is irrelevant in Manhattan if you don't follow the pre-pre-pre-application rules. **What you are about to read is all true.**

For nursery-school applications (that is to say, when your child is in his second year) (of life), you must call each individual nursery school on the one day (Tuesday) after Labor Day. Only. You will spend the morning nervously dialing the admissions numbers at the (average of eight) schools you have heard about to be able to get an application sent to you. You will have not ever seen these schools before, unless you have older children. You must dial and redial (and get your spouse, your assistant, your spouse's assistant, your assistant's spouse) on speed dial until you speak to an admissions officer. No sense getting huffy; it won't help. The answer to your next question is: no. If you show up in person—sensible, since the line is constantly busy—you will be turned away without an application, and by then all the applications will be spoken for. At some schools, if you don't get through their lines until midday, your child will not be eligible to attend the morning session, and you will have to satisfy yourself with the hope of a spot in the less-desirable afternoon session.

It is estimated that there are approximately 2,500 places altogether in a year's entering class in Manhattan nursery-school land. Of those, perhaps half will be lost to children who are legacies or siblings. Still, there are no sure things. If you get through on your Tuesday morning, you might have leveled your playing field, and won the opportunity of sending your child to a wonderful nursery school, costing anywhere between $16,000 and $25,000 per year.

Prepdom's Most Vintage School.

When we think of the seventeenth century, we mostly think about Europe, don't we? According to various sites online (what's a library again?), 1628 was a busy, event-filled year: The Massachusetts Colony was founded. Cardinal Richelieu became prime minister. Louis XIII occupied La Rochelle. Emperor Ferdinand demanded that Austrian Protestants convert to Catholicism. Rembrandt, twenty-two years old, painted his self-portrait. Construction began on the Taj Mahal, and the Collegiate School in New Amsterdam (Manhattan) was established, "the oldest day school in North America."

Funny, that. Look up the Boston Latin School wherever you "look up things." Five signers of the Declaration of Independence are alumni (Adams, Franklin, Hancock, Paine, and Hooper). Founded in 1635, it shares its birthday with that of the painter Tintoretto and the scientist Robert Hooke (he coined the term "cell"). It was also the year that Bernini completed the Palazzo Barberini in Rome, and that Connecticut opened for business as a colony. When Boston Latin was founded, it was known as the English High and Latin School.

Now on to Roxbury Latin. Although it was founded much later, in 1645, it wasn't a dull year. That was when Sweden and Denmark signed a peace agreement, as did the Dutch and Indians. It was also the year that both pirate William Kidd and explorer Louis Joliet were born. And although tapestries were still popular, the year marked the beginning of wallpaper.

Kerry P. Brennan, the twelfth headmaster of Roxbury Latin (and formerly the twenty-sixth headmaster of the Collegiate School), maintains he is "the youngest and most handsome" of all the antique boys' school heads. We would agree. The founder of RLS, John Eliot, was a "Protestant divine, who was an apostle to the Indians," meaning he translated the Bible into Algonquin in order to convert the Algonquin. Since Harvard was already established, Eliot opened Roxbury Latin to be its feeder. (He had a son.) While Brennan does admit that Collegiate is the older institution, it did educate girls for a time—dodgy—and closed during the Revolutionary War. And while Boston Latin is older, it is public and it also shut down for part of the Revolutionary War. So Roxbury Latin—young Roxbury Latin—is "the oldest boys' school in North America in continuous existence." It not only stayed open during the Revolutionary War, its patriotic students "hurled appropriate patriotic invectives, and the schoolmaster, to spite the Tory troops, would not call off school for even one day."

Consider it official.

GOOD VALUE.

The average tuition for a private day or boarding school for academic year 2009–2010 was $37,341.60. Lest you think this is a high price to pay for mere social connections, allow us to make the case for the education that comes along with them. The following may make you think you're reading a college course catalogue.

Dalton School, founded in 1919 as the Childrens University School, in Manhattan, has 1,285 students from kindergarten through twelfth grade. Some of the classes offered might include Contemporary Dance and Improvisation; Zen Dance; American Literature: Gender and Sexuality; and The Sixties and the American Prophetic Voice. Always strong in the arts, the school maintains a "composer in residence." Alumni include Jennifer Grey and Tracy Pollan.

Episcopal High School, Alexandria, Virginia. Founded in 1839 as the first high school (for boys) in all Virginia, it has been coed since 1991. One hundred percent of its students board on campus. Between 1861 and 1866, school buildings were used as a Union Army Hospital. (Walt Whitman served as a nurse there.) Today's students, 30 percent of whom receive some aid, can study Religious Thought in Music; Honors Multivariable/Vector Calculus; Salvation, Judgment, and the End of the World; and The Philosophy and Literature of Medicine. Beloved pediatrician T. Berry Brazelton and Sen. John McCain are both graduates.

Gilman School, Baltimore, Maryland. Founded in 1897 as The Country School for Boys (and the first "Country Day School" in the United States). Now home to 1,015 boys in grades K–12, Gilman offers a solid college prep curriculum, in addition to being famous for lacrosse (whose home is Baltimore). Sophomores have a required year-long course in Art History/Music History. Other offerings include Dreams and Disasters in Western Literature; European Ideologies; Comparative Legal Systems; and History of Anti-Semitism. Graduates include Frank Deford and Ty Ruff. Upperclassmen may take electives at all-girls' Roland Park Country Day School (alumnae include Julie Bowen and Adrienne Rich) and the all-girl Bryn Mawr School, whose first headmistress was Edith (*Mythology*) Hamilton.

The **Hockaday School,** Dallas, Texas. Founded in 1913. Hockadaisies, which is what all 1,083 students at all-girls Hockaday are called, are able to study Classical Genetics; Science and Pseudoscience, or How We Know What We Know; and Military History: Terrain, Tactics, and Technology. Recent speakers on campus included astronaut Sally Ride and Soviet poet Yevgeny Yevtushenko. Fewer than 100 girls board at Hockaday.

Lakeside School, Seattle, Washington. Founded in 1919, merged with St. Nicholas in 1971. Coed, grades 5–12, 785 students. The alma mater of high-tech royalty Bill Gates, Paul Allen, and Craig McCaw, among others, Lakeside now caters to their children. Besides Mrs. Steve Ballmer, other trustees include a Skip and a Whimsy. Offerings include Race Matters: A (Fairly) Contemporary Intellectual History of African America; Infectious Disease: Culture and Science; Salmon Behavior and Ecology (this is the Northwest, after all); and Linear Optimization. Outdoor education is stressed in Middle School, tremendous study abroad available to juniors.

Marin Academy, San Rafael, California. Founded in 1971 by a group of parents and faculty, Marin Academy is a coed day school of 400 students in grades nine through twelve. With a diverse population from all corners of the Bay Area, students study Field of Dreams: Baseball Lit; Russian History: From Vladimir to Vladimir; and Why War? (English dept.); Every January MA offers week-long mini-courses, just like some colleges do. Past courses have included the Marin AIDS Project, Southwest Archaeology, Whale Watching in Baja, Marine Biology, Raku Ceramics, Theater in Ashland, Skiing and Singing, Vision Quest, and the Cuisine of China and the Caribbean.

Milton Academy (also known as MA by some) was established in 1798, and then again in 1884, in Milton, Massachusetts. With about 960 students on 125 acres, the Upper School enrolls about 670 students, half of whom board. It is coed. Jazz Improvisation; Microeconomics: The Power of Markets; and Advanced Latin: Lyric Poetry are a few of the classes offered, in addition to an extensive semester- and year-away program. Each dorm has its own tradition, taken seriously by all the campus. Buckminster Fuller and Governor Deval Patrick are both alums.

64

School'd: Boarding School Books.

Imagine our surprise at learning that the canon of books and movies that examine the world of prep schools is a legitimate genre. Even better, it forms a syllabus at the Hotchkiss School. **Sam Prouty** (Worcestor Academy, Swarthmore BA, Middlebury MA), an English instructor there, has been teaching this course every spring term since 2005. "This class is available to seniors only, as a college-style elective. The students are on the downside of their careers here, and in the beginning of their nostalgia period. I'm hoping this will help them process what it has meant to them." School'd is popular, and ends with students reading and analyzing recruitment materials published by America's boarding schools themselves to see what messages are beginning to define the prep experience.

SHORT STORIES

The Palace Thief
  Ethan Canin
The Lie
  Kurt Vonnegut Jr.

NOVELS

The Catcher in the Rye
  J. D. Salinger
A Separate Peace
  John Knowles
Black Ice
  Lorene Cary
Prep
  Curtis Sittenfeld
Outside Providence
  Peter Farrelly
New Boy
  Julian Houston,
  Hotchkiss graduate

"OTHERS THAT WE SOMETIMES LOOK AT, BUT THAT I SKIP IF TIME GETS TIGHT"

The Sixth Form
  Tom Dolby,
  Hotchkiss graduate
The Upper Class
  Hobson Brown, et al.,
  Hotchkiss graduates

The Prime of Miss Jean Brodie
  Muriel Spark
Never Let Me Go
  Kazuo Ishiguro
When the Moon Turns Away
  Tracy Ma

NONFICTION

The Headmaster
  John McPhee
Selections from Hotchkiss:
  A Chronicle of an American School
  Ernest Kolowrat, ed.

PLAYS

The History Boys
  Alan Bennett
Six Degrees of Separation
  John Guare
Tea and Sympathy
  Robert Anderson

FILMS

Outside Providence
The Emperor's Club
Dead Poets Society
Six Degrees of Separation
Igby Goes Down
Goodbye, Mr. Chips

TEACHER OF THE MONTH:
MRS. RADCLIFFE.

Patient, or at the end of her rope?

A Van Cleef & Arpels choker. Teachers should be well accessorized. It makes their students respect them.

Well-cared-for copy of Pride and Prejudice, bought at the Bryn Mawr bookstore nineteen years ago.

Calvin Klein classics.

Has a master's degree in Ferragamo.

Name: Alice Anne Swanson Radcliffe
Hometown: Rutland, Vermont
Subject: English, Drama, touch typing
Husband: Timothy J. Radcliffe, insurance salesman/mortgage broker
Children: One daughter, Darcy Elizabeth Radcliffe, eleven years old
Pet: Persian cat, Emma
Favorite Spot: The beach at Hilton Head with a good book
Favorite Season: Summer
Hobbies: Needlepoint, antiquing (rare editions of Austen, a specialty), Anglophilia
Alma Mater: Trinity College (Connecticut)
Favorite College Memory: Semester abroad, St. Andrews (That's where I met my husband!)
Favorite Food: Chicken enchiladas
Favorite Drink: Diet ginger ale
Favorite Book: *Pride and Prejudice*
Favorite Movie: *Pride and Prejudice*
Favorite Actor: Colin Firth
Favorite Actress: No one who's ever played a love scene with Colin Firth
Favorite Designer: Calvin Klein (see photo!)
Fantasy: To sit on the beach at Hilton Head with Colin Firth

MR. KENT.

ONE-FOURTH OF A PERFECT PERSON.

Graham Kent is a science teacher. Unfortunately, very few of us at Pine Coast Country Day speak "science." We don't speak its dialects, "Physics," "Chemistry," or "Biology." If Mr. Kent spoke to us in English, it might help. But we barely can concentrate. It's not because Graham Kent is so cute (you know . . . for a teacher). His lab is on the fourth floor, and it's hot up there. (Wasn't it in first form that we learned about heat rising? Or was that in that *People* story about Justin Timberlake?)

Which are the elements of the particles? The particles of the elements? Anyway, word is that Mr. Kent and Miss Zuckerman . . . ? The calculus teacher? We can't believe it; it's pretty upsetting. Miss Pierson—at least they have something in common. They both coach cross-country and went to UVA, but Miss Zuckerman? Doesn't she, like, play chess or cello? She probably doesn't even ski. It's bogus. If she likes science people so much, why doesn't she play duets with Mr. Srinivassa? He's quiet, too. They could sit in the Commons and think their deep thoughts and not even say anything.

But to make a perfect person, you'd have to take parts of Mr. Kent, Miss Pierson, Reverend Watson, and Coach Jones, and put them in a blender. You'd get a smart, cool distance athlete who sings karaoke and does community service, and who could get into UVA. And has green eyes. But for now, we'll take Mr. Kent, and his Vineyard Vines ties and matching belts. Even if we don't understand him.

Saying something smart, but we don't speak Physics. Sorry!

Hair: boyish.

Tie: so coordinated.

Belt: Vineyard Vines. He has at least three of these, by our count.

Trousers: Nantucket Reds look fine all year long.

Yes, they did.*

King Abdullah II al-Hussein of Jordan	*Deerfield Academy*
Trey Anastasio	*Taft School*
Bob Balaban	*Latin School of Chicago*
Elizabeth Berkley	*Cranbrook Schools (x)*
Mike Birbiglia	*St. Mark's School*
Ivan Boesky	*Cranbrook Schools (x)*
Humphrey Bogart	*Trinity School (x) Andover (x)*
Judge Robert Bork	*Hotchkiss School*
Dan Brown	*Phillips Exeter Academy*
Joy Bryant	*Westminster School (CT)*
Paul Butterfield	*U. of Chicago Lab Schools*
Truman Capote	*Trinity School (x)*
Mary Chapin Carpenter	*Taft School*
Steve Carrell	*Middlesex School*
Dov Charney	*Choate Rosemary Hall*
Daniel Clowes	*U. of Chicago Lab Schools*
Roy Cohn	*Horace Mann School*
Chris Collingwood	*The Hill School*
Joseph Cornell	*Phillips Academy Andover*
Philippe Cousteau Jr.	*St. George's School*
Buster Crabbe	*Punahou School*
David Crosby	*Cate School*
Paul Dano	*Browning School*
Jamie Dimon	*Browning School*
Adam Duritz	*Taft School*
T. S. Eliot	*Smith School*
Daniel Ellsberg	*Cranbrook Schools*
Helen Frankenthaler	*Dalton School*
Ana Gasteyer	*Sidwell Friends School*
Henry Geldzahler	*Horace Mann School*
Stefani Germanotta (Lady Gaga)	*Convent of the Sacred Heart*
Paul Giamatti	*Choate Rosemary Hall*
Matt Goldman and Chris Wink	*Fieldston School*
Betty Grable	*Mary Institute*
Temple Grandin	*Hampshire Country Day*
Fred Gwynne	*Groton School*

*Though (x) means they didn't graduate

Yes, they did.

Larry Hagman	*Trinity School*
Anne Heche	*Francis W. Parker School*
Ed Helms	*Westminster Schools*
Howard Hughes	*Fessenden*
Linda Hunt	*Interlochen Arts Academy*
David Henry Hwang	*Harvard-Westlake School*
Rashida Jones	*Buckley School, CA*
Kim Kardashian	*Buckley School, CA*
Michael Kinsley	*Cranbrook Schools*
Werner Klemperer	*Cate School*
James Franciscus	*Taft*
John Lahr	*Riverdale Country School*
Sherry Lansing	*U. of Chicago Lab Schools*
Tom Lehrer	*Loomis Chaffee*
Alan Jay Lerner	*Choate*
Huey Lewis	*Lawrenceville School*
Lisa Loeb	*The Hockaday School*
Stacy London	*Trinity School*
Jon Lovitz	*Harvard-Westlake School*
Allard K. Lowenstein	*Horace Mann School*
Lois Lowry	*Packer Collegiate Institute*
Seth MacFarlane	*Kent School*
Stephen Malkmus	*Cate School*
Sally Mann	*The Putney School*
Reginald Marsh	*Lawrenceville School*
Dr. William Masters	*Lawrenceville School*
Roger McGuinn	*Latin School of Chicago*
Jan Miner	*Beaver Country Day*
Margaret Mitchell	*Washington Seminary*
Elizabeth Montgomery	*Harvard-Westlake School*
Frank Morgan	*Trinity School*
Dmitri Nabokov	*St. Mark's School*
Matthew and Gunnar Nelson	*Harvard-Westlake School*
S. I. Newhouse	*Horace Mann School*
Bill Nye	*Sidwell Friends School*
Keith Olbermann	*Hackley School*
Claes Oldenburg	*Latin School of Chicago*

Yes, they did.

Jennifer O'Neill	*Dalton School*
Princess Leila Pahlavi	*Rye Country Day School*
Alexandra Paul	*Groton School*
Elizabeth Perkins	*Northfield Mt. Hermon*
H. Ross Perot	*St. Mark's School of Texas*
Generoso Pope	*Horace Mann School*
Zac Posen	*St. Ann's School*
Keshia Knight Pulliam	*The Foxcroft School*
Bob Rafelson	*Horace Mann School*
Gov. Bill Richardson	*Middlesex School*
Joely Richardson	*The Thacher School*
Sally Ride	*Harvard-Westlake School*
Tom Rush	*Groton School*
Edward Said	*Northfield Mt. Hermon*
Aram Saroyan	*Trinity School*
Boz Scaggs	*St. Mark's School of Texas*
Richard Mellon Scaife	*Deerfield Academy*
Ilyasah Shabazz	*The Masters School*
Wallace Shawn	*Dalton School*
Duncan Sheik	*Phillips Academy Andover*
M. Night Shyamalan	*Episcopal Academy (PA)*
Eliot Spitzer	*Horace Mann School*
Dr. Benjamin Spock	*Phillips Academy Andover*
Sufjan Stevens	*Interlochen Arts Academy*
Taki Theodoracopulos	*Lawrenceville School*
Gene Tierney	*Miss Porter's School*
Rachel Uchitel	*Nightingale-Bamford*
Mark Sinclair Vincent (Vin Diesel)	*Dwight School*
Rufus Wainwright	*Millbrook School*
Joss Whedon	*Riverdale Country School*
Olivia Wilde	*Phillips Academy Andover*
Thornton Wilder	*The Thacher School*
William Carlos Williams	*Horace Mann School*
Sean Wilsey	*St. Mark's School (x)*
Carnie Wilson	*Oakwood School*
Reese Witherspoon	*Harpeth Hall School*
Jeffrey Wright	*St. Albans School*
Eli Zabar	*Fieldston School*

Here are two friends, Callie and Parker. Callie and Parker have known each other for years. They have never dated each other. Didn't he once like Polly, Callie's sister? (Hard to remember. Ninth grade?) Things they say about each other: "He's like a big brother to me." "She's way too young. Forget it!" "He's practically engaged to that Margot Spooner." "She's not my type." "He's not a jock." "She's into jocks."

But that winter weekend, when they both need someone to bring to the Christmas formal, they go together. It's nice when things work out the way they're supposed to.

Hampden-Sydney College.

Fact: Hampden-Sydney College, in Prince Edward County, Virginia, is the tenth-oldest college in the United States (besides being the oldest continuing all-male college in this country). It is the oldest private college in the South as well. It has been a regional secret these many years.

While this sinks in, allow us to assure you, in no uncertain terms, that Hampden-Sydney is, without equivocation, the preppiest college in the United States.

Some will whimper and whine and debate us. Please don't. We've visited hundreds of colleges and universities, in all fifty states. We've been to Greek Weeks and homecomings, to tailgate parties and candlelight rituals. We've been throughout New England, throughout the South, and this is no casual verdict. (Sweet Briar and College of Charleston, we're talking to you.)

Whereas: Single-sex schools are—de facto—way preppier than coed colleges. They are modeled after our first schools, they are more traditional, and their alumni/ae and trustees like it this way. (See us after class, Connecticut College.) While one could argue that New England or the mid-Atlantic states, with their heavy load of original colonies, seem older, require more layers to be comfortable, and look more British in that tweedy woolen way, we have found that Virginia, home of FFV (First Families of Virginia) and Jefferson's aura, is the real deal. The students at Hampden-Sydney refer to themselves as "gentlemen." They are frequently sons of Hampden-Sydney gentlemen.

Whereas: In the class of 2009, the number of classical-studies majors equaled that of computer-science majors. Take that, preprofessionals.

Whereas: Students often wear freshly pressed shirts to class. Because they feel like it.

Whereas: Students wear coats and ties to home football games.

Whereas: It is a small school, with approximately 1,128 students.

Whereas: Many students minor in military history.

Whereas: James Madison and Patrick Henry sat on the college's first board of trustees.

Whereas: In 1775.

Whereas: Each freshman receives a copy of the vital student etiquette handbook, *To Manner Born, To Manners Bred: A Hip-pocket Guide to Etiquette for the Hampden-Sydney Man.* No other college in America places such a high value on good—no, exemplary—manners.

Whereas: Each student needs to pass a Rhetoric Exam as part of the college's rededicated mission to pay "a more particular Attention . . . to the Cultivation of the English Language than is usually done in Places of Public Education."

Whereas: There is no student unrest at Hampden-Sydney.

Therefore: We rest our case.

Thomas Shomo and the Long Memo.

When former dean and now director of public relations Thomas Shomo answers his phone at Hampden-Sydney, one feels all is right with the world—or at least, nothing has changed, which is almost the same thing.

This Hampden-Sydney graduate, class of 1969, has spent, at this point, twenty-nine years of his life on campus, as a student and in various administrative positions. It is home. In 1978, Diana Bunting, wife of then president Josiah

To Manner Born
To Manners Bred

A Hip-pocket Guide to Etiquette for the Hampden-Sydney Man

Bunting, complained to her husband that students were not responding to her invitations to dine at the president's house. So Tommy Shomo was pressed into action and began writing a memo. "I used the college library's copy of Emily Post, though it was from 1929—now de-accessioned—and a copy I had of Amy Vanderbilt. I tried to write it for our students."

This memo grew beyond the impor-tance of responding to invitations and ex-panded to include table settings, holding doors open for women, and encouraging appropriate attire for all events, up to and including Buckingham Palace . . . just the sort of thing that gentlemen at Hampden-Sydney should know. The title comes from *Hamlet*, Act 1, scene 4:

*"But to my mind, though I am native here
And to the manner born . . . "*

The first edition was published in 1978, and ever since, a copy has been given to every single freshman when he ar-rives at school. Subsequently, the book has been reprinted, rewritten, revised, and up-dated. Shomo estimates that about 8,000 books are in print (and for sale at the Hampden-Sydney College bookstore). As Shomo updates his *Hip-pocket Guide to Etiquette for the Hampden-Sydney Man* he "tries to keep up with social changes. We used to tell the boys to light their dates' cigarettes. Now we hope they don't smoke. Cell phones, e-mails, answering machines . . . It's amazing."

But is the book read? "I don't know if they read it; I know they get it," Shomo says, chuckling. "But eventually I think they do read it," he adds, "before the din-ners." The Etiquette Dinners are a Shomo specialty, the kind of thing you would not find anywhere else. The Career Services Office hosts an etiquette dinner for seniors who are hoping to interview in corporate America. In case recruiters are inviting anyone for a meal, Shomo talks them through a somewhat elaborate meal (semiformal attire required), including such obscure implements as fish forks and knives. Young women from Sweet Briar are invited as well. Table settings re-create what one would find at the White House (the twenty-first century's version of Buckingham Palace). Besides dealing with complicated flatware, students hear about how to leave their place settings when they get up from the table, how to network gracefully, and more. Shomo patrols the dinner of about fifty participants and "gently" corrects them, if need be ("nothing too embarrassing in front of their dates").

The Society of 91 (which is short for 1791, natch) also has a formal Etiquette Dinner. Members of this leadership organization attend their dinner in black tie, and invite dates of their choosing. No trick utensils or foods are served, though one year Cornish hens (not easy to cut) were accompanied by finger bowls.

How have the gentlemen changed since 1965, when Shomo first arrived at Hampden-Sydney? "They are the same as when I was a student. They never change. Sometimes we go through a shaggy period, when there is a little facial hair, but," he says with a laugh, "even that is nicely trimmed."

Around 1985, a writer described Hampden-Sydney as "an affront to the whole twentieth century." It was, and remains, utterly unto itself: indifferent to the world's opinion, quietly sure of itself—assured that its habits and culture are faithful to the ideals of its progenitors (among them James Madison and Patrick Henry); that mind without character, like knowledge without wisdom, is ignoble, and that there remains a need, still, in the United States, for *gentlemen*. The campus ambience is well-bred understatement, easy camaraderie, quiet mischief and gaminerie, unstated pride in a searching academic regimen in which grade inflation has made not the merest dent, and a devotion to honor in all things. It is an affront to the twenty-first century—so far. Hampden-Sydney incarnates the wisdom of a forgotten English peer: when it is not necessary to change, it is necessary not to change. If it ain't broke, don't fix it.

—JOSIAH BUNTING III
The Hill School (x), Salisbury, Virginia
Military Institute, Christ Church, Oxford
(President, 1977–1987)

I Say Alumna, and You Say Alumni.

We have a problem. It's not on the scale of global warming, childhood obesity, or the worldwide recession, but it is a problem nonetheless, and it is this: The appropriate terms denoting graduates of schools, programs, or rehabilitation facilities are Latin words that have gender and cases. If many preppies can keep these four words straight (even in the midst of a reunion tailgate free-for-all), then so can you.

To wit: A female graduate of, let's say, Emma Willard School is called an alumna. The plural, or more than one graduate of Emma Willard, are called alumnae. (This can be pronounced either "alum-nay" or "alum-nee," depending on how old your Latin teacher is.) A graduate of the all-male Episcopal Academy is an alumnus ("alumnus"). Put several of these fellows together and you have a room full of alumni ("alum-nigh"). Lucky you, if you are a single girl with straight hair and good legs.

If your school or program (Suffield Academy, Trinity College, the Rhodes Scholarship program) admits both males and females, all together you are still alumni, though individually you remain either an alumna or an alumnus. Casually, of course, you can refer to yourself or others as an "alum," but if the above isn't absorbed thoroughly, you could embarrass yourself one day, and that would be dreadful. So please practice your vocabulary now. Life is full of pop quizzes.

Truth and Cotton.

An Interview with David Coolidge, the
Muslim Chaplain of Brown University.

It just so happens that almost anyone can assimilate into our world of prepdom. The desire to be prep is the most important factor. The desire to embrace Allah as your god and Mohammed as his messenger (in front of two witnesses) is the most important criterion in choosing to practice Islam.

The Muslim chaplain at Brown is named R. (for Robert) David Coolidge. He's known as Dave. What's even more unusual about his nonstereotypic Muslim name is his whiteness. He is a serious, well-spoken, thoughtful, joyful midwestern WASP who converted to Islam a few years ago, when he was a Religious Studies major at Brown. He returned to campus in the fall of 2009, when he was thirty, to be part of the University chaplaincy and to be the adviser to the Brown Muslim Student Association. He arrived in Providence with his wife, Sumaiya.

Raised in suburban Chicago, Coolidge intended to explore faith in college, as he looked for a deeper meaning. "I was comfortable about being agnostic, so I was surprised that I was drawn into the process of conversion. For me, it was a search for the ontological truth. Then through Islam I felt I found Truth with a capital *T*—not a small thing. I was excited."

It took a number of years to "find my place within the cultures and histories of Islam. As a white Anglo-Saxon, I didn't want to feel my conversion was an act of cultural apostasy," he explains. White Christian Americans are not the preponderant converts to Islam, which seems to reach more to the African American and Latino populations. "As a white Muslim, I had to be myself with my background and proud of those things, and proud of Islam, even though there are not a lot of people like me." Furthermore, "most white Muslim converts try to become Arab," meaning they study the Arabic language and move to the Middle East for an extended or even permanent stay. But Dave Coolidge wasn't comfortable with that approach. "Last night I went to a mosque in jeans and a Brown sweatshirt. I suppose I looked like a stoner," he says with a little laugh. "I look like anyone, but I wear a short chin beard, kind of the minimum requirement, that is my outward symbol of being Muslim. (I know I'm very Muslim on the inside.)"

Could he imagine a Muslim student striding across the quad in a Lacoste shirt and khakis? "I like it. They are the clothes of my people. I'm biased. I like it when people dress preppy. If a Pakistani student wore a button-down or Lacoste shirt, no one would blink. But if he wore an argyle sweater, his collar up, and a pair of Nantucket Reds," that would be too much. "I have a friend, who is also a white Muslim who converted, who graduated from Amherst, and she and I have talked about having a Muslim preppy party." It would be, needless to say, alcohol-free.

The Children's Table.

A THANKSGIVING TRADITION.

PORTER.
Seventeen-year-old fresh-man at Vassar. Was in-vited to roommate's house in Dominican Republic and will not let us forget it.

MUFFY.
Thirteen going on twenty-five; have you seen her Face-book page? It's a scandal.

DRYDEN.
Has had a fake ID since she was fourteen, but she gets A's in math and science. (Doesn't take after us.)

ANDERS.
No complaints here. (Well, he could sit on a chair, but that would be asking too much.)

One never knows how many people will show up for Thanksgiving until the last minute, and our children just have to be willing to be flexible. We were perfectly happy to sit at the children's table—a long-standing tradition—at our parents' Thanksgiving . . . not like our darlings. This is a time to be thankful, after all. We are thankful that Crosby was given a "withdrawn" rather than an "expelled" from Woodberry Forest. We are thankful that Sallie's marriage to her surfing instructor was annulled. We are grateful that Evans will be living in the halfway house soon. We are grateful, of course, that Daddy opened the special bottle of Bâtard Montrachet.

And we're sure the young people at the table feel the same, or will when they think about it. We are not going to let their attitudes spoil our lovely Thanksgiving. Look at Porter twirling her hair with daggers in her eyes, Muffy texting all day long; you couldn't pry that thing out of her fingers if you tried. And you know Dryden and Larkin are just going to run to the bathroom again. Thank goodness for Spencer. He's a perfect angel. (Should we be concerned that he hasn't moved a muscle since the soup was removed? It's a little odd. No matter!) What happened to Anders's shoes? Speaking of which, where is Henry?

Happy Thanksgiving. It's wonderful to be together again.

LARKIN.
This is how she looks after two espressos. What's up with her? At nineteen you're supposed to have energy to burn! A sophomore at Cornell.

SPENCER.
Our little mystery man. Five years old. Loves Sudoku, Charlie Rose, and rice.

Hair: An Education.

As of now one cannot major in hairstyles in an accredited college, but one can always dream. A syllabus of style: The politics of tortoiseshell hair accessories. Whither the flip? Biomed ethics on how the brain is affected by hair-color chemicals, and how blond is dangerously blond? (Not to mention the prep male follicle seminars: What your part says about you. Just because you don't grow a beard doesn't mean you can't. The preppy hairline.)

We arrive as freshwomen—intimidated by cool and experienced upperclass women—not realizing that we actually threaten them. We are new, unspoiled, unknown, young, but not too young to get involved with seniors.

FRESHMAN.

"I'm just going to leave it down. I had to go to class this morning with damp hair. It looked weird, so I had to leave Poli-Sci and go brush it for a while, during the slide show, which was b-o-r-i-n-g! Texted Franny from the bathroom. She is still half asleep, the sloth. No matter what I do with my hair, it pretty much looks the same all the time. Maybe it's my shampoo."

SOPHOMORE.

"Can't decide: to cut it off or keep it long? What about bangs? I might have gained three pounds over the break, and maybe I should change my hair as a distraction? Should I take History and Literature of the Riviera pass/fail or keep my B? So many questions. I'm so stressed. Kip just told Anson he loves my hair; that's it! I'm keeping it long. Should we go to Boston for the weekend? What about Hanover?"

1.　　2.　　3.　　4.

JUNIOR.

"I am going to Berlin for a semester, and I have to write this damn paper as part of my application. Get my hair off my neck to concentrate. Concentrate. How has globalization affected my education? Just concentrate, Sophie. I don't mind it in a ponytail. It's simple and neat, and with my pearl studs, it's a look. Do I look too much like my mother? Eeeww. Clark likes it this way. But he likes Mummy, too. Gross."

SENIOR.

"I swear, I'm just going to cut it. No, I need to keep my options. That's why I'm applying to law school and Teach for America and Condé Nast. And Google. And anything else I can think of. The career counselors here seem totally clueless. I should have Daddy speak to them. He could straighten them out and get them all real jobs. (Just kidding!) I'm serious about my future, Daddy. But you promised me I could travel with Brophy to Greece after graduation. You promised!"

4.
I JUST
FOUND IT
IN MY
CLOSET.

WARDROBE.

*I was a failure in Boston because they thought I was too fashionable to be intelligent,
and a failure in New York because they were afraid I was too intelligent
to be fashionable.*
—Edith Wharton, *A Backward Glance*

FASHION RULES.

We know that many of you understand the principles of preppy style. But just to be sure, let's review them again.

We wear sportswear. This is because it is easier to go from sporting events to social events (not that there is much difference) without changing.

We generally underdress. We prefer it to overdressing.

Your underwear must not show. Wear a nude-colored strapless bra. Pull up your pants. Wear a belt. Do something! Use a tie!

We do not display our wit through T-shirt slogans.

Every single one of us—no matter the age or the gender or sexual preference—owns a blue blazer.

We take care of our clothes, but we're not obsessive. A tiny hole in a sweater, a teensy stain on the knee of our trousers, doesn't throw us. (Remember, we are the people who brought you duct-taped Blucher moccasins.)

We do, however, wear a lot of white in the summer, and it must be spotless.

Don't knock seersucker till you've tried it. (Between Memorial Day and Labor Day, unless you live in Palm Beach or southern California, or the southern Mediterranean, please.)

Bags and shoes need not match.

Jewelry should not match, though metals should.

On the other hand, your watch doesn't have to be the same metal as your jewelry.

And you can wear yellow gold with a platinum wedding band and/or engagement ring.

Men's jewelry should be restricted to a handsome watch, a wedding band if American and married, and nothing else. If a man has a family crest ring, it may be worn as well. For black tie, of course, shirt studs and matching cuff links are de rigueur.

Nose rings are never preppy.

Neither are (shudder) belly-button piercings.

Nor are (two shudders) tongue studs.

And that goes for ankle bracelets.

Tattoos: Discouraged. Men who have been tattooed in a war have them, and that's one thing. (Gang wars don't count.) Anyone else looks like she's trying to be cool. Since the body ages, if you must tattoo, find a spot that won't stretch too much. One day you will want to wear a halter-necked backless gown. Will you want everyone at the party to know you once loved John Krasinski?

Sneakers (aka tennis shoes, running shoes, trainers) are not worn with skirts.

Men may wear sneakers with linen or cotton trousers to casual summer parties. We like.

Women over the age of fifteen may wear a simple black dress. Women over the age of twenty-one must have several in rotation.

High-heel rule: You must be able to run in them—on cobblestones, on a dock—in case of a spontaneous footrace.

Clothes can cost any amount, but they must fit. Many a preppy has an item from a vintage shop or a lost-and-found bin at the club that was tailored and looks incredibly chic.

Do not fret if cashmere is too pricey. Preppies love cotton and merino wool sweaters.

We do not wear our cell phones or BlackBerrys suspended from our belts. (That includes you, President Obama.)

Real suspenders are attached with buttons. We do not wear the clip versions.

Learn how to tie your bow tie. Do not invest in clip-ons.

Preppies are considerate about dressing our age. It is for you, not for us.

Men, if you made the mistake of buying Tevas or leather sandals, please give them to Goodwill.

You may, however, wear flip-flops to the beach if your toes are presentable. Be vigilant!

Pareos (sarongs) are for the beach, not for the mall. (Even if it is near the beach.)

Riding boots can be worn by non-riders; cowboy boots may be worn by those who have never been astride a horse. However, cowboy hats may not be worn by anyone who isn't technically a cowboy or cowgirl.

You may wear a Harvard sweatshirt if you attended Harvard, your spouse attended Harvard, or your children attend Harvard. Otherwise, you are inviting an uncomfortable question.

If your best friend is a designer (clothes, accessories, jewelry), you should wear a piece from his or her collection. If his or her taste and yours don't coincide, buy a piece or two to show your loyal support, but don't wear them.

Every preppy woman has a friend who is a jewelry designer.

No man bags.

Preppies don't perm their hair.

Preppy men do not believe that combovers disguise anything.

You can never go wrong with a trench coat.

Sweat suits are for sweating. You can try to get away with wearing sweats to carpool, to pick up the newspaper, or to drive to the dump, but last time you were at the dump, the drop-dead-attractive widower from Maple Lane was there, too.

And finally:

The best fashion statement is no fashion statement.

We're a-frayed so.

WHY OLD IS BETTER THAN NEW.

As you know by now, it's a brand-new old world. Meaning, of course, that showing one's age is not a bad thing, necessarily. Observe the threads hanging down from Jeremy's khakis. Using our prep carbon 21 (our forensic dating isotope), we can deduce that these trousers (100 percent cotton, from the look of things) are at least eight years old and appear as if they've been thrown into the washing machine approximately forty-four times per calendar year. The elongated threads wave freely from the correct cuff. There is no need to "train" them or snip them. They are not embarrassing, and no, these trousers need not be replaced. (Nor are they worn for city business appointments, but Jeremy knows that.)

Look closely: Elliot's collar shows wear. But of course it also is softer than a new shirt, is more comfortable than a new shirt, and presents itself as an old friend in the closet. Most people would not even notice the way the top layer of fabric has separated from the underlayer. You can continue buying shirts all you want—each year the stripes become bolder, the checks become checkier—but you can also wear the oldies with impunity. (And under a sportcoat—and especially with rakishly long hair—no one would notice.) The gentle parting of the fabric only demonstrates to the trained eye that you are no Johnny-come-lately.

ABOVE: A frayed chino cuff is the pant equivalent of a trusted friend. BELOW: Ditto the collar of your favorite dress shirt.

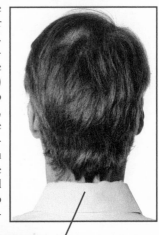

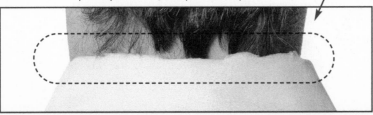

Breton stripes.

Hotchkiss and Yale man Gerald Murphy—*artist, F. Scott Fitzgerald muse, and heir to Mark Cross— first discovered the jaunty appeal of the striped sailor top. Summering in Cap d'Antibes in 1923, he wore his Marseilles market find so well that soon such fellow beachcombers as Pablo Picasso and Coco Chanel were sporting them, too. Then came devoted Americaphile the Duke of Windsor, who wore his even during his brief reign as King of England while yachting with soon-to-be-twice-divorced girlfriend Wallis in 1937. After World War Two, the striped top went through its rebellious phase, worn by the likes of Jean Seberg, Andy Warhol, and Joan Baez before settling down as favored prep unisex garment during the 1970s. Its next incarnation, embodying fashion with a capital F, came courtesy of Jean Paul Gaultier. With its navy-on-cream stripes, the iconic Breton fisherman's sweater is as significant a part of the French clothing vocabulary as the beret.*

— CAROLINE RENNOLDS MILBANK
St. Catherine's, Bennington

THE BIGGEST CHANGE IN THIRTY YEARS.

If, in 1980, you had whispered to a few friends that within the next few decades, America would elect a thin, black, preppy basketball-playing lawyer to be President, they would have laughed at you and exhaled in your face, *inside* the restaurant or club where you were sitting. And if you predicted that one day, all our children would have little portable phones stuck in their pockets so that they could not answer us when we called them from our little phones, we would have, again, exhaled in your face—indoors— and said you were talking science fiction.

Still, to our minds nothing is more sci-fi than the fact that preppies in the twenty-first century all wear the unnatural fibers we collectively refer to as "fleece." We always thought our reliance on natural "guaranteed-to-wrinkle" fibers was our right and our trademark. If it's hot or humid, we'd just roll up our all-cotton long-sleeved shirts. But now we wear polyester fleece, and its offspring, recycled water bottles.

THE REVOLUTION began in 1981, at a company then called Malden Mills, in Lawrence, Massachusetts, manufacturer of textiles, including the wool for bathing suits around 1910–20, and that for uniforms in World War Two. A place like Malden Mills is populated by textile engineers, who spitball, "mess around with fabrics," and then refine, according to spokesman Nate Simmons. They work collaboratively with clothing manufacturers, as they did in this case, with Patagonia. What came off the looms in the early '80s was pure synthetic, and it was soft, quick-wicking and quick-drying, and machine-washable. It did not fade, and it changed the wardrobes of athletes forever. Its Malden Mills' name was Polarfleece; its Patagonia name was Synchilla.

Throughout the 1980s Malden Mills continued to invent new versions of its fleece and to make constant improvements. And the fleece was picked up by The North Face, L.L. Bean, and Lands' End, among others. In 1991, the fleece was renamed Polartec, and Polartec 100, Polartec 200, Polartec 300, and Polartec 1000 (windproof) were introduced.

As each iteration came to market, new ones were being tested in the wings by the "athlete teams" used by Patagonia, REI, The North Face, et al., as well as by Malden Mills itself. But if you think that the corporate culture at

Malden Mills (renamed Polartec in 2007) is all outdoorsy and people roughing it, you'd be mistaken. "It's really smart fiber and fabric people who love to make amazing fabrics," says Simmons. And let us not forget that Polartec continues to manufacture in the United States, employing approximately 700 in its Lawrence headquarters, and another 300 or so worldwide, as the fabrics are popular the world over.

"Our athlete advisory board is getting stuff now for 2012," says Simmons in early 2010.

The board is made up of specialized "niche names," well known within their worlds but unknown to most—for example, "the top telemark skier and a well-known adventure racer, who is very credible." But don't you have to test the materials on ordinary people who have to work outdoors in terrible weather? "Our biggest test group is the military, and soldiers give us feedback. The military pays us to do research, and when they pick a product, we work with manufacturers who are approved vendors." Every single step of the manufacturing process must be approved and must occur within the United States. Simmons says that a new yarn, Unifi, is loomed in North Carolina, shipped in trucks to Massachusetts, sewn into garments in Michigan, and then packed and sent from Virginia Beach. Polartec is proud of all the jobs they've created or saved here.

Some preppies have worried that their zippered tops originated in bottles of things we do not drink, like grape or orange soda, or diet root beer. Fortunately, Polartec is using "single-use clear plastic water bottles." Phew.

And despite entries in Polartec's timeline which are utterly un- prep, i.e., "Polartec introduces biomimicry fabrics that imitate animal fur, and body-mapping fabrics that seamlessly vary density, loft, and breathability," the company still makes textiles with merino wool, among other fibers. "Sometimes wool just works better."

CASUAL FRIDAY.

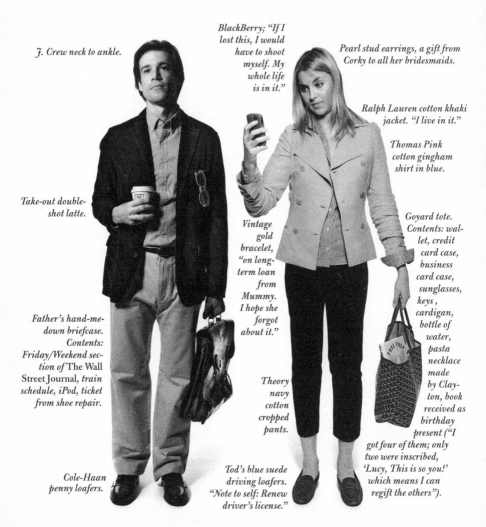

J. Crew neck to ankle.

BlackBerry; "If I lost this, I would have to shoot myself. My whole life is in it."

Pearl stud earrings, a gift from Corky to all her bridesmaids.

Ralph Lauren cotton khaki jacket. "I live in it."

Thomas Pink cotton gingham shirt in blue.

Take-out double-shot latte.

Vintage gold bracelet, "on long-term loan from Mummy. I hope she forgot about it."

Goyard tote. Contents: wallet, credit card case, business card case, sunglasses, keys, cardigan, bottle of water, pasta necklace made by Clayton, book received as birthday present ("I got four of them; only two were inscribed, 'Lucy, This is so you!' which means I can regift the others").

Father's hand-me-down briefcase. Contents: Friday/Weekend section of The Wall Street Journal, train schedule, iPod, ticket from shoe repair.

Theory navy cotton cropped pants.

Cole-Haan penny loafers.

Tod's blue suede driving loafers. "Note to self: Renew driver's license."

It just seems wrong to have to go to work on Friday. There are only a few hours before the weekend officially begins (at noon, Prep Standard Time), and it will take the morning to get packed, finalize plans, have coffee with Pip, and then get on the road. Yes, you are correct in assuming that what the world regards as "summer hours" we regard as "prep hours." Friday afternoons year-round are redundant. They are use-less. We cannot concentrate. They're just like the second half of senior year of high school after you've been admitted to Middlebury.

Thus, a wise person invented Casual Friday to raise employee morale in bridging this most jarring of weekly transitions. Many give credit to the carelessly dressed denizens of the dot-com bubble, which, before it burst, left tieless shirts and khakis in its wake.

SATURDAY.

In total relaxation mode. Work is out of sight, out of mind.
Hair: deliberately uncombed.
Sunglasses: I'm outdoors, or on my way outdoors.

Tennis racquet: for weekly doubles game at club. Have a backup racquet in my locker, too.

G&T: I'm taking a break from my break.

J. Crew head to ankle.

Cole-Haan penny loafers.

BlackBerry; "If I lost this, I would have to shoot myself. My whole life is in it."

Tod's blue suede driving loafers. "Note to self: Renew driver's license."

Pearl stud earrings, a gift from Corky to all her bridesmaids, etc., etc., etc.

PORTABLE CHILD
Four-year-old son, Clayton.

Lacoste heather-grey traditional polo.

Crewcuts khaki shorts and leather belt.

Tiny desert boots, unlaced, because Thats. How. Clayton. Likes them.

Vintage Lego.

One doesn't have to work in the high-tech world to appreciate a dressed-down workday. And in fact, many people in service industries choose to dress casually when meeting with customers isn't on the day's schedule. In truth, preppies are well supplied with Casual Fridayabilia. This is what we wear when we're not at the office, anyway. Dressing this way makes us more comfortable, as we recognize the sweater with the hole at the elbow as an ally, or enjoy our shoes even more when we're not wearing socks with them.

Even private schools have adopted Casual Friday into their sartorial agenda. Schools with dress codes or uniforms either routinely lift them or charge students $1 to wear blue jeans on Fridays, with the money going to charity.

Is Casual Thursday next?

Logology.

Sometime in the 1980s the cart began leading the horse. Don't look at us; preppies were certainly not to blame. Fashion followers mistakenly thought the logo was the point. (This is when we would write LOL, except we *loathe* LOL.)

2.8 centimeters

1.

Logos have gotten a lot of people into a bit of trouble: Those who are tempted to re-create them without proper license; those who go in search of the great counterfeits by traveling to Southeast Asia, New York's Upper East Side's street vendors, or Chinatown, or by trawling the Web; those whose original work has been stolen. But worst of all, wearing a logo-laden outfit or accessory points to the wearer's confusion about his or her identity or insecurity. If you think you are being ironic, think again.

Here's the rule of thumb: The first logo that preppies loved was the Lacoste crocodile (1). It belonged to the French tennis star Réné Lacoste, whose nickname was Le Crocodile. (See W. Averell Harriman, p. 28) It was an authentic, since he himself wore *la chemise* in 1927, after having been the top tennis player in the world in 1926 and 1927. (He won seven Grand Slam singles titles in France, Britain, and the United States. In 1961 he also invented the first metal tennis racquet, which was sold in this country as the T-2000 by Wilson.)

The shirts, made by La Société Chemise Lacoste, became an international sensation in 1933. Initially made just for men, they had long tails, green (always) crocodiles of 2.8 centimeters width, and embroidered labels with the sizes in French: Petit Patron, Patron, and Grand Patron.

And since 1933, the fabric, called "Jersey petit piqué," has not changed. Up until that time, tennis was played in long sleeves. The shirts were made only in white until 1951, since it was the sole color one could wear at Wimbledon, the French Open, and the U.S. Open. The United States is the largest consumer of Lacoste shirts, which have been available in children's sizes and women's sizes since 1959 and the 1960s, respectively.

Fred Perry, the British tennis champion of the 1930s, introduced his laurel-wreath logo (2) onto white polo shirts in 1952 (a few years after inventing the sweatband). Fred Perry shirts were successful immediately.

Brooks Brothers introduced its Golden Fleece logo (3) as its company's symbol in 1850, but for casual sport shirts, it sold the chemise Lacoste until the 1960s. Then Brooks Brothers made its own men's polo-styled shirts with the golden fleece embroidered on them. These shirts were more subtle than the others as the logos were embroidered in the same colors as the shirts that bore them. And until 1969, the sheep suspended by golden ribbons was made only in men's sizes.

Ralph Lauren was already making menswear when, in 1971, he embroidered a little man astride a polo pony (4) on the cuffs of some women's shirts. The ponies, 1¼" high, moved onto his many-colored cotton polo shirts for men in 1972. The logo, now one of the world's best known, sometimes grows up to 5 inches high ("Big Pony") and sometimes stays small.

.875 inch

2.

.875 inch

3.

1.25 inches

4.

Vineyard Vines' little pink whale (5) appeared in 1998 (see p. 92), and so far, the whale has shown admirable restraint in staying 1.05 inches wide by .43 inch high (as per their universal style guide).

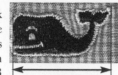

1.05 inches

5.

When Gucci, Fendi, Dior, Chanel, Louis Vuitton, and then Prada began to understand the strong appeal their logos offered, they went wild. Gone were the subtle stripes, woven ribbons, tiny metal trademarks, and interior decoration that had been prized. Now the logos took growth hormones, and there seemed nothing too big or crass to sell. Gucci sold jeans with its logo plastered all over them, as did Dior. Then came some Chanel bags with logos larger than Karl Lagerfeld's head. The clientele for these designer goods changed, and the original customers had to move on to more discreet brands like Bottega Veneta, Tod's, Loro Piana, and VBH. Today's customer is more discerning. Removing logos has become something of a hobby for purists.

When Juicy Couture arrived, emblazoning bottoms with the word "juicy" on its pricey sweatpants, we were dismayed that our daughters thought they wanted them. We steered them back to sanity. We believe that the Juicy Couture tracksuit phenomenon signals the end of civilization as we know it. Nothing less.

TRUNK SHOWS.

Berry and Daisy do not like to go shopping anymore. The stores are crowded and noisy. The sales staff doesn't know if they can order your size from another branch. That Indian-style tunic looks shopworn. Wouldn't it be nicer if you could have some privacy, work with a salesperson who is familiar with your wardrobe, have a glass of chardonnay or an espresso, and relax?

Welcome to the trunk show. Here, in a lovely hotel suite or somebody's lovely living room (you have the same taste in window treatments!) is all of next season's offerings (and a few special items no one will see after this week). Trunk shows, once the domain of specialty shops importing a famous designer to the New York suburbs (like Dallas), is now a cottage business (in the Newport, Rhode Island, sense of the word "cottage") all over our world.

PAPO D'ANJO is an exquisite (but not too precious) line of children's clothing made in Portugal and sold in the living rooms of nice mummies all across the country. Designed by Catherine Connor Monteiro de Barros, they are the clothes that remind us of how our mummies dressed us when we were children. "I like children to look like children." (And weren't we children for a bit longer than chil-

dren get to be now?) "I had clothes made for my [four] children when we lived in Portugal," says Wisconsin-born Monteiro de Barros, "and I was a little bored. I did the cliché thing of doing children's clothes as a business. My first show was on 72nd and Madison at the apartment of an Andover classmate in 1995. We sold $10,000 worth of merchandise," she says with a laugh, "but I don't give up."

Peter Pan collars, cotton piqué, Liberty of London prints, and now a first: a collaboration with Liberty and MacIntosh to make some great rubberized raincoats for little J.R. and Alison. Many mummies volunteer to run the twice-yearly trunk shows in their homes, both to provide the right clothes to all their friends and to earn deep discounts on their Papo clothes for their own children. "It's a cult," says more than one at the big spring show at New York's Hotel Carlyle. Prices range from $14 for a headband to $229 for a smocked Liberty party dress.

Cathryn Collins's I PEZZI DIPINTI sells lots of cashmere, silk slippers, jewelry, boots, and one-of-a-kind furs. Her prices range from $150 to $45,000. Yes, she also sells daily from her SoHo office, over the phone, and via e-mail, but twice a year in London, Los Angeles, San Francisco, Jackson Hole, Detroit, and New York, she sells in person "as an excuse to communicate with all our clients." While the trunk shows bring in only a fraction of her "3,500-plus real shopping clients, hundreds more shop around the show. It is always a vigorous period of activity." She hosts all of the trunk shows herself. These intense two- to three-day spurts represent "fifty percent of the year's business." Collins's hotel sales, like Papo's, are about real buying, not eating, drinking, or schmoozing. Otherwise, customers call to ask what's new—her Web site is not an e-commerce site, and there is no catalogue.

William Rondino more or less invented the fashion trunk show in 1980, when he started the CARLISLE COLLECTION, a kind of Tupperware party for Junior Leaguers. In the '70s, Rondino, a designer on Seventh Avenue for various companies, had the idea of designing a line that he could sell himself without depending on retailers. He launched his first collection in 1982 by inviting friends of his who were past presidents or "sustainers" of Junior Leagues "around the country, who were organized and had lots of tentacles. They weren't the principal breadwinners in their families; no one needed to do it." Ninety-seven "consultants" received the entire wardrobe, "say, 200 pieces. We made 100 sample sets, and said, 'It's yours for a week.' " The consultants, "influencers with social clout and pull," then invited their friends over for a look. Carlisle developed a devoted following, and word of mouth brought more consultants. That's how Mummy earned her quiet six figures per annum, though her family did have to adjust to her new career: no dinner on the table for a week, no living room to hang out in, and so forth.

In the posh showroom Carlisle maintains in Midtown Manhattan, consultants can meet their customers to show them the line in situ—and clients can bring their older pieces in to see what goes with what. Prices for jackets range from $395 to $695, and pants and skirts cost $195 to $250. Nothing goes on sale, and e-commerce isn't possible, because then Carlisle would compete with its ladies.

Today there are between 3,000 and 4,000 Carlisle (and its sister brand, PER SE) consultants who receive samples four times per year.

Lisa Fine, the co-owner of IRVING & FINE, says that as she travels the country checking on her trunk shows, she visits stores where everything is always the same wherever you go. The daughter of Hattiesburg, Mississippi's largest local retailer, Fine has seen the economic model of shopping change from stores like her daddy's to the shopping mall, and to the discount store. Her trunk shows are held in people's homes in cities and resort communities. Irving & Fine manufactures beautiful Indian and Indian-inspired tunics and blouses. Prices range from $150 for a cotton block-printed tunic to $1,600 for a one-of-a-kind Ikat tunic she bought in Uzbekistan and had hand-embroidered in India.

The social component is a draw at Irving & Fine's shows. For one thing, Fine and her partner, Carolina Irving, often invite other designers to join them. Outside of New York, where she holds two shows a year, drinks and nibbles are offered, because "people are more comfortable that way." Instant gratification is here: "We like cash and carry. You don't have to worry about orders, and you don't have to worry about stores paying you."

SOME TRUNK SHOW SOURCES.

CARLISLE COLLECTION

ELIZABETH GAGE

I PEZZI DIPINTI

IRVING & FINE

KULE

LEONTINE LINENS

PAPO D'ANJO

→

IRVING & FINE TRUNK SHOW, San Antonio 2010.

FINLEY AND ABIGAIL SHOPPING AT A PAPO D'ANJO TRUNK SHOW FOR SOMETHING TO WEAR TO THEIR MONKEY'S BIRTHDAY PARTY.

SHEP AND IAN: THE BOYS FROM VINEYARD VINES.

Shepherd Paul Murray, left, born in 1971, and his brother Ian Charles Murray, four years younger, grew up in Greenwich, Connecticut. They both graduated from The Brunswick School, the boys' day school there. Their childhoods (with another brother) sound idyllic—school terms in Greenwich, and for a change of pace, summers on the Vineyard. (Same people; no air-conditioning.) After they graduated from Skidmore and Lafayette, respectively, they joined the great commute, traveling between Connecticut and Grand Central Station every day to work at careers that never thrilled them.

In 1998, Shep quit his job at Young & Rubicam within minutes of Ian quitting his job in travel PR at Evins Communications. They wanted to sell ties. Taking cash advances on credit cards (think: indie film), the Murray brothers ordered yards and yards of custom-printed silk, designed by an art-director buddy. By July 3, 1998, they had 800 ties, which they showed to a few retailers on Martha's Vineyard.

The next day, July 4, 1998—considered "day one" of Vineyard Vines—they began selling their ties out of their Jeep for $65 apiece. Their first account, The Fligors in Edgartown, sold them for $60 each. All the ties were sold out within a few weeks. It looked like the brothers' hunch was correct.

The boys reordered, paid off their debts, and in 2001 they passed the $1 million mark in sales. Now, though the Murrays almost never wear ties themselves, they have approximately 430 patterns and colors on offer.

Hanging with them at their Stamford headquarters or over lunch in downtown Greenwich, you think: I know these guys. I really know them. They are the two brothers who grew up on your block, or were a grade ahead or behind you in school, or rode the same bus, took the same tennis clinic, or played on your brother's hockey team. They are familiar, easygoing, sometimes finish each other's sentences, enjoy what they do, and are replicating their upbringing for the next generation of Murrays.

Bain Sans Soleil.

It is indisputable that overexposure to the sun will cause premature aging, and worse. (Hold on! What could be worse?) At the same time it is inconceivable that preppies would live entirely indoors or remember their sunscreen and follow the prescribed rules for skin care. That just doesn't sound like us.

Call us casual; call us cavalier. But we just love the sun: Lead us to a chaise on a sunny day, and we're happy. As children we were shooed outside the minute the sun appeared. And as outdoor creatures, we will develop a suntan while skiing (that's us in the Rockies over spring break), playing tennis (we play every week), golfing (ditto), sailing (that's us waving from our sloop off Barbados), or gardening (but not our hands; we are wearing gloves). It can't be helped. Not to mention that the sun provides lovely doses of vitamin D—essential to our collective well-being. (Sun deprivation is a grave problem. We're serious! People get depressed, and in northern climes where the sun shines for only half the year, that can lead to homicidal and suicidal impulses, and worse.)

What's a sporty Lilly Pulitzer-wearing college graduate to do?

It is a fact of modern life that a suntan helps you radiate well-being and health. To use an overused word du jour, we have a conundrum. Slather on your sunscreen when you arrive at the beach, and thereafter remember to re-apply . . . if you can. (It's hard. We empathize.) Or wear a hat in the middle of a sunny summer day. Or sit under an umbrella or a canopy.

Since most people have "some color" by midsummer, your hue won't make too much of an impression. A tan in the winter months is more memorable, because it means you've been traveling and most likely on holiday (or recently returned from a stint as a beach vendor in New Zealand).

The twenty-first century has brought the increased efficacy of self-tanners. Some of them merge with your skin's chemistry to make you look tan, not orange. There are sprays and creams that can start you off or prevent your natural tan from fading too fast. But there has been a proliferation of dangerous tanning salons. Too-deep fake tans achieved through tanning beds never look real and are seriously dangerous. (Your local news runs stories about the perils of tanning salon addiction. Check back here for rehab.)

By the time they hit their sixties, if they have avoided melanoma, preppy men and women have adjusted to their sun spots and wrinkles. They regard them as souvenirs of summers well spent. Their freckles remind them of their own mummies and daddies, in the days when bad news was a day without sun.

BOOK BOOK.

In the new old-world department, add the Book Book to your virtual shopping list. Introduced on January 21, 2010, it is a laptop case that looks from the outside like an antiquarian book, and from the inside like a . . . laptop case. Andrew Green designed it for TwelveSouth, the company he operates with his wife, Leigh Ann, which makes accessories for Apple. Based in preppy mecca Charleston, South Carolina, TwelveSouth can barely keep up with the demand for the classic cover, which sells for $79.99. "I enjoy the juxtaposition of something old containing the most modern technology." So do we.

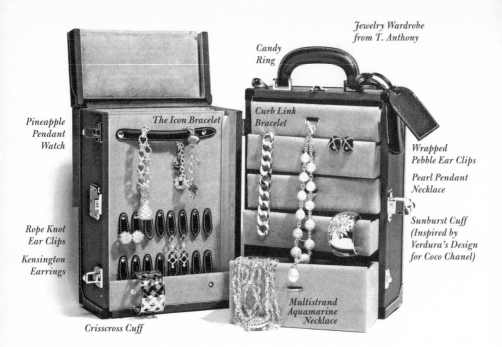

Jewelry Wardrobe
from T. Anthony

Candy
Ring

Curb Link
Bracelet

Pineapple
Pendant
Watch

The Icon Bracelet

Wrapped
Pebble Ear Clips

Pearl Pendant
Necklace

Rope Knot
Ear Clips

Sunburst Cuff
(Inspired by
Verdura's Design
for Coco Chanel)

Kensington
Earrings

Multistrand
Aquamarine
Necklace

Crisscross Cuff

Verdura.

Your ship has come in. You want something (or you want to buy your wife something) that is substantial but not vulgar, daytime and not too sparkly, but not one of those things you see on everyone else at lunch. Definitely not.

Someone you read about and whose style you admire—was it Mona Bismarck?—was a fan of Fulco Santostefano della Cerda. Or you may have heard of his other name, the Duca di Verdura.

Born in Palermo, Sicily, in March of 1898, Fulco grew up at the Villa di Niscemi as the cosseted and adored son surrounded by animals that he loved and a 4,000-volume library. He started school at age eleven. Accustomed to being addressed by his titles, when the teachers called him Fulco, he often forgot to respond.

As a young, fun-loving man in his early twenties, Fulco spent every summer in Venice, where European and American society came to play. Two of his playmates, Cole and Linda Porter, urged him to move to Paris, where he could take his artistic talents more seriously,

though dukes weren't expected to work. In 1927, he joined the world of the already successful Coco Chanel, who first popularized the look of mixing precious and fake jewelry. It was Verdura who designed many of Chanel's iconic jewels, like her white cuffs with the Maltese cross. He sailed to America in 1934, and by 1939 he had established his shop in Manhattan. His unusual settings and designs included shells, seahorses, bees, swans—a nod to his love of animals and the sea. He was a pioneer in the use of multicolored stones, both gems and semiprecious all together.

One of his biographers said of Verdura that he was "determined to downplay the glitz—flashy gems were to him like wearing 'checks around one's neck.' A friend said, 'The important point about Fulco is that . . . his jewelry, like him, was totally unpretentious.'"

No new designs are sold at the luxe, jewel box–like Verdura salon high up in a deco office building on Fifth Avenue. Everything comes from his archives, yet everything somehow looks original, fresh, and compelling. Even the diamonds are set with wit.

What has to go?*

Deciding on the exact amount of jewelry that can be worn at any time is an important chore. Lots and lots of things have to be considered: Is this something you wear all the time no matter what (the friendship bracelet handmade for you by Cissy, your wedding band, your family crest pinkie ring, your good-luck horseshoe charm Daddy gave you when his filly won)? Is this something you need to wear because

Lose the signet ring, Allegra. Too much!

you're about to see the person who gave it to you (Aunt Lucy's pearls, the engagement ring your fiancé gave you, those hoop earrings from your best friend, the paper-clip necklace made by Byron Jr., your son)? If you have even the teensiest fear that you are overdoing it, then you probably are. Trust that impulse. Take off one thing. (A pair of earrings counts as one thing. Especially if your ears are pierced more than once.) And though we love sparkly things as much as the next magpie, gilding the lily is not refined. You can always wear your new Cathy Waterman earrings to the next session of your book club.

On Day Diamonds.

We are sighing here in Central Command over the dilemma about diamonds. Surely we are not alone in our concern about the sudden increase in rocks and—ahem—"boulders" over the last fifteen years. When engagement rings (or the new trend, engagement rings 2.0, 3.0, etc.—the new and enlarged diamonds that arrive with big anniversaries or birthdays) are too enormous, they become distracting. When new brides of old husbands enter the 2.0, 3.0, 4.0 iterations, it is annoying to see rings that turn out to be much larger than those of their predecessors. Not to mention in bad taste. A fine compromise is the diamond wedding band. This goes everywhere without calling too much attention to itself, a long-held preppy tenet. If you keep your diamond band clean, it will sparkle. Black diamonds, newly popular in the twenty-first century, are subtle enough for daytime as well. Wear diamond studs during the day, too . . . if they are under one carat each. Wear bigger ones at night if you like.

Watchmakers now put diamonds around the bezel on all kinds of watches, even those made of steel. A leather strap is truly preppier than a metal one, but don't tell that to the overwhelming numbers of preps who wear or rather live in their Rolexes. (Diamonds on Rolexes are less prep than diamonds on Cartier or Bedat or Pateks. You have questions; we have answers.)

Pearls.

These gifts of the sea are right anytime.

VIRGINIA.
(Georgetown)
Always multitasking: reading the paper, looking svelte in her trench dress (and she's probably cleaning her oven, too).

MARGOT.
(Amherst)
Yes, we see your sassy lining! Get a grip! You have four more hours till your blind date!

BRETON.
(Connecticut College)
"What do you call it when it's not quite a 'sext' but not just a text?"

EMILY.
(Boston College)
"Can't believe I had enough time to run home and take Jackson for a quick walk!"

SPRING FEVER.

It's going to be a looong lunch hour today. Whee! It's the first warm day of the year, and it's torture to stay indoors when it's delicious outside: not humid, a tiny strain of crispness in the air. Oh, just say it: It's a great hair day, too.

Life downtown changes when spring briefly alights. We wear fewer layers and have more energy. All the guys sit outside now to stare at girls, though they pretend they're just getting some fresh air. They don't fool anyone for a second, but it's motivational, and so the heels are higher and the posture straighter. We should meet out here again for coffee around four. Maybe an errand or two? Doesn't someone need something from the post office?

And later, how about meeting at that place with the tables? You know which one? Yes, the one with green-striped umbrellas.

See you there.

ASH.
(Bowdoin)
Was just minding her business, when all these people started hanging here. Good eavesdropping.

TREVOR.
(Colorado)
"Found this jacket after the party last night. I don't think it's mine."

FORREST.
(Harvard)
Listening patiently to misguided skiing advice, with his ironic but understated personalized bag.
Yes, he went to Groton.

97

Swing into any of the vintage shops we've recommended to you (see opposite), and look at the jewelry counters. By and large, costume jewelry. Hattie Carnegie, Miriam Haskell, and Kenneth Jay Lane have always been popular and collectible. Why? Because if it looks as good as the real thing and costs much less, why bother buying the real thing?

Wear it until it tarnishes, and then you can redonate your faux jewels to the thrift shops whence they came. You might even get a tax deduction.

Our tunic is wearing an extraordinary selection of costume jewelry. It was Coco Chanel herself who first made fakes chic, and there are some impressive copies of important jewels here. Quite a lot of David Webb, we see. We spy with our little eyes something like Barbara Bush's pearls. Jackie Kennedy was a fan and a customer of KJL, who provided these pieces, and she remains our singular style leader to this day.

VINTAGE STORES.

WE JUST WANT TO GO ON RECORD: We knew about and appreciated vintage a long time ago—in fact, before it was rechristened vintage and was just plain *used*. We learned, through trial and error (and an embarrassing yearbook picture we'd rather not discuss anymore), that vintage Bakelite pins look great on school blazers, there's a reason gaucho pants are obsolete and faded chamois "cowboy" jackets—if you can carry off the fringe—are fab. Herewith, a country-wide listing of great places to check out to incorporate vintage looks with your basic uniform. These shops have had their tires kicked by Ivy Baer Sherman (Friends Seminary, Barnard College), editor in chief of *Vintage Magazine*.

CALIFORNIA

Beverly Hills
Lily et Cie. 9044 Burton Way (310) 724-5757

Los Altos
Repeter Consignment. 308 State St. (650) 949-1323

Los Angeles
America Rag. 150 S. La Brea Ave. (323) 935-3154
Decades. 8214¼ Melrose Ave. (323) 655-0223
Jet Rag. 825 N. La Brea Ave. (323) 939-0528
Resurrection. 8006 Melrose Ave. (323) 651-5516

San Francisco
Jr. League Next-to-New + Consignment Boutique. 2226 Fillmore St. (415) 567-1627
Seconds to Go. 2252 Fillmore St. (415) 563-7806
Town School Clothes Closet. 1850 Polk St. (415) 929-8019

CONNECTICUT

Darien
Double Exposure. 1090 Post Road (203) 655-8799

Green Farms
Roundabout Designer Consignments. 170 Post Road West, Westport (203) 227-4334

Greenwich
Consign Designs. 115 Mason St. (203) 869-2165
Second Time Around. 6 Greenwich Ave. (203) 422-2808

New Canaan
Thrift Shop of New Canaan. 2 Locust Ave. (203) 966-2361

Southport
Twice Is Nice. 3519 Post Road (203) 259-7627

DELAWARE

Wilmington
Rags to Riches. Centreville Square, 5801-B Kennett Pike (302) 654-5997

FLORIDA

Gainesville
Junior League of Gainesville Thrift Shop. 430-A N. Main St. (352) 376-3805

Jacksonville
The Clothing Warehouse. 1010 Park St. (904) 356-5003

Palm Beach
Classic Collections. 118 North County Road (561) 833-3633
Fiore's Fine Men's Wear. 116 North County Road (561) 655-9965

GEORGIA

Atlanta
The Clothing Warehouse. 420 Moreland Ave. (404) 524-5070

East Point
The Clothing Warehouse. 2824 Church St. (404) 766-3432

Savannah
The Clothing Warehouse. 217 W. Broughton St. (912) 233-2034

ILLINOIS

Barrington

Double Exposure Elite Resale. 706 S. Northwest Highway (847) 756-2702

Vintage Faire. 113 S. Hough St. (847) 842-9719

Evanston

Classy Closet. 701 Washington St. (847) 475-0355

INDIANA

Carmel/Zionsville

Goodwill. 10491 Walnut Creek Drive, Suite 100 (317) 876-0096

LOUISIANA

New Orleans

Junior League of New Orleans Thrift Shop. 4645 Freret St. (504) 891-1289

MAINE

Portland

Good Cause Thrift Store. 16 Forest Ave. (207) 772-4903

Second Time Around. 28 Exchange St. (207) 761-7037

MARYLAND

Baltimore

The Wise Penny. 5902 York Road (410) 435-5521

Gaithersburg

Chic to Chic. 15900 Luanne Dr. (301) 926-7700

Rockville

The Ritz Boutique. 5014 Nicholson Lane (301) 230-2167

Takoma Park

Polly Sue's Vintage Shop. 6915 Laurel Ave. (301) 270-5511

MASSACHUSETTS

Boston

Second Time Around. 176 Newbury St. (617) 247-3504

Cambridge

Second Time Around. 8 Eliot St. (617) 491-7185

Marblehead

Rags to Riches. 41 Atlantic Ave. (781) 631-3379

Nantucket

Consignment Shop. 62 Old South Road (508) 228-1408

MICHIGAN

Bloomfield Hills

Treasure Trunk of Birmingham. 33277 Woodward Ave. (248) 645-5465

Grosse Pointe

Neighborhood Club Thrift Shop. 17150 Waterloo St. (313) 885-0773

NEW JERSEY

Princeton

Nearly New. 234 Nassau St. (609) 924-5720

Summit

Junior League of Summit Thrift Shop. 37 DeForest Ave. (908) 273-7349

NEW YORK

Brooklyn

Odd Twin. 164 5th Ave., Park Slope (718) 633-8946

Beacon's Closet. 88 N. 11th St., Williamsburg (718) 486-0816

Housing Works. 122 Montague St., Brooklyn Heights (718) 237-0521

Long Island

Junior League of Long Island Thrift Shop. 1395 Old Northern Blvd., Roslyn (516) 484-0485

Manhattan

Amarcord. 252 Lafayette St. (212) 431-4161

Edith Machinest. 104 Rivington St. (212) 979-9992

Ellen. 122 Ludlow St. (212) 471-0080

Encore. 1132 Madison Ave. (212) 879-2850

The Family Jewels. 130 W. 23rd St. (212) 633-6020

Housing Works. 130 Crosby St. (646) 786-1200

Housing Works. 245 West 10th St. (212) 352-1618

Housing Works. 306 Columbus Ave. (212) 579-7566

Housing Works. 143 West 17th St. (718) 838-5050

Ina Men. 262 Mott St. (212) 334-2210

Laurel Canyon Vintage. 63 Thompson St. (212) 343-1658

Michael's. 1041 Madison Ave. (212) 737-7273

Patina. 451 Broome St. (212) 625-3375

What Comes Around Goes Around. 351 West Broadway (212) 343-9303

And Do Make Note: Lighthouse International, formerly known as the Lighthouse for the Blind, sponsors what fashion insiders consider the ultimate sample sale, called the POSH sale, now in its thirty-seventh year. Held over four days in New York every spring, POSH sells both new and "almost new" high-fashion clothing and accessories at about 80 percent off. Fancy people shop there by going to the preview sale, tickets for which sell for $175. Otherwise, admission is $10 per day. (The part of socialite Nan Kempner's wardrobe that didn't go to the Fashion Institute of the Metropolitan Museum is rumored to have ended up at a POSH sale.) POSH Palm Beach has happened every February since 2007.

NORTH CAROLINA
Chapel Hill
The Clothing Warehouse. 109 E. Franklin St. #101 (919) 933-9926

OHIO
Columbus
One More Time. 1521 W. Fifth Ave. (614) 486-0031

OREGON
Portland
My Girlfriend's Closet. 4443 NE Fremont St. (503) 281-4459

PENNSYLVANIA
Ardmore
Junior League of Philadelphia Thrift Shop. 25 W. Lancaster Ave. (610) 896-8828

RHODE ISLAND
Newport
Closet Revival. 30 Broadway (401) 845-0592

SOUTH CAROLINA
Charleston
Butterfly Consignments. 482 King St. (843) 577-8404

Greenville
The Clothing Warehouse. 123 N. Main St. (864) 467-1238

TENNESSEE
Memphis
Junior League of Memphis Thrift Shop. 3586 Summer Ave. (901) 327-4777

VIRGINIA
Falls Church
Unique Thrift Store. 2950 Gallows Road (703) 992-6560

Reston
Vogue to Vintage. 11414 Washington Plaza W. (703) 787-5700

WASHINGTON
Bellevue
Your Sister's Closet. 11810 NE Eighth St. (425) 223-2100

Seattle
Alexandra's Designer Consignment Boutique. 412 Olive Way (206) 623-1214

Crossroads Trading Company. 325 Broadway Ave. East (206) 328-5867

WASHINGTON, D.C.
Georgetown
Annie Cream Cheese. 3279 M St. NW (202) 298-5555

Second Time Around. 3289 M St. NW (202) 333-2355

Secondhand Rose of Georgetown. 1516 Wisconsin Ave. NW (202) 337-3378

BROOKS
BROTHERS

BURBERRY
MINI

CALVIN KLEIN
WOOL TWEED

L.L. BEAN
SIGNATURE

BURBERRY
RUCHED SILK

IN THE TRENCHES.

Who designed the trench coat? No one is quite sure whether it was Mr. Burberry or Mr. Aquascutum (actually, John Emary). Both invented water-repellent materials: Burberry named his gabardine; Emary's was a "shower-proof" wool, and he renamed his tailor shop Aqua-scutum, Latin for "watershield." This much is certain: The jacket Burberry designed for soldiers in the Boer War in South Africa at the very end of the 1800s was nicknamed a "Burberry." By World War One, they were quite the thing. Mr. Burberry's first trench coats were made for

CORDINGS
OF PICCADILLY

ARMANI
LEATHER

BURBERRY
TRENCH DRESS

BURBERRY
MODERN PLAID

BROOKS
BROTHERS

British officers, when wool serge was unavailable. The coats were not required uniform, but were so durable in the trenches that officers would pay for them out of their own pockets. Between 1914 and 1918, perhaps half a million Burberrys were worn by officers. Aquascutum outfitted World War One as well. By 1918, *Harper's Bazaar* was recommending them for stylish women. Given their English provenance and their unisex, sturdy appeal, preppies claim the trench as our own. The D-rings, loops, and funny flaps (originally for map holders, grenades, and water bottles) only add to their preppiness. Now, of course, everyone makes a trench, at all prices and in all kinds of fabrics. There's a trench coat for everyone.

HERMÈS.

It's French, chic, and CRAZEEE expensive. But it's also understated. It's Hermès, and this time around, it must be recognized for its long-standing attraction to preppies around the world. We don't love it for the prices or for its snob appeal. Men love the ties because within the tightly designed patterns are whimsical animals. And the leather pieces—especially the wallets, agendas, and little this-and-thats—come in every possible color you can imagine. Hawkins cannot decide on what today's investment will be: Happily, it will come in its well-constructed thick orange box, which she will reuse for lost buttons. Should it be a scarf? She already has half a dozen. The wallet is great. Maybe a clutch? Maybe another tie for Tommy? He has quite the collection, but he goes weak for little monkeys.

Not Your Mummy's *School Ring.*

Proust had his madeleine. Kane had Rosebud. Jessica Mindich has her Kingswood Oxford School (West Hartford, Connecticut) class ring. "With the fleeting nature of memories, I look at my jewelry box as a place for my souvenirs: my class ring, my sorority pin, my grandmother's pearls." And she saw that the high-school kids in her neighborhood weren't wearing their school rings. Too expensive.

Now Jessica makes silver or enamel charms of school crests and shields, and she threads them onto cotton cords. She sells them wholesale to private schools (often through the parents) and colleges. The institutions then sell them for whatever price they like to raise money for a cause. That's why her company is named Jewelry for a Cause.

BELTED.

A young man from Northern California named Taylor Llewellyn was raised by easterners outside of Oakland. They urged him to go east for college. He chose Colgate, a hotbed of cool preppies, and like everyone else there, he "had a blast." Properly indoctrinated, he was engaged in private equity in Washington, D.C.

But Llewellyn had a dream: to bring "hand-stitched needlepoint belts that wouldn't break the bank" to people all across America. It was a specific dream, to be sure. In October 2007 he quit his job and went to China, armed with the four needlepoint belts in his closet. One day, while walking to a trade fair in Guangzhou, eating a dumpling from a street vendor, Llewellyn thought, "I'm either great, or I've lost it. What the hell am I doing?"

As he met manufacturers, he whipped the belt off his waist and snipped it into ten segments, to give to ten "sourcing" companies. "They replicated them perfectly." Was he worried that this wouldn't work, and he'd be out some money and his cherished belt?

"The risk of not doing it was worse than the fear of it failing."

Cut to spring 2010. Llewellyn's company, Tucker Blair (family names, both), is turning a profit on "hand-stitched needlepoint belts" and flip-flops, headbands, key fobs, and dog collars "that don't break the bank." They are sold on his Web site, through sales reps at college campuses, and at Sperry stores. The young man from California is twenty-eight.

BELTS BY VINEYARD VINES, CK BRADLEY, KENNETH JAY LANE,

TIFFANY, AND ONE CUSTOM NEEDLEPOINT.

107

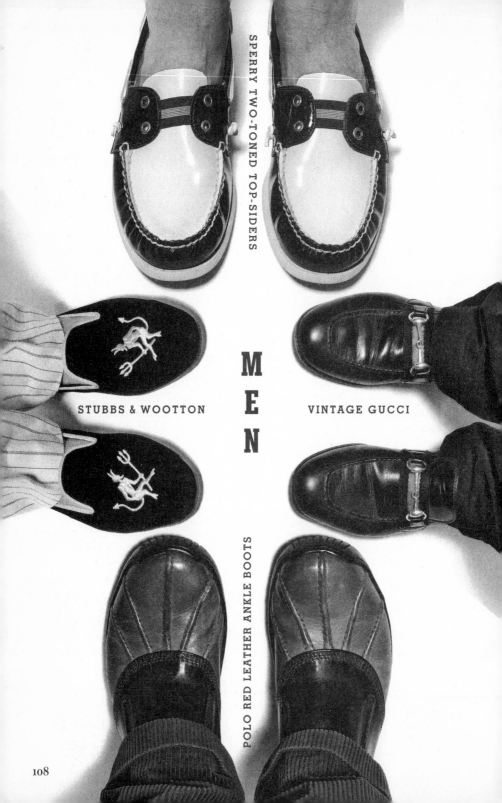

SPERRY TWO-TONED TOP-SIDERS

MEN

STUBBS & WOOTTON

VINTAGE GUCCI

POLO RED LEATHER ANKLE BOOTS

BASS

TANINO CRISCI

PRADA

TOMMY HILFIGER

MEN'S LOAFERS.

So many loafers, so little time. And just when you think you've seen (and bought) the *ne plus ultra* of slip-on footwear, a new variation on a theme comes out that you need. Here are a few we like. There are plenty of others scattered about in the book for the observant among you.

RALPH LAUREN DRIVING SHOE

J.M. WESTON ALLIGATOR

RALPH LAUREN BELTED

BROOKS BROTHERS TASSEL

MANOLO BLAHNIK

CELINE

COLE-HAAN

RALPH LAUREN

WOMEN'S LOAFERS.

Women's loafers started out as smaller, narrower versions of men's shoes. Now some come in unusual materials and even with heels and pointed toes. They are a so-called "sensible shoe" but with a dash of sex appeal.

BURBERRY

BROOKS BROTHERS

FERRAGAMO

BASS WEEJUNS

STUBBS & WOOTTON

WOMEN

JACK ROGERS

PRADA

SUPERGA

One Man and His Outerwear.

Anderson Flatto has it all: a degree from Trinity College, several trips to Europe under his belt (including a junior semester abroad; don't ask), and a 2008 Audi A4 Cabriolet convertible. Andy's got nice parents, a decent sister, and signing privileges at his parents' club. But what he has—really has—is the wardrobe. This is our idea of having it all: the perfect clothes for every occasion, from the car wash to Pammy's debutante ball.

Spring or fall, Anderson's ready for action in his perfect, unchangeable ensemble. Whether he's twenty-two or eighty-two, he will look just right: a little stodgy in his youth, and quite boyish in his dotage.

SPRING: Topping the look is his bottle-green oiled-cloth Beaufort jacket from Barbour. It's hovering nicely over a Henri Lloyd vest and a classic button-down oxford cloth shirt from Brooks Brothers. A CK Bradley embroidered belt holds up Flatto's wide-wale red

cords, embroidered with whales from J. McLaughlin. Sperry Top-Siders complete the look. As always, he's wearing his Taft school ring and the Rolex he got for graduation from Trinity. (Don't mind telling you, it was touch-and-go for a while.)

FALL: Whether it's Homecoming weekend or any other weekend, Andy's classic Brooks Brothers duffel coat is the perfect casual topper. He can wear this one for the next twenty years. (He probably will not, he's not a slave to fashion.) While looking for Reed and Jasper in the tailgating area, Andy wears his Norwegian sweater from L.L.Bean with panache. Corduroy trousers with fox heads (J. McLaughlin) scream fall, and his Wellies by Hunter are smart for the mud. (Flatto's carrying his overnight bag made of an old sail—Re-Sails—in case he has to blow his particular Popsicle stand a night early.)

BROOKS BROTHERS: NOW.

Tom Davis, at Your Service.

When Tom Davis was a teenager, he was a member of the Merchandise Club at the High School of Commerce on the West Side of Manhattan. Drafted after graduation, he got out of his Georgia MASH unit in 1967. Upon discovering that the president of the Merchandise Club had become an assistant buyer at Brooks Brothers, Tom called him, and he got an appointment with the head of personnel on a Thursday.

"She said, 'Would you like to start today?' but I didn't think I was so well dressed, so I asked her if I could start on Monday." He pauses. "I came to Brooks Brothers on November 27, 1967, a Monday." By 1976 Davis had been promoted to the main floor, where he stayed until 2009, when the made-to-measure shirts—his area of specialty since the '90s—moved back up to five. He still works there full-time.

In those years, Tom sold shirts to David Rockefeller, Richard Widmark, William F. Buckley Jr., and his brother Senator James Buckley. As a child, John-John Kennedy would come in with his Aunt Lee Radziwill. It is well known that Gianni Agnelli bought his shirts from Brooks Brothers in New York, but it was said that he wore his shirts once and then disposed of them. Davis set the record straight. "Mr. Agnelli was a practical man. He didn't wear them once, but he didn't like to travel with luggage, so he'd order many shirts at a time to send to his various houses. He'd buy two dozen or more at a time, only in white, beige, and blue." How did he customize them? "He didn't. He bought them right off the table. Pima oxford cloth button-down shirts. No monograms. Never."

Davis is particular about what he wears, but he denies being a clotheshorse. "I don't have closets full of clothes. I buy out of need, and the clothes last. The last suit I bought was in 1993. The store would lose money on me," he says, grinning.

Made-to-measure pin-striped grey suit, Anglo-English style, from 1985.

White shirt with tennis collar.

Pocket square.

Brooks Brothers tie, with tie bar.

Trousers 19-inch width at bottom.

Cuffs 1¼ inch.

Brooks lace-ups.

AND NOW.

Thom Browne, Tweaking Tradition.

Grey wool suit by Thom Browne.

White cotton oxford cloth button-down shirt by Black Fleece.

Thom Browne grey wool necktie, 2.5 inches wide.

Thom Browne V-neck cashmere cardigan with red, white, and blue grosgrain trim.

Two side vents on jacket.

Ankles by Thom Browne.

Thom Browne black leather wingtip shoes.

Thom Browne, the fourth of seven children raised in Allentown, Pennsylvania, by two lawyers, grew up wearing hand-me-downs, mostly from Brooks Brothers and L.L.Bean. He didn't lead a life in which fashion was the predictable outcome. After studying business at Notre Dame, he had no idea what to do. It was while pursuing acting in Los Angeles that he began buying himself suits at vintage shops and cutting them down to a shrunken (almost Pee Wee Herman–esque silhouette) size: trousers are 38 inches long from the top of the waistband, and the hem falls 2 inches above the top of his shoe; jackets nip in at the waist and fall to the tops of his hips. "I wanted it to look cool."

In 2002, when Browne started dressing his way, the L.A. dress code was jeans and T-shirts, on everyone. "Suits weren't done. They connoted old men."

A stint as a designer of menswear for Club Monaco was short-lived, as Browne's ideas did not sell. As he continued to refit old suits for himself, Browne met Rocco, his old-fashioned Italian-trained tailor. "I learned everything from him." The pair designed a few samples, which they showed to the men's store of Bergdorf Goodman. Bergdorf scooped up the whole line, as did the legendary Paris store, Colette.

When Browne was a runner-up for the CFDA Fund awards in 2006, Anna Wintour asked him what he'd be interested in doing besides designing his own "fashion-forward" line. "I thought to do a collection for Brooks Brothers—where I had grown up—would be cool. It's the iconic American brand." Wintour made the connection, and Black Fleece, the men's and women's lines created by Thom Browne exclusively for "B Squared," was created.

Browne's signature is "taking classics and making them provocative," a favorite word. Browne himself wears only his Thom Browne–brand suits. He wears no jeans, and only wingtips, sockless until the weather gets cold.

And Black Fleece? It's somewhere in between what Brooks Brothers has always done and what Browne does for his own line. Luxurious fabrics, quirky details, and something that pushes it over the edge. Don't wear it if you don't want to be noticed.

5.

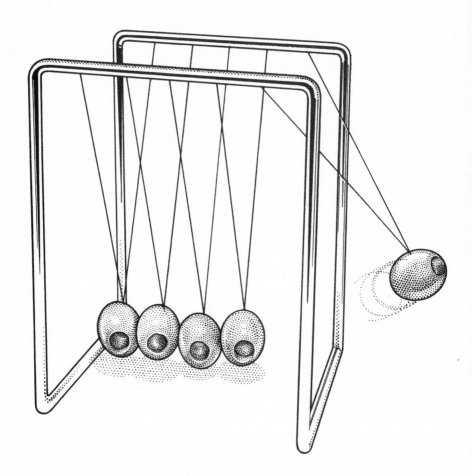

UNHAPPY HOURS.

WORK.

The worst of doing one's duty was that it apparently unfitted one for doing anything else.
—Edith Wharton, *The Age of Innocence*

Preppies realize society's need for enterprise. They go to college with the idea of a career—or should we say, their parents' idea of a career—planted firmly in their minds. This is why so many of them attend law school. They also understand their need for income. One gets a bad reputation if derelict with one's club dues. As the twenty-first century unfurls, herewith a vital list of jobs that are prep-proof, others that are defunct, and some that will always help preppies maintain their rightful positions in their world.

PREP CAREERS FOR THE NEW MILLENNIUM.

Alumni Director. *For the good of your school.*

Development Officer. *Ditto.*

Dog Walker Entrepreneur. *Accommodates Lake Forest, Rollins, and drop-outs.*

Party Planner/Publicist. *The perfect job for girls who won't be working after they get engaged.*

Nursery-School Assistant Teacher. *But not over the age of thirty.*

Contributing Editor, *Vogue. Consuela's mother works for* Anna.

Senator. *For policy wonks.*

Entrepreneur (Serial). *One day, one of your ideas will take off.*

Ne'er-do-well. *Uncle Tony.*

Caterer. *Use Mummy's recipe for chicken pot pies as your signature.*

Decorator. *Who doesn't love chintz?*

Residential Real-Estate Broker. *Sell Bradford a lovely house; marry Bradford and decorate your new house.*

Golf Pro. *Self-evident.*

Art Restorer. *Very good for part-time artists.*

Divorcée. *'Nuff said.*

Anchorman or -Woman. *Remember to remove your makeup when you meet friends after work for drinks.*

Curator. *Requires many trips to Europe.*

Au Pair. *How Princess Diana got her start.*

President. *Good perks; bad hours.*

Vineyard Owner. *Ultimate career move.*

Tennis Pro. *Will keep you fit through your thirties and forties.*

CIA Operative. *Yalies, in particular.*

Decorative Painter. *Learn how to make anything faux bois.*

Ski Bum. *Self-evident.*

FORMER CAREERS WE WON'T BE SEEING AGAIN SOON.

Assistant Editor. *It's called the Recession, Greer.*

Media Escort. *No more book tours; therefore, no more escorts.*

Fund-raising. *Should rebound by 2015.*

Investment Banker Trainee. *Might rebound by 2020.*

Travel Agent. *Expedia.*

PREPS NEED NOT APPLY.

Doctor. *Presumes caring about strangers; exception: orthopedic surgeon (see p. 207).*

Research Doctor. *Atrophies your God-given social skills.*

Computer Scientist. *No.*

CPA. *Really no.*

Missionary. *See "Doctor."*

Sex Worker. *See "when pigs fly."*

Any job requiring the question "Any fries with that?" *Only at the club during the summer before junior year. Of high school.*

Governor. *Possibility of sex scandal too great.*

Engineer. *Choo-choo or the other kind.*

Fact-checker. *Facts, shmacts.*

Manny. *NOKD.*

Meteorologist. *Too science-y.*

THE WAR ROOM.

Daddy hasn't worked this long and hard to have to spend time in a plain vanilla office space. No longer a slave to institutional furniture, he has made his office a reflection of his likes and idiosyncrasies. The memorabilia Mummy won't allow in the house shares shelf space with toys he can play with when he is experiencing some downtime. The furniture is antique and (some) reproduction antique. The leather club chairs have been with him forever. The message: A real man works here. And plays here.

Daddy loves and collects cars. The real ones are in his garage at home and his garage in the country, but it's comforting to have toy models of them in the office. (Good for breaking the ice with new clients.) Of course, he uses his computer, Black-Berry, and the thingy, but he still keeps his Rolodex, just because.

The humidor is over there, wet bar is over here. His assistant mans the espresso maker.

The floral curtains? Reminds him of his childhood house in Massachusetts. You know what Daddy always says? "My office, c'est moi."

1. *To wet bar.*
2. *Wooden tennis racquet belonging to an American player during the 1936 Berlin Olympics. Really.*
3. *Cute flat-screen TV. Keeps it on CNBC, mostly.*
4. *Daddy's desk chair is on wheels so he can swivel when he gets bored.*
5. *Daddy's collection of hats he bought in former Eastern European Socialist countries.*
6. *Nice chintz fabric that Mummy had left over from the breakfast-room banquette.*

7. *Daddy. He's talking to his Italian tailor,
   ordering his bespoke bathrobe.
   (Hand gesture gives that away.)*

8. *Daddy's desk: reproduction period English
   desk from Mill House in Connecticut.*

9. *In & Out Box, purchased at Bentleys in
   London. Probably came from a clerk's
   (pronounced "clark's") office, "not landed
   gentry desk material." Until now.*

10. *1948 Ford Woody wagon. Gift.
    Almost as cool as Daddy's real-life
    1940 vintage Woody.*

11. *Model of a late-1930s Pan Am Clipper.*

12. *Daddy's 1,500 closest friends.*

13. *So many invitations!*

14. *Leather club chairs, purchased fifteen
    years ago. Manly.*

15. *To humidor.*

BANKERS: WHAT DO THEY DO ALL DAY?

Explaining what bankers and traders on Wall Street actually do all day is a bit like watching the proverbial sausage being made at the slaughterhouse: There are some things better left unexplained. But since you asked so nicely, unlike the House Committee on Oversight and Government Reform and the Financial Crisis Inquiry Commission, here's your answer.

For the record, bankers and traders help allocate capital around the globe, wherever it is needed, twenty-four hours a day, seven days a week. For instance, for Apple to develop, manufacture, and market the iPad, the company requires access to capital around the globe (and especially in Asia, where the product is assembled). Steve Jobs long ago gave up the practice of funding Apple's capital needs himself. So whether he wants to or not, he has to turn to a bank or to a Wall Street firm to raise the money needed for his company to make things.

Capital can be raised in many forms—among them, loans from banks, bonds raised from public investors, or equity from private investors or people like you and me with a Merrill Lynch brokerage account—and whenever this happens, bankers and traders always manage to take a slice of the pie. This is what Wall Street is really after: fees. Fees for raising money, fees for advising on mergers and acquisitions, fees for taking companies private, fees for taking companies public, fees for allowing us to open a brokerage account and trade with our own money, and fees on the difference between the cost of borrowing money and the price they can charge for lending it out. For instance, one of the ways Goldman Sachs made a Mount Everest–sized amount of money in 2009 was by borrowing so cheaply from the Federal Reserve and then turning around and charging much more to lend it out to its clients. Nice work if you can get it.

Off the record, though, we used to say on Wall Street that investment banking was good one day a year: the day bonuses are paid. In what other profession on the face of the earth can people make so much money for taking so little risk with their own money? The answer is "Nowhere." Of course, bankers and traders take plenty of risks with other people's money, and when those bets pay off they get huge bonuses, and when they don't they—apparently—get bailed out by taxpayers.

During the rest of the year—while bankers and traders are waiting for that special bonus day—they preen, they politick, they suck up, and they backstab, and occasionally they help their clients raise capital, invest money, or buy and sell companies.

Community bankers don't do what investment bankers do . . . They make loans in their communities for businesses and for mortgages, and yes, they want fees, but they also want the interest paid on the loans as well as the loans back themselves. Commercial banking and investment banking have been scrambled together like an egg yolk and an egg white, thanks to the repeal of the Glass-Steagall Act. Good luck unscrambling.

All "too-big-to-fail" banks do pretty much the same thing, although Goldman Sachs doesn't take deposits from you and me—too petty, lowbrow—but most other banks do, either in the form of deposits at ATMs or in brokerage accounts or both. The beauty of this method of collecting money is that it is an incredibly cheap form of gathering cash. (Even though you wouldn't know it, Goldman does have a small bank in Utah.) They can lend out and get those big fees I described before. How much does your bank pay you for your savings? Like zero, right? Well, add up all those deposits, which cost close to zero, and then lend all that money out at high interest rates and—bingo—you have massive profits. That's banking—in many different forms.

In what other profession on earth could one imagine becoming a millionaire by your thirtieth birthday without putting any capital at risk? It's one thing for Gates or Jobs to be a billionaire by the time they are thirty or forty—they took huge financial and career risks and became huge successes and got rich. No such personal risks exist on Wall Street, except the risk of a stupid boss who fires you because he decides you haven't done enough sucking up. That's the real risk on Wall Street.

The simple truth is that investment banking became the black hole for the best and brightest preppies because it paid by far the most money to people without any particular gift. If you are Roger Federer, you play tennis and make a billion; if you are Michael Jordan, you play basketball and make a billion; if you are Oprah, you are Oprah and you make a billion. But these highly talented people are very few and far between. If you are Skip Powell IV, you go to Wall Street, work hard, do what you are told, and—bingo—you have a house in the Hamptons and a co-op on Park Avenue.

—William D. Cohan
Phillips Academy Andover, Duke, Columbia Journalism School, Columbia Business School

"I can't believe 411 can't find Cowtan & Tout. How long will this robot keep me on hold?"

"Hello? I need a human being! Cowtan is with a C. Cow as in bovine, tan as in what you look like when you've spent a week at Round Hill."

"Is this what killed Sister Parish?"

"My short leather jacket proves I'm stylish but safe."

"I'm so glad Geoffrey bought me this Birkin bag. It holds all my swatches and paint chips."

Mummy is suddenly so busy. Wasn't she happy in her book club, playing her weekly squash game, and taking care of us? She's suddenly got bits of fabric and samples of wallpaper on the dining-room table (which means we eat in the kitchen, even for dinner), and she couldn't bring our Spanish workbook to school yesterday when we forgot it, because she was "meeting a client."

She's decorating Aunt Henny's pool house and thinking of redoing our breakfast room. It's kind of cool that Mummy's working. Instead of telling us to do our homework or take our baths, she's kind of distracted. But it was nice when we came home from school and she would be home, too. If only we could have gotten her attention.

WHY NOT-FOR-PROFITS ARE MORE PREP THAN PRIVATE-SECTOR JOBS.

Any job that has a kind of mysterious benefactor is preppier than a job that has an obvious salary source.

Any job that has a vaguely helpful purpose is preppier than a job that is just about earning money. (Earning lots of money is fine but a little bit obvious and therefore embarrassing.)

Any job that helps people really far away (microfinancing in Africa, feeding children in Haiti, and so on) is incredibly prep.

You need to feel you are contributing to our nation's good, à la John Adams, John Quincy Adams, Thomas Jefferson, FDR, Jane Addams.

You are not doing it for the money.

Writing grant proposals is in itself a thankless preppy task, like writing endless papers.

Research in, say, a think tank is prep. Because there is no real "finish line" or "end user" for your research.

Working in obscurity is prep. No one really knows what you do, which is perfect—your privacy is intact, as are your online Scrabble scores. Remember, in the best of situations, your kids have no idea what you do beyond going to an office.

It means you are working for one of those earnest preppies who care so much about something arcane: You are preserving the musical rhythms of the Mayan people. You are conserving the textiles of the ancient Aborigines. You are protecting the traditions of the Lost Kingdom of Mustang, the indigenous language of Antarctica. Whatever it is, no one can really check up on you because you go far away for long periods of time and cell phones don't work in the jungle, the brush, on the equator, at the South Pole, or wherever it is you go for three months at a time.

You can do this (whatever it is) forever.

WHERE THE GIRLS ARE.

If you are like us (and you are getting closer), you will read the social announcements in your Sunday paper or in *The New York Times*. (It goes without saying that you read them first—before the Front Page, before Sports.) We won't mention it again.

As you graze about, looking at the delightful couples, you might see a pattern amongst the young ones. Yes, many of them met at college. Except for those who met during high school. And plenty met in elementary school. And many of the brides are nursery- or lower-school teachers. Why is that?

Several reasons.
• Alex loves children. She adores them! She can't wait to have some of her own.

In fact, she's planning on leaving education ASAP to get on with it and move to the suburbs and let Trevor do all the earning from now on.
• Alex is a self-starting preppy. She didn't grow up this way, but she has reinvented herself in the image of some of the younger mummies. She immerses herself in a milieu where she will meet preppy families who will introduce her to a preppy dreamboat.
• Alex has a trust fund. She does not have to earn her keep. (Martinis at the Four Seasons?) Theory and Roberta Freymann clothes? Not on this salary.
• Alex wants her summers off.

UH-OH #2: MUMMY JUST PASSED HER REAL-ESTATE EXAM.

"Mrs. Coe will say the house is too narrow, but she's wrong. Especially for her budget."

"Sunglasses for sun, waterproof jacket for rain. I've just the best wardrobe for being a broker."

"Where is my co-broker?"

"Mrs. Coe can't take her eyes off my ring. Maybe she should look at the moldings instead."

Mummy got bored with decorating. She said she never knew how difficult and indecisive her friends really were! Bailey changed her mind every day or twice a day after she saw Ripley's wainscoting and Ba's moss-green silk curtains. She even thought Mummy was trying to gouge her! The nerve! So . . . sit down. Mummy just took her real-estate exam. And passed it the first time! Mummy says it's easier to work with strangers than with friends, but how is any-

one going to know she is a broker? Daddy says it's a giant waste of time, but he says he will support her whatever she does. (Does that mean financially?) Mummy says she wants "her own money," whatever that means. She can finally buy me a horse! The Masons had to visit that house on Newcomb Street three times and still can't decide. Mummy says Jill Mason will be the death of her. But that's better than when she said we would be the death of her . . . sort of.

UH-OH #3: MUMMY IS NOW A DOCENT.

"Do I look like a docent in my cashmere twin-set? I feel like one. I think I'm getting a headache from my daughter's headband. Didn't realize she had such a small head."

"The coat check is to your left in the Great Hall. Next to the huge sign that says COAT CHECK. *Jesus, these people . . ."*

"How old was Holbein when he painted this? Am I supposed to know? I'll try to Google it on my Black-Berry."

"They never told me I had to know the artists' ages. What do they do with docents who didn't major in Art History?"

Well, Mummy is over real estate. This market was pretty stressful. Is Mummy really made for work? She had some kind of job when she met Daddy but quit it after they met. Now she's a docent at the museum. She always knew her Art History major from Wellesley would come in handy one day. "Excuse me, miss. Why did van Gogh cut off his ear?" How should Mummy know? She tells them, "Listen to the song!" Except for all the tourists who make her shout (she doesn't raise her voice) and all the people who ask her where the bathrooms are, being a docent is fulfilling. And Mummy still has time to play doubles, read her book club books, and get a manicure.

First it was Didi, now Flossy, and it wouldn't surprise us if Mopsy, Topsy, and Cottontail all joined in, too. No, they are not becoming sales consultants for Carlisle; they are all writing books. Or to be perfectly correct, they are all *thinking* of writing books. Or they are *thinking* about thinking about writing something booklike.

Being a pre-writer is a preppy career choice, perhaps the choicest one of all. It has no timing, no deadline—nothing but intellectual aspirations and cachet. It's a great save for when you socialize with "doers" who have interesting projects and jobs to report about; your life of needlepoint, book club, tennis club, dog walking, naps, and vacations doesn't exactly garner a lot of interest at cocktail parties (though the story of the Stanfords trying to steal your caretaker was marvelous).

Now that we've established you will contemplate a book project—Ooh! You sound more interesting already!—what will it be?

You could put together a book of photographs about a theme. Let's see: Swimming pools? (Been done.) Flowers? Everyone always loves flower pictures. You were an art history major at Wellesley—maybe you could expand your final art paper on Caillebotte? (No. You just remembered how positively ex-cru-ciating it was writing the eight pages twenty years ago.) What about a cookbook? What about a dog book? Maybe like the president's dog, you could write a memoir in Henry's voice? How you get it published is another matter altogether, and practically irrelevant, because you may lose interest in this particular book before you write or finish writing your proposal.

What about your grandparents? Didn't they have an interesting life? Wasn't your grandfather's uncle the mayor of Grosse Pointe? What about all that traveling you do: That could be fodder for something. The point is to announce that you are working on a book. And when you change your mind on this subject, you can start working on another. Maybe even a series of them. You have a laptop that you use for e-mail and 1stdibs. Now you can use it for your "book."

I AM BUNNY. I HAVE A CLIPBOARD.

Many of the cute young women who used to teach in nursery schools and kindergartens have put aside their childish dreams and are now the gatekeepers at swell parties. Not prep parties but trendy catered events that are held for the benefit of the press and publicity.

This is counterintuitive for preppies but undeniably popular in the early twenty-first century. What makes no sense is that these are the girls who want to be attending the events sans clipboard. And working at night? Ick. What is going on?

For one thing, a simple phone call from Mummy (she's on the permanent guest list) can get Bunny a short-term job at the publicist's office. From there, Bunny knows the girls who work for the designers' PR firms. It's just a baby step to getting a job with the designer. Then Bunny gets photographed when she attends an opening wearing the designer's clothing. Within a year she's doffed her clipboard and met Tad. Soon they will put their down payment on a starter loft downtown in escrow.

GETTING YOUR DEGREE IN GETTING YOUR DEGREE.

A grand prep tradition is sadly coming to an end. You may remember that son of your parents' friends who was a perpetual student. Each time you heard about him, he was still doing "fieldwork." Well, now due to the exigencies of living in a recession, no longer is it possible for a young(ish) man or woman to stay in graduate school forever. Universities don't have those little stipends to hand out. Fellowships subsidized through endowment funds have dried up, and now this: Without demonstrating "satisfactory progress in the degree program as determined by both the program" and the graduate school, Columbia and other great American universities are terminating students after their eighth or ninth year. This means instead of languishing in the stacks and teaching a couple of classes, you must actually complete your dissertation and distribute it. You can petition, you can whine, and perhaps you can swing a tenth year. Cheers.

UH-OH #4: MUMMY IS NOW A YOGINI/HEALER/SHAMAN.

"I know I'm not a 'licensed healer,' or whatever they're called, but I think I'm really making a difference."

"Breathe in. Now exhale slowly. Focus on something that isn't moving. Morgan, I think you are focusing on my string of pearls. I'm glad I left them on."

"I kind of like Daisy's yoga top. Wonder where she got it."

"Note to self: Cut down on morning cappuccinos before yoga. I'm feeling hyper."

"Oh, damn! I forgot to call the butcher!"

It was while taking yoga and feeling, you know, really *still* and *centered*, that Mummy decided to be a healer. She was always amazing when we had bloody noses, and now she is helping others. Sometimes she even forgets to charge her customers. "Gandhi didn't charge, and neither will I," she says in this weird, dreamy way. Mummy says her "clients love and trust her." Sometimes she tries to interpret their dreams. Other times she makes them drink wheatgrass juice. If it weren't for her diamond watch, we'd think someone replaced Mummy with Mummy Lite—a mellower version of the woman we knew and loved. She barely touches the mojitos anymore. Where is our Mummy?

127

6.

WE CALL IT HOUSE.

WHERE WE LIVE.

The XYZs have decided, they tell me,
to have books in the library.
—Edith Wharton, quoted by Daniel Berkeley Updike,
in *Portrait of Edith Wharton*

Why a house is not a "home."

Just because you inherited that old Stanford White house doesn't mean you're house-proud. Just because your unmarried great-uncle's Hepplewhite secretary is in your library doesn't mean you care that much about your library. You either are domestic or you are not.

One reason we call it "house" instead of "home" is that preppies are not bred to cosset others. We have been raised as if at scout camp: cold showers, threadbare blankets, lumpy pillows, dry toast. We're just following patterns set by our ancestors, who somehow accomplished more in their thirty-two years than we have done in our forty, so far.

We would be remiss if we didn't point out that "home" is a bit pushy. "Welcome to our home" is uncouth. "Welcome to the house" is unpretentious.

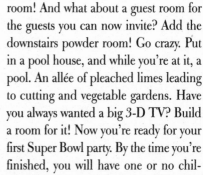

As preppies love tradition, even ugly pieces are excusable if they have been inherited or have an interesting backstory. You can revel in their ugliness if their anecdotes are good enough.

If you are not inclined to make your dwelling comfortable, stylish, or inviting, maybe you'll find someone who can—a decorator, an aunt or Mummy, or a closeted gay husband. They will be the ones to choose wallpapers and backsplash tiles. The ones to cruise tag sales. The ones to refinish the bureau. They will be the ones returning to Restoration Hardware again and again, looking for the perfect brass drawer pulls. They will enjoy all this, and you won't have to lift a finger except to write checks.

As preppies make more money, they can't help but be swept up in the wave of the new materialism. This is so sad; *triste*, really. It starts with the lower-school cocktail party in your living room—so you might reupholster your wing chairs and put some fringe on the ottoman. Then someone might want to publish a story on your herb garden. You order a new set of dishes on the DL. One thing leads to another, and you are suddenly the Nan Kempner of Wilmington. (There are worse things, Dotsie!)

If you happen to be one of the fortunate who has so much money you might as well spend it on the house, you can expand it. Let every child have his own room! And what about a guest room for the guests you can now invite? Add the downstairs powder room! Go crazy. Put in a pool house, and while you're at it, a pool. An allée of pleached limes leading to cutting and vegetable gardens. Have you always wanted a big 3-D TV? Build a room for it! Now you're ready for your first Super Bowl party. By the time you're finished, you will have one or no children left at home, but you will have a showpiece.

THE MUDROOM.

1. *To the eat-in kitchen. More master-pieces from Prudence and Constance's lower-school art classes await.*
2. *Daddy's boots. And an extra pair; no one seems to know where they came from.*
3. *Ski poles should be in the ski rack.*
4. *Who put the skis here? They belong in the ski rack, too.*
5. *Connie? Where are your ski boots? Did you leave them in the car again?*
6. *Every time the keys fall off, Mrs. Gibbs picks them up. Not because she's a stickler for neatness but because she's afraid Henry will eat them.*
7. *We bought this Union Jack banner when we were in India after grad school.*
8. *Ditto the Berber rug we haggled over in the souk in Marrakesh. Always reminds me of our first walk-up.*
9. *This paddle doesn't belong here at all. Tyler should put it back in the boathouse.*
10. *Henry in his "Sphinx" pose.*
11. *His water bowl and toy positioned to trip us.*
12. *Ernesto, the gardener, likes to sit on a swing and smoke a cigarette now and then. Not that we've noticed, but he's the only one around who uses it.*
13. *Umbrella stand from our old apartment on 74th between Park and Lexington. Doesn't really belong here, but where else do we put our golf umbrella and butterfly net?*
14. *The girls were so proud of winning their ribbons. Now they've forgotten what horses are.*
15. *Extra-large Goldfish box. Someone's been to Costco!*
16. *Potting table. For potting.*
17. *Old radio. Should bin it, but it works so well. Does anyone listen to it?*
18. *Drawing, untitled, circa 1994.*
19. *North Face, Pendleton, foul weather slicker by Carhartt, L.L.Bean barn jacket, Barbour quilted vest.*
20. *Bean duck boots and Prudence's Uggs.*
21. *Assorted important hats.*
22. *Boat tote from L.L.Bean. One of seven in this family.*

English houses have long had mudrooms. Where else would you keep your Wellies after a tramp in the mud, or your Barbour jackets, walking sticks, racquets? Mudrooms can be wood-paneled and quite grand, depending. For us, where else would we find the keys to the twelve-year-old Land Rover? And where would Henry go for his REM sleep? Preppies are now focusing their domestic attentions on a room that was previously humble and misunderstood. This one is rather simple. But it will do fine for us.

THE STARTER APARTMENT.

Here's the problem with decorating your first apartment: You don't really know your style yet. So as soon as you're done, Crate & Barrel or Pottery Barn will come out with a couch and an area rug you way prefer to what you got. Or Design Within Reach will put everything on sale. Or you changed your mind entirely about yellow walls in the living room, as every other living room you've been in is yellow. Or your Aunt Lucy's couch looks very dingy next to your lithograph.

Just know that you will not be graded on your first attempt to feather your nest. It will always be a combination of hand-me-downs and floor samples from reasonably priced manufacturers. And let's be perfectly clear. Your style has been influenced by the reruns you've just seen of *Friends*, the displays at Anthropologie, the final issue of *Domino*, and the headmaster's office at the Millbrook School. It's a working marriage between the whimsical and the institutional.

DECORATING WITH BOOKS.

The problem with wallpaper is you get sick of it. Or you find your friends the Taylors put your living-room paper in their powder room and that spoils it for you. What to do about all the walls? Even if you have a decidedly unliterary bent, you might want to consider designing a library. How to fill the empty shelves? Aunt Lizzie's frog collection? When this problem surfaces, increasingly people call Nancy Bass Wyden, the co-owner of the Strand Bookstore with its "18 miles of books" in New York City, who has three people just to put together various "books-by-the-foot" schemes. "People with money are increasingly decorating with books, which pleases me, since often the TV is now the library's centerpiece," says the bookseller. Strand also kits out private libraries and movie sets. Both Ralph Lauren (Triple RL stores) and J.Crew now stock vintage books from the Strand in some of their stores. Many hotels and lodges also order books from the Strand, as both decorative and recreational elements for their guests.

"Typically, we do a lot of houses in the Hamptons. And we'll ask the people or their decorator a lot of questions. What are the people like? Do they have kids? What do they like to read? What are their hobbies? And we start to pull books for them."

"Glamorous, preppy, aspirational"—these are some of the adjectives Nancy uses to describe the books that often get recruited for the Hamptons. Biographies of rich, successful people—she mentioned the Vanderbilts and the Astors, the Slim Aarons books of photographs of WASPs at leisure (see Master Reading List, p. 180), lots of oversized volumes for the coffee tables. "Some classics; books about sports cars, hunting, old money, horses, architecture and art books."

Hardcovers cost $75 to $100 per foot, "but they're great books," says this booster of the old print medium. Leather-bound books cost between $300 and $400 per foot. Bass Wyden is grateful that people want books for their homes, even if they themselves are not readers. "Maybe they're not for [the home owners] but for their kids and their guests." When decorators make the call, they will often look for spine colors that coordinate with the room or with one another. "Both the content and the look have to be right."

We inherited loads of books from both sides of the family. And Winslow can't physically pass a bookstore without going in and adding to the collection. He can't! It's not so adorable now that we are running out of room. Both fiction and nonfiction books serve equally well as coasters, leaving room for one's thingies. Family pictures can be propped up against books on the shelves. Our little chair was painted by Mrs. Templeton (mother-in-law) when she studied finishes at Isabel O'Neill's studio. All her friends painted little red chairs, too. The coral pillow reminds us we'd rather be snorkeling.

Q: What to do with all the family photos?
A: Buy a piano.

When you visit your friends who are further ahead in child begetting, you start to notice that there are framed photographs sprouting up on all their horizontal surfaces: There's Poppy with Jack (the Irish wolfhound); Poppy, Lemon, and Jack; Jack and Lemon; Lemon and Poppy in the car; Poppy and Jack on the dock at Dark Harbor; Poppy and Jack and Lemon in the pool with Whit in Southampton; Whit and Jack on the beach in Mustique with Mrs. Wood; and George on a hunter in Middleburg. On the next table, you have the same idea. Before your house is taken over by the endless picture frames, and there's no place on an end table on which to put your telephone, your book, your thingy, and your coaster, consider buying a grand or baby-grand piano. You won't regret it.

You can consolidate the family gallery on one large surface. A piano solves the problem of how to arrange the furniture in the living room. It makes for a cozier sitting arrangement. And it is likely you can encourage your children to take piano lessons—maybe all the way through Middle School. If not, you might think of hiring a pianist for cocktail parties, and after your kids graduate and move away, you can think (and think and think) about finally learning the piano. You've always meant to, and now you can. (You might have to remove some of the photographs, though, when you start banging around.)

1. *After Pookie's christening, 1999.*
2. *Thanksgiving, 2002.*
3. *At the beach, Outer Banks, 2006.*
4. *Palmer and Maisie, 1988.*
5. *Christmas, 2003.*
6. *Portugal, September 2000.*
7. *Betsy, student-athlete dinner, 2001.*
8. *Christmas, 2000.*
9. *Christmas, Vermont, 1988.*

I was minding my own business in the hills of Toledo—a kind of hang for boars like me. A few of the other guys were there: Nosy, Speed, and Tiger—inside joke; would take way too long to explain now. The sun was bright and the air was cool. It was a good hair day, and a good snout day, that's all I really remember. Because once I saw her, everything was a blur.

She was beautiful. She was graceful. She had that long white-gold hair we rarely get to see (I'd say it was natural, but Raúl says I'm too naïve). She was not running; she just suddenly appeared in front of me.

I had to blink a few times, her presence was so blinding. Tiger and Speed said I should move out of her way, but I couldn't take my eyes off her. We just had one of those instantaneous connections, you know? It was like I was glued to my spot.

It hurt my feelings that she shot me; I can't deny that. But my hope is that Hadley (isn't that a perfect name for her? I read it on her luggage tag) just wanted to make sure we would always be together. So in a few months, I'll be moving to a wall in Locust Valley. It sounds awful—those are angry bugs. I'd only do it for her.

—*As dictated by Hugo the boar*

How much of the house belongs to the dog?

All of it.

Collections.

Margot collects turtles. Sloan collects hedgehogs. Sasha collects Scotties. Carol collects borzois. This is a prep pastime that allows us to feel whimsical whenever we shop, and to shop and scour the Internet whenever we want. And it's quite considerate of you to have a known collection, because it makes life easier for your friends at birthday and holiday time. Martha does ducks? Easy. We buy her some duck magnets and mugs for her birthday. Maybe we'll throw in a decoy. Lakey collects whales? That's a home run for us. Even if some of your collection is a bit commercial or junky, the mass of it placed together in an area of your kitchen cupboard or on the shelves in your library will look substantial and neat.

It's not too late to become a collector yourself. Stamps and coins are not prep. Why? Because. Neither are teaspoons or thimbles: too olde gifte shoppe. Cats are less prep than dogs, ducks, frogs, turtles, whales, and swans. Again, it's because.

Here are some fresh new ideas for collections: flamingos (a little showy, and almost too pink), fish, kangaroos, koala bears, otters, ostriches, piglets. Armadillos for Texans. Little architectural models, those staircases, and Eiffel Towers in all sizes. If you start now, by August you will be obsessed.

Monogramania.

Who would have thought that the monogram could make such a huge comeback? One reason is the abundance of commercial logos that make us interested in our own brand. Suddenly, a sweater, a tote bag, or playing cards with your own initials look fresh and, yes, kind of original. But you knew that already. You used to have sweaters with your monogram, and you always had stationery, of course. Your golf clubs can have socks with your initials. Your luggage should be imprinted with your initials. Your books can have bookplates.

What about your house?

You will have your monogram (or yours and your spouse's) engraved on your silverware. You can monogram your napkins, tablecloths, bed linens, and towels. (White on white works with any decorating scheme.) Needlepoint pillows or throws with embroidered monograms on your chaise or couch will dress up the furniture. (Even prep living rooms like to be well accessorized.)

Glass wine carafes are nice places to put your monogram. Water carafes in the guest room are perfect, too. Candy dishes, formerly known as ashtrays, can bear a monogram, although when they're filled it won't show. (If smoking is not allowed in your house, hide any ashtrays that have depressions for cigarettes, or give them away.) Avoid planting your monogram or insignia on your walls, your headboards, or your car windows: it's supposed to look effortless and casual, like you.

BEACH HOUSE

FORCED FAMILY FUN

POOL

ROADIE

Mr. & Mrs. F. Scott Fitzgerald
Est. 1920

HAVE YOU SEEN MY CONTRACTOR?

B LIST

Vacation House Matching Quiz.

*ON THE LEFT YOU WILL SEE THE NAMES OF WONDERFUL PLACES TO HAVE A SECOND
HOUSE. LUCKY YOU. ON THE RIGHT YOU SEE THE PROPER NAMES OF THE KIND OF HOUSES
THAT ARE INDIGENOUS TO THESE LOCATIONS. MATCH THE PAIRS THAT GO TOGETHER.
WE WISH WE COULD OFFER YOU A PRIZE, BUT YOU CAN'T BUY A VILLA IF YOU DON'T
KNOW WHERE TO FIND A VILLA. CONSIDER YOUR KNOWLEDGE A GIFT UNTO ITSELF.*

---

1. House on Lake Thompson in Maine.
2. Ninety-two acres in Rhode Island.
3. Old farmhouse set in an orchard outside Siena, Italy.
4. Lighthouse off Nova Scotia.
5. Running water and electricity but no Internet or cable, in a beach house in Todos Santos, Mexico.
6. Three hundred acres outside Missoula, Montana.
7. Two bedrooms plus den in Beaver Creek, Colorado.
8. Two bedrooms and an outdoor shower in Chilmark, Massachusetts.
9. Seven hundred acres, including watering hole for elephants, in Kenya.
10. Stucco-and-stone house in Zermatt, Switz.
11. One-room apartment on the Île de la Cité.
12. Studio apartment in Islington, London.
13. Cluster of houses, stables, and assorted other buildings in Argentina.
14. Arts and Crafts–style house in Pasadena, California. One level. Dark and overpriced.
15. Forty rooms in New Jersey, owned by a rap artist.
16. Sixteen rooms in Greenwich, Connecticut, with tennis court, pool and pool house, and brand-new everything.
17. One-room dwelling with sink near bed.
18. Post-office box in the Cayman Islands.
19. Three-fourths acre north of Sunset in Beverly Hills, California.
20. Eight-hundred-acre farm in Australia.

A. Pied-à-terre.
B. Estancia/Finca.
C. Rhode Island.
D. Ranch. Small.
E. Condo.
F. Estate.
G. Mansion.
H. Shack.
I. Chalet.
J. Bungalow.
K. Maid's room.
L. Cabin.
M. Tax shelter.
N. Cottage.
O. Station.
P. Folly (we never use it).
Q. Old farmhouse (trick question).
R. Bedsit.
S. McMansion.
T. Ranch: a big one.

Answers: 1. L, 2. C, 3. Q, 4. P, 5. H, 6. D, 7. E, 8. N, 9. O, 10. I, 11. A, 12. R, 13. B, 14. J, 15. G, 16. S, 17. K, 18. M, 19. F, 20. T.

Do It Yourself.

Now that Minnie is engaged to be married, Mummy and Alfred expect her and Trey to spend time with them at the family house. And here is Minnie's lovely old bedroom! Mummy and Alfred pretended to be offended when Minnie suggested that at twenty-seven she and her boyfriend (that would be Trey) shared a room everywhere else. We are all pretty excited; it's a good way for Trey to become assimilated into the family. Soon there will be command performances: Thanksgiving—"Trey, you carve"; Easter—put out the eggs for the cousins; occasional weekends, and even weeks, when no one else is using the house, so Minnie and Trey can have some grown-up fun without the grown-ups.

It's not really a problem, as in a *problem*, but there is the matter of Minnie's bedroom. It's kind of Miss Havishamesque—nothing has been changed since Minnie was in the seventh grade. The ceiling is cracked, and there are two single beds separated by a very old white dresser from the Greenwich Hospital Thrift Shop. It probably should have been repainted after Minnie and her friend Boots were caught smoking True Blues and left those big burn marks. The stained Kent School felt banner (yuck) still shares a wall with the Duran Duran poster, curling at the edges. Three huge piles of cassette tapes (two copies of a Destiny's Child album; was Minnie such a fan?) share an étagère with all different kinds of horses: glass (the adorable ones with the broken legs), ceramic, a wool one,

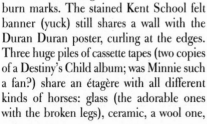

stuffed animal ones (Aunt Kitty's from the '40s). Has anyone even been in this room since Minnie moved to that apartment off Beacon Hill? Has it become some kind of shrine? "Here lived a typical twelve-year-old girl. Her favorite color was dusty pink, as in pink with real dust on it." Is that Minnie's diary? Better move it before Trey finds out she had a huge crush on Topher Grace. The only non-girly thing is the signed football her Daddy brought back from the Super Bowl that time.

The plan is to transform Minnie's bedroom from an adolescent time capsule into an adult room for her and Trey. They will be living in or visiting this house for many years to come. They will need to push those little twin beds together, and get a king-size feather mattress, mattress pad, and good 400-thread-count cotton sheets.

The white dresser is not ideal either, but if it were stripped and stained, it might work. Maybe wooden floors are lurking under the (put politely) "vintage" wall-to-wall. Trey can work on it, but it's more likely he'll ask someone else. He might be allergic to physical labor. We'll buy Minnie a new blanket from an outlet store as a room-warming gift. (Also remind us to buy some new irregular towels when we go. They're just as good as anything at Neiman's.)

• Give Trey a spot all his own: the back of a chair and maybe a drawer or two.

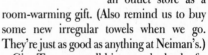

• Clean white walls—good-bye, Simon Le Bon.

• Good-bye, horses.

7.
POOR MRS. ASTOR.
TRUE PERPS.

It was the old New York . . . the way of people who dreaded scandal more than
disease, who placed decency above courage, and who considered that nothing was
more ill-bred than "scenes," except the behaviour of those who gave rise to them.

—Edith Wharton, *The Age of Innocence*

As in every other facet of a preppy's life, when it comes to scandal, we are appropriately dressed. Think of Dede Brooks, the former CEO of Sotheby's, under house arrest in a sedate knee-length skirt, pearls, low-heeled pumps—and anklet.

Think of Anthony Marshall strolling to court in a fine suit, his wife wearing her Belgian shoes and Barbour jacket—as if antiquing for the afternoon.

Remember, best of all, Mrs. Jean Harris, who had the decency to wear her headband even while incarcerated.

We have always had our fair share of scandals. Somehow, the world is surprised and intrigued by the details of ours because we all look so cool, calm, and proper. The contested will of Lois DeSoto, the widow of Frank, a humble and talented plumber, is not of the same interest as the contested will of Brooke Astor (to pick a name out of a chapeau) because there might perhaps not be (delicately phrased) as many assets, as many socialites, as many Impressionist paintings, or as many beneficiaries of the DeSoto fortune as there are of the Astor fortune. Just saying.

We are equally ashamed, ashen, and astonished when news of our unseemly doings becomes public knowledge and yet from the beginning of time, unseemly doings have been the stuff of newspapers, books, movies, plays, and hushed meetings at the Carlyle hotel.

We don't mean to be bad. Just like other people, we intend to be good. Sometimes, though . . . temptations rear their irresistible heads. Mostly, like Homo sapiens of every other stripe, we do not want to be caught.

PREP CRIME WATCH.

MINOR WRONGDOINGS, Bad.

LYING.

This begins in childhood. Early. As when Mummy asks you if you know where the five-dollar bill that was lying on the kitchen counter went. She left it there for the laundress's carfare. Did you take it, Gordo? Did you? What about the box of Ritz crackers that is now on the floor of the den, being eaten by Wesley, your four-year-old Wheaten terrier? Who left the box in the den? Lindy? Was that you? These are the stuff of early wrongdoings. To suggest that these lies lead to a life of Ponzi schemes or insider trading would be overdoing it, but they remain good "teachable moments" for parents, in any case.

MINOR WRONGDOINGS,
Less Bad.

WHITE LIES. These are the lubrication of polite society, without which we would all hurt one another needlessly. Obviously Charlotte doesn't look like she is a pregnant fourteen-year-old. Of course you will tell the Clarks that their Oktoberfest beer thingy was fun, even though you and Duck decided on the way home you will never again attend a party where beef jerky is the main food group and your thirty-eight-year-old host is wearing lederhosen. Faults in tennis and mulligans in golf are part of this purview as well. The well-bred prep (a redundancy) knows when to look the other way, when to laugh off a teeny infraction, and when to get red in the face. Some of it is DNA. Some of it is learning by example.

If Pops famously ended up in the Barrington (Rhode Island or Illinois; it hardly matters) slammer for trying to steal the street sign of the block where his ex–starter wife, Calla, lived, your family has a more laissez-faire approach to civil disobedience than perhaps the Morgenthau family, which eschews such foolish troublemaking. Or indeed views it as a felony.

SHOPLIFTING. A crime for beginners or lost ladies (elderly Hedy Lamarr and Bess Myerson come to mind; Winona Ryder, your name goes here) but not one of which preppies partake. Perhaps it is the overly appealing displays, the tempting cornucopia of goods that are to blame. Don't look at us?

MAJOR WRONGDOINGS, Bad.

DRUGS, USING/SELLING.
We wholeheartedly condemn the use of drugs, and consider those who vend them to be dreadful criminals. Those whose marketplace is filled with minors are beneath contempt. End of story.

FORGERY.
This is a serious problem, and one that we hope to help eradicate. If you are faking your résumé for your wedding announcement, stop right here. You will be caught, and the humiliation of fake degrees, hidden early marriages, etc., will render you unfit for print. If you are faking your past in order to have a better present (hello, *Mad Men*), you too will be discovered. One word: don't.

If you are forging a Cézanne for over the bench in your hallway, please tell people it's a fake. They will be impressed by your artistic bent as well as your honesty. And if you are exceptionally talented, they might not believe you. (And if it happens to be an authentic Cézanne you possess, you would be allowed to say it was a copy. You don't want to encourage major larceny.)

When it comes to your parents' signatures on your terrible report card, or a permission slip from school that slipped your mind when you were home—well, we've all done it, and because you are essentially an honest and good soul, you will have to confess it one day. Maybe at your bachelor party, or at your twenty-fifth birthday party, when it will seem like proof of your innocent dearness. On the other hand, your parents may want you to sign for them at the club or the market, so make sure you can do a credible job with both their signatures. Do not forge your elderly relatives' signatures on new codicils of their wills, especially when those relatives are showing signs of dementia. That's just—and this is strongly worded—not nice.

SEX SCANDALS.

Obviously the most dishy of all crimes: Sex sells papers, papers sell ads, ads sell product. Everyone profits. (How this profits Google or Bing or Whatever-Dot-Com remains to be seen, but we recognize the power of the Interthingy.) Since the dawn of pornography, women who look scrubbed, innocent, virginal—nay, particularly actual virgins—have been a potent part of the fantasy. So when one of our women turns out to be an insatiable tiger (it *could* happen), this becomes a bonanza for the press.

Sex is at the core of the Dr. Tarnower murder, the Preppy Murder, and the lubricious life of Mrs. Pamela Digby Churchill Hayward Harriman, not to mention the social-climbing successes of men and women from California to the New York Island.

ADULTERY.

Particularly popular in the twenty-first century, adultery has been with us since time immemorial. The onus must belong to the preppy who strays; his (mostly his) accomplices may not realize to what extent the hale fellow is married. (It's a spectrum, just like sexuality.) Is he separated? Separated yet still living at home? Separated in his mind but not in the mind of his wife? Unhappily married and looking for an escape hatch? Happily married but looking for some adrenaline-providing ex-

citement? Living with his girl- or boyfriend yet still shopping around?

One way or another, most women will detect a change in their husband if he strays. Even if she doesn't care much for him. It is the public humiliation that hurts, not the betrayal. Life is enhanced by the appearance of a successful home life, even if it isn't exactly happy behind closed doors. A couple may be living a pleasant-enough but sexless life. Coco certainly doesn't want to sleep with her husband, but she doesn't want everyone she knows to know that Eggy doesn't want to sleep with her, either. The lesson here is how to respond to a known cuckolding: Suffer it in relative silence (preppies are genetically suited for this) and dignity, and most of all, move on, your head held high. Think of Norma Shearer in *The Women*. (The part before she gets her husband back.)

When things go awry with her husbands, one attractive dowager tries to meet and subsequently marry men who carry the same last initial, so that her monogram can remain the same. You might be looking for a Pisces; she is looking for an *M*, what with her Frette towels, her James Robinson silver, and her Mrs. John L. Strong stationery. It's quite understandable.

THE NOUVEAU RICHE.

It is amusing how no one wants to think of his or her money as "new." Even if they just cashed in their stock options to the tune of seven figures, somehow that money has been percolating in an old vault for years and perhaps decades. That is fine with us. However, if you persist in throwing your weight around because of all your dough, you will call undue attention to it. Buying your way onto boards is done, but then you must be of use to the board that has taken you on. (Give extra money, underwrite something, invite other rich people to donate to a fund drive, etc.) *Do not* flaunt. Keep the sable for opening night, not for board meetings. Learn to give anonymously. Insisting on signage everywhere is an admission of insecurity and proof that your lucre is brand spanking new. If you splash your name around, your behavior must be first-rate; now we know who you are. Catch our drift?

HARD-CORE BAD STUFF.

Evangeline Crowell was born in Pittsburgh, Kansas, in 1915. She fled to Kansas City, reinventing herself as Ann Eden. In 1941 she made her way to New York, becoming a showgirl at FeFe's Monte Carlo. She met William Woodward, heir to Hanover Bank, and soon was dating his son, Billy. Though shunned by society at first, she married Billy and bore him two sons. When Billy asked Ann for a divorce in 1947, she refused. In 1955, Ann said she thought she heard a burglar in her house. She fired a shotgun twice and killed her husband. Now the really bad guys: She was Dominick Dunne's inspiration for *The Two Mrs. Grenvilles* (see Master Reading List, p. 180). Although she was acquitted of murder, society fully turned its back on her. In 1976, her son James and, in 1999, her son William "Woody" committed suicide.

When it comes to fraud, nothing approaches the brazenness of one Christian Karl Gerhartsreiter, who played the role of the forgotten Rockefeller, Clark. He wooed a successful, accomplished businesswoman, to whom he was married for twelve years. Perhaps if Mr. Gerhartwhatever had picked a less illustrious name, not boasted of arriving at New Haven to begin his college education at fourteen, not kidnapped their daughter, and had generally been less of a creep, he might have had a longer run as a fake.

Finally, poor Brooke Astor, who barely knew what hit her, and if she had, might have perished sooner than her 105th year. It seems that after marrying hungry Charlene, the wife of the local Episcopal priest in Northeast Harbor, Maine, Brooke's son Anthony Marshall, already well accommodated by his mother's generosity, was having her lawyers rewrite and rewrite her will, even when his mummy was non compos mentis. As the Marshalls were siphoning more and more from Mrs. Astor, friends and other relatives suspected Anthony of depriving his mother of proper care. He was found guilty, but whether he ever serves time in lockup remains to be seen.

How Do Preppies Emerge from Their Scandals?

Always tastefully. We get spiritual but not too spiritual. We go to church or synagogue . . . for a while. We keep a lower-than-usual profile. We do community service. We make appropriate donations (anonymously), and we have no comment at this time.

Then—after a reasonable interval—we move on.

FIRST SIPS.

Drinking is the centerpiece of what we do as teenagers. Whether it's chugging forties in the park, pregaming (drinking before) a movie on the way to the theater, or playing beer pong on a kitchen table, alcohol will likely be the key to that evening's plans. Or, starting around tenth grade, it *is* the evening's plans; at first, kids get their beer from the few celebrated stores that do not card. Once a group of friends discover such an oasis, they will return again and again, and will probably end up on a first-name basis with the store's benevolent employees. If we can't find such Good Samaritans, we'll use our fake IDs to buy our beer. Everyone has them.

When kids have access to an "open house"—one without parental supervision—they will often play drinking games. There are more types of drinking games than there are stripes on a seersucker jacket; they are the entry point into the world of drinking for many of us.

By the time we arrive at college, drinking will be old news. Yes, we have more freedom. Yes, we have much more time. Even so, some find we drink less compared to what we did in high school.

For us, drinking is not primarily an act of rebellion. The thrill of the forbidden may be seductive for some, but most teenagers drink simply because it gives them something to do together on a weekend night.

— *James Thunderberg*, Collegiate, Cornell—class of 2013

Beirut for Boston Brahmins.
Or the Do's and Don'ts of Harvard Beer Pong.

It's not about who wins but how you play the game. Because Harvard Beirut is more about community than competition, real preppies leave behind the sophomoric stratagems they may have employed in secondary school. One of these tactics, bouncing, or taking advantage of a distracted adversary by ricocheting a Ping-Pong ball off the table and into an opponent's cup, is shrewd, and forces one's rival to eliminate a total of two cups. This technique, however, is not appropriate for polite settings, especially if Wellesley girls are providing the distractions. A Harvard gentleman also makes sure to "kiss" his cups together, that is, readjust the formation in order to eliminate space between cups.

Showing grace, saving face. Some of the more complex Beirut rules involve a challenging (if not impossible) set of acrobatics. The prudent prep believes that it is better to have never attempted these maneuvers than to have failed in their execution. For example, only the beer pong virtuoso should attempt behind-the-back throws, in which a player, already having missed his shot, retrieves his Ping-Pong ball and attempts this more difficult move. Rather than take this risk, it is best to stay aloof and allow your opponents to have their turn.

The nightcap. Beirut is a win-win game: Either you drink the elixir that is sweet victory or you drink yourself to oblivion. In the latter case, try to prevent yourself from peeing on the John Harvard statue or, at least, not in front of those Wellesley girls.

— *D.F.*, The Bishop's School, Harvard

REHAB:
The New Boarding School.

Where you attend (and possibly get booted from) boarding school is one of the most important elements of your pedigree. And just as important is where you go to rehab to lose your addictions—the dangerous behaviors your parents sent you away to avoid, but you still managed to pick up anyway in the safety of the middle of the woods somewhere in deepest New England or outside Santa Barbara.

Like boarding schools, rehabilitation centers are exclusive and expensive. The traditional **Betty Ford Center**—where patients have to make their own beds and are forced to do grueling manual labor, such as emptying their trash—is the Exeter for alcoholics and drug abusers. It's serious, and if you're caught breaking rules or backsliding, you're tossed out faster than you can say Larry Fortensky. Like Exeter, Betty Ford boasts a high-profile student body, and the administration is fastidious about staying in touch with its alumni through regular newsletters. Some patients spend thirty days ($26,000) at Betty Ford, but the center prefers ninety-day ($44,000) treatment courses. Like at Exeter, men and women have separate

living quarters with roomies, and are situated around Betty Ford's Main Campus Quad. There is even a campus bookstore, where you can buy required reading like *Healing and Hope* by Betty Ford herself. Though Betty Ford, like Exeter, is not like ninety days at an Aman resort, patients (even ones who enter the program ashamed of their addictions) often call it enlightening and make friendships that last a lifetime. Distinguished Alumni: Peter Lawford, Kelsey Grammer, and Margaux Hemingway.

The St. Paul's of rehabs, Hazelden, in Minneapolis, is also no-frills, offering the added benefit of mental-health therapy to address issues like Pop's second family or Mummy's setting the Christmas tree on fire after too many bloodies and sedatives. Hazelden is seen as the template for hard-core recovery programs, and patients pay $27,700 for a twenty-eight-day stay. There are three women's units and five men's units, with twenty-two beds each. Best of all, Hazelden accepts insurance. Expect to have a roommate, and as at St. Paul's, you'll be eating in the campus cafeteria. Distinguished Alumni: Eric Clapton and Matthew Perry.

Silver Hill Hospital (aka "Silver Spoon" or "Silver Pill Hill"), located in a white clapboard house in ultra-preppy New Canaan, Connecticut, looks just like a real boarding school or perhaps someone's multimillion-dollar house on Further Lane in East Hampton. Forty-five acres of pristine rolling green hills, commons-like yards, an outdoor tennis court, a fitness center, and an admissions office will make you feel like you're at Pomfret, not the loony bin. There is a five-day intake program (insurance accepted), requiring a deposit of $7,500; then patients go on to a twenty-eight-day program costing $26,000 (insurance not accepted). The five-day program has twenty-one beds for men and women, and the twenty-eight-day rehabilitation program has fourteen women's beds and nineteen men's beds. The process here is rolling admissions, so fresh faces crop up at different times, when spots become available. Distinguished Alumni: Edie Sedgwick, Truman Capote, Tatum O'Neal, and Joan Kennedy.

Out west, movie and pop stars being weaned off drink and the pills—why are all these young people prescribed painkillers in the first place?—head to Promises in Malibu and Cirque Lodge in Utah (conveniently overlooking Robert Redford's Sundance Lodge). They are the Hyde Schools of rehab—rustic and tough but with a loving touch. Cirque Lodge requires patients to pack hiking boots, so expect to sweat out those gin and tonics. The Lodge itself (a building higher up on the mountain and with fewer people) has a thirty-day program that can take in sixteen people for $47,850 each; there are two private suites available ($77,000 for thirty days) when money doesn't matter. The Studio's thirty-day program at Cirque Lodge is $29,850, and the ninety-day is $44,000; both have room for forty. And bring your yoga clothes to Promises in Malibu, where tennis, swimming, and Zen activities (Japanese brush painting!) are incorporated as well to help rich preps and stars like Britney Spears kick pill habits. Distinguished Alumni at Promises: Ben Affleck and Selma Blair. Distinguished Alumna at Cirque Lodge: Kirsten Dunst.

Après-rehab, patients attend daily/weekly reunions, also known as AA meetings. How fun to mix your Concord school ring with your Reed field hockey T-shirt and a Betty Ford baseball cap! While drinking your latte with your Marlboro (red) cigarettes, you can reminisce about the good old days—of afternoon sports and weekly mixers, and the bad old days of detoxing from vodka in your water bottles—over a game of backgammon on the porch of The Meadow Club.

—Peter Davis
Pomfret, Bennington

When Sunny Got Blue.

Social chronicler Dominick Dunne called her "Sleeping Beauty." When the striking blond heiress Martha "Sunny" Crawford von Auersperg von Bülow was found lying on the marble bathroom floor of Clarendon Court, her twenty-room Newport house (the location for the original *Philadelphia Story*), on December 22, 1980, she was unconscious. Had her second husband attempted to inject her with a fatal dose of insulin, or had she overdosed by accident on her own? She had fallen into a brief coma one year earlier, after allegedly downing just two spiked eggnogs. Tales were told of his mistresses and her self-medicated melancholia. Von Bülow might have had a motive; Sunny had all the money.

Claus von Bülow was accused of attempted murder. The trial was as absorbing as any ratings-period story arc on a soap opera (like *Dark Shadows*, the one Claus's mistress had acted in). Sunny's longtime maid, Maria Schrallhammer, testified about a black leather bag in which the master of the house kept syringes. Sunny's older children, Alex and Ala von Auersperg, firmly believed that their stepfather had caused their mother's death (which created a schism between them and their half sister, Cosima von Bülow). Claus von Bülow was found guilty, but in his appeal—one of the first trials ever covered gavel to gavel on TV—he was defended by Alan Dershowitz. It ended in acquittal, not to mention the movie *Reversal of Fortune*, based on

Dershowitz's bestselling account of the case.

By now, Sunny was living at Columbia-Presbyterian Hospital in Manhattan, in a room with a view. Sunny was attended to as if she were napping. Her bed was made with the Porthault sheets she loved. Several paintings from her Fifth Avenue apartment were hung there. A police guard was posted outside the door to ensure privacy. Fresh flowers were delivered regularly. Manicurists, hairdressers, and makeup artists arrived twice a week to keep Sunny groomed to perfection.

After eighteen years of this idyll, and a $500,000 annual cost for the room alone, the family moved Sunny to the Mary Manning Walsh nursing home on East 79th Street. Her two oldest children continued to visit often, sometimes bringing their respective children to see their grandmother, still comatose. Framed pictures of the grandchildren she never knew decorated Sunny's room at the nursing home.

By the 1990s Claus von Bülow was living in London. His life consisted of attending parties, visiting his club, and spending time with his daughter, Cosima, and her children. He was divorced from Sunny, and in exchange for waiving a settlement, Cosima was reinstated into the family will.

Sunny died on December 6, 2008, almost twenty-eight years after her collapse. Her three children finally reconciled. It is a kind of fairy tale, but not the kind you read to your children.

Alibis for where you've been for the last three to five years.

You don't know how it happened. Maybe it didn't happen. Maybe it's just a bad dream. You thought your taxes were filed properly. Or you didn't realize it was pot you bought (though it was rather expensive for manure). Or you didn't mean to trash the clubhouse that night; indeed, you think you were framed, as you have no recollection of it whatsoever. And then the matter of those stock transactions . . . How were you supposed to know that what Teddy said it was privileged information? He told you in the steam room, for God's sake . . . and Vickers was there! Vickers isn't being held responsible. Is it because of your family's glorious name and your provenance the court is making an example of you?

Yes, they're nodding gravely, all up and down the East Coast: Life isn't fair. How could this have happened to JB? You are actually heading up the river to the slammer, where you will live in confinement in the clink. Good-bye, yacht club; hello, rack. Good-bye, trading floor; hello, pokey.

Is there consolation in the knowledge that other Wharton men have landed in the brig, too? Not to mention a couple of women from Wheaton? While you consider your plight from your Cadillac (big-house slang for inmate bed or bunk), you need to come up with an alibi to use when people ask you where you've been the last few years. (Happily, by the time they see you, some will have forgotten you were

doing time. And you will look much better and much more toned after your stint in the pound.)

• You've been exploring the Amazon. Sure, it's possible. Of course, you might have come home for Cassie's graduation from Francis Parker School, but it was hard to get home from South America. And *very poor* cell service. (The Amazon alibi might explain the crude-looking tattoo you now have on your shoulder. It will require an effort, but don't say, "It's from my jointman," meaning an inmate who behaves like a guard; say, "It's from my shaman." Practice.)

• You entered a religious retreat. Hmm. Weird. Perhaps you could link it to a midlife crisis, for more believability. And instead of mentioning your sweet kid—an inmate who allies with an older, more experienced inmate, possibly for protection or knowledge—you could discuss your spiritual mentor, who aided you in your transition to monastic life.

• You joined a not-for-profit think tank in Eastern Europe. (Wasn't that Dash's cover?)

• You decided—without telling anyone in advance—to go to law school. This doesn't work if you are already a lawyer, but lots of jailbirds end up getting law degrees by correspondence course. And you can, too! And if you are well behaved, you might get a pardon or commutation of your sentence, or "a lifeboat," as it's called in the stir.

KIDS, DON'T READ THIS:
SEXUAL MATERIAL.

When our own David Duchovny (Collegiate School, Princeton BA, Yale MA) portrayed a man with very bad habits on his cable TV program, no one thought that he was performing in a reality show. But when he announced that he was a sex addict and going to rehab for it, we felt just terrible. We felt terrible for his wife, Téa Leoni (née Elizabeth Téa Pantaleoni—Brearley, Putney [x], Sarah Lawrence [x]), and we felt dreadful for their children, but we weren't sure we understood exactly what this newish syndrome was. Is it a real disease? Some define it as kind of compulsivity. Some call it an "excessive drive."

The latest edition of the *Diagnostic and Statistical Manual of Psychiatric Disorders* (DSM), which our doctors keep on a shelf in their offices, puts sex addiction under this category: "Sexual disorders Not Otherwise Specified." The text goes on to describe it as "distress about a pattern of repeated sexual relationships involving a succession of lovers who are experienced by the individual only as things to be used." Like it or not, Duchovny is not our only sex addict. You've heard of Eliot Spitzer, the new guy at CNN.

Central Command wonders at the sudden spread of this malady. One day it's just Michael Douglas (Allen Stevenson School, Choate, UCSB), and then a decade later, the clinics are flooded. It's like an X-rated peanut allergy.

Because a good-looking preppy fellow can be persuasive when he wants to be, young women must be prepared for the charm offensive that can be irresistible. Behind those aviators and that bright smile could lurk a womanizer. Yesterday's wolf has become today's predator; or has he? We will keep you posted.

THE FIRST WIVES' CLUB.

It might surprise you to learn that there are quite a few preppy women who, despite having never taken a class in economics or computer science, have figured out a way to hack into their husbands' financial accounts, e-mails, and cell phones.

Sometimes this investigative work takes place tremblingly alone late at night while their husbands are out of town. (It could just as easily take place tremblingly during the light of day. These wives do not work.) Sometimes a group of them get together and share their techniques and secrets along with cocktails and cigarettes. These sessions resemble their halcyon days at boarding school, when they learned how to blow smoke out the bathroom windows. They are most always first wives for whom the red flag of doubt has been raised.

They proudly admit they discovered discrepancies this way but are resolute in not sharing their methodology. There's always a chance that their second husbands are reading this book.

UH-OH #5: WHAT HAPPENED TO MUMMY'S FACE?

Mummy, what are you looking at? Why do you always look so surprised?

Oh.

Face-lifts were once the property of Hollywood and those whose appearances were crucial to their livelihoods. Now every woman over the age of thirty-five (outside of Las Vegas, Miami, Los Angeles, and Brazil, where they start much younger) has to confront her softening skin, her drooping parts, and consider seeing the doctor. Even preppies are not immune.

Dr. Alan Matarasso, a highly regarded plastic surgeon on Park Avenue, has a practice filled with an eclectic constituency, "one day a senator, the next a schoolteacher." He has seen enough preppies to draw several conclusions.

"From the first consult to when we remove the sutures, these women are more understated, in the way they dress, in the way they behave with us, and in what they do. Everything is on a different scale; they'll do one step less." He has many patients whose pictures adorn the society pages, who start at the same age as non-preppies, "late thirties, early forties. They stare at themselves at the hairdresser and say, 'That's not me.' Then they go back to the hairdresser, look in the mirror, and say, 'That's not me.' The third time, they say, 'That's me,' and then they make an appointment for a con-sult." Botox injections and fillers like Restylane are usually the first step.

Matarasso's preppies are far less voluble than his non-preppies. They are not sharers. They don't chat about what their friends had done, or what their husbands think of their necks. "They come alone. They might say, 'You operated on my friend, but don't tell her I was here.' They are less open. They ask fewer questions. They suck up the drugs and don't complain to your face."

Surgically, they have certain genetic advantages over the general population. "They're thin. These are women who jog six miles every day, have a carrot and a glass of water for lunch," the doctor explains. "They're not here for liposuction." Also, this is not the crowd looking for nose jobs.

Although some of the name-brand surgeons in Manhattan live in the same social milieu as their patients, they can experience a professional backlash, since their patients don't necessarily want to go out and see "the man who cut open their faces. And even Dr. Michael Hogan, famous for performing one of Jackie Kennedy's face-lifts, said, 'They often treat you like you're the help.'"

Finally, it is less likely that Mummy will go overboard and have the plumped lips and breasts of the ladies across town. She still wants to look like Audrey Hepburn, after all.

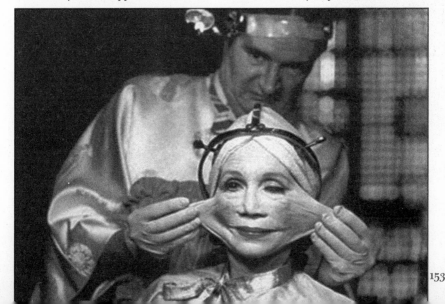

8.

DRINKS BEFORE DINNER.

WHAT WE EAT.

I despair of the Republic! Such dreariness . . . such crass food, crass manners,
crass landscape! What a horror it is for a whole nation to be developing without
the sense of beauty, and eating bananas for breakfast.
—Edith Wharton, letter to Sally Norton

How we think about food.

Give us an E for effort, won't you? We used to consider Velveeta its own food group. Now we are all little foodies-in-training. Edwina spent a postgraduate year in Tokyo and now considers wasabi the world's most important condiment. Corby took a cooking course when he was separated, and he and his girlfriend talk endlessly (read: boringly) about "fusion this" and "fusion that." Blue is "into" artisanal teas, Cobb apprenticed for that famous butcher in Dutchess County, and Daisy is a vegan . . . or so we've heard. (Is that pronounced "vee-gan" or "vay-gan"?)

And on top of that, everyone's allergic! Gluten, lactose, shellfish! It's an epidemic, or a punishment, isn't it? Family suppers with the roast and potatoes just aren't what they used to be—someone's always complaining; too many questions (Is there lard in this crust? Peanut oil on the haricots verts?); it's become quite an effort. The only thing everyone can agree on is a simple salad.

There's no denying our palates have expanded in the last few years. We used to eat when we remembered to, or chew a few Triscuits, Wheat Thins, or Ritz crackers before cocktails. Now we think about food; we actually *think* about it.

It's probably because of Martha, a woman who looks like Mummy, dresses like Mummy (though Mummy wears skirts, too), and cares about food. She made us feel bad that we didn't care enough about food, so we follow her, and try, though it may be futile, to copy her. Some of our number are obsessed with Martha, of course, and become disconsolate when their attempts at making wrapping paper from scratch, carving their hedges into topiaries with a pair of garden shears, or assembling her rainbow sorbet cake fell short of the Stewart level of perfection. But look at the bright side: Our homemade pesto is decent (though store-bought is better), our holiday cookies are prettier, and we now make interesting centerpieces using gourds, flats of grass, and metallic twine. We will never—repeat, never—run out of votive candles.

The legendary Julia Child, icon (see p. 25), is also on our minds thanks to writer-director Nora Ephron. We tried out her boeuf bourguignon. (Wash those cubes of beef first, everyone!)

In addition to the exotic food we now attempt to cook, we go out to ethnic restaurants. We love cold sesame noodles and Peking Duck, burritos and fajitas—even fish tacos are now a comfort food. Pad Thai, coconut soup, tikka masala, curried goat, sashimi, and *crudo*. We eat parts of animals we don't want to know about, know what shapes are denoted by various pasta names (farfalle, rotelle, orecchiette), and yes, that black pasta has squid ink in it. We've branched out, and we're a little proud of ourselves. Let's celebrate with a *tiramisù per tutti*!

THE COOK'S DAY OFF.

Poor Mrs. Gibbs. She's just called in and suddenly has to go with her husband to get his green card. Of course we understand, and we wouldn't *dream* of docking her, but that's not the issue. Dinner's in only a matter of hours, and now it's practically an emergency.

We'd been meaning for ages to get her recipe for that lovely thing she does with the peas and the pearl onions and the bits of meat, all swimming in that divine sauce. But she's not answering her cell. We *can't* order pizza—again.

Let's see what she keeps in the cupboard. Oops, that's the liquor cabinet—well, serendipity! We need inspiration, so why not? What's in the fridge? Lemons. An excellent start. Limes! Ooh! My, there's all *sorts* of things in here. And there's the *Junior League Cookbook* to the rescue! We're all set. We may not exactly be Martha, but even *she* had to start somewhere. Come to think of it, it was near here, wasn't it?

One thing we know for sure: No meal was *ever* ruined by mayonnaise. Or martinis.

"Do I slice the lime first, or the lemon? It doesn't say, dammit."

THE ULTIMATE NEW CANAAN NIBBLE.

INGREDIENTS.

ONE KRAFT INDIVIDUAL SHARP CHEDDAR
SINGLE, CELLOPHANE REMOVED

SHOT GLASS

ONE BOX OF RITZ CRACKERS, OPENED

FRENCH'S MUSTARD
(OPTIONAL)

Place the sheet of cheddar on a flat, clean surface. Using a shot glass, set the rim flat on the cheese square and twist it around carefully. Lift, and voilà! A perfect circle. Place perfect disk of cheese on one Ritz cracker and serve. If you're feeling especially festive, affix flawless dairy coin to the cracker with a dab of mustard.* *Très bon!*

Six sheets yields six pieces, which ought to be enough for anybody. We eat to live, not vice versa.

"Hmm. If I crumble these in the salad, that's like croutons, right?"

*Tip: If it's a special occasion—say, a holiday or a funeral—top with a thin slice of olive, perhaps from your martini glass.

Two perfect preppy drinks you've never heard of.

THE MIXED MARRIAGE.

BABY PINKY.

Cocktail hour demands drinks with brio. Not for us a bananatini or a lollypop-flavored frozen margarita. Simple daiquiris, gimlets, and cosmos are okay for some, but the basic prep cocktail is a martini.

Those Who Know have discovered that traditions need shaking up (or is it stirring?) from time to time. A vodka martini can seem boring, a gin martini can taste medicinal. Conventional wisdom dictates we never mix our liquors, but now and then we have to take a leap away from complacence. Let us propose the Mixed Marriage: the Lucy and Desi of adult beverages and its colorful offspring, Baby Pinky.

TWO JIGGERS PLYMOUTH GIN	TWO JIGGERS PLYMOUTH GIN
TWO JIGGERS SMIRNOFF VODKA	TWO JIGGERS SMIRNOFF VODKA
ONE CAPFUL NOILLY PRAT VERMOUTH (YES, WE SAID A CAPFUL. IT'S A *COCKTAIL*.)	ONE CAPFUL NOILLY PRAT VERMOUTH
OLIVE OR TWIST, FOR GARNISH	ONE DROP GRENADINE SYRUP, TO INTRODUCE THE IDEA OF ANTIOXIDANTS

Pour into your favorite cocktail shaker with plenty of ice. If tiny shards of ice shimmer on the surface after pouring, they are properly mixed. Remember our rule of thumb: One is not enough, and three are too many.

Post-hangover Ham and Cheese.

Stratas are grilled ham and cheese "sandwiches" for breakfast. I assemble the dish the night before if I think we're going to be drinking, and then I bake it for a delicious breakfast remedy the next day. Feel free to improvise and add bacon instead of ham; add interesting sausages, such as chicken-apple or spinach-feta; or vary the cheese to your tastes.

SERVES 8

6 1-inch-thick by 5-inch-wide slices French or
Italian bread
6 ounces Virginia ham, finely diced
4 ounces Gouda cheese (about 1 cup)
4 ounces Jarlsberg cheese (about 1 cup)
8 large eggs
1¾ cups whole milk
1 tablespoon Dijon mustard
¼ teaspoon freshly grated nutmeg
Salt and freshly ground pepper to taste
¼ cup freshly grated Parmesan cheese
1 tablespoon unsalted butter, diced and
softened

1. Lightly butter an 8x11x 2-inch baking dish.
2. Break up the bread into little pieces and place in the prepared baking dish. The bread pieces should cover the bottom of the baking dish.
3. Top the bread with the ham, Gouda, and Jarlsberg.
4. Combine the eggs with the milk in a large mixing bowl and whisk until smooth. Add the Dijon mustard, nutmeg, and salt and pepper, and continue to whisk until well combined.
5. Pour the mixture over the bread, making sure the bread soaks in the liquid. Scatter the grated Parmesan and tiny pieces of the butter on top. Cover and refrigerate overnight.
6. Preheat the oven to 350°F. Remove the strata from the refrigerator 30 minutes prior to baking.
7. Bake the strata, uncovered, for about 45 to 55 minutes, or until puffy and golden and the center is set.
8. Remove from the oven and allow to sit for 5 to 10 minutes. Serve hot, cut into squares.

Laurie Burrows Grad
University of Pennsylvania

BEROCCA: MORNING-AFTER NECTAR.

Be Sharp! Be Ready! Be Somebody!

If you've lived in Australia, New Zealand, or South Africa for any length of time—even for a week's holiday—you've probably heard of Berocca through its many catchy commercials. B-B-B-Berocca gives you B-B-Bounce.

Berocca is an effervescent tablet that is said to prevent hangovers if dropped into a glass of water before drinking. If drinking has occurred (and you will probably know if it has), you could drink your bubbly Berocca water when you've rolled home, and hope for the best. In the worst case, drink your Berocca the next morning when you awaken, and your hangover will be cured or reduced.

It tastes citrusy. It's got a lot of vitamins ("vit" rhymes with "wit"). It can't hurt you, and in fact could very well put the pep in prep.

Manufactured now by Bayer HealthCare, the product's Web site recommends that it be taken daily (drinking or not drinking) by every adult over twelve, to increase brain function and energy, reduce stress, and, of course, eliminate hangovers.

WHAT'S IN THE PANTRY?

PEANUT BUTTER

JAR OF KEILLER DUNDEE ORANGE MARMALADE (PURCHASED IN THE '80S)

TIN OF DRY MUSTARD

BOXES OF TWININGS TEA BAGS

MAYONNAISE

BOX OF MELITTA COFFEE FILTERS

STALE SALTINES

6 CANS OF TUNA PACKED IN WATER

JAR OF CAPERS

OLD JAR OF SANKA (FOR GRANDMOTHER)

JAR OF BOVRIL

CHEERIOS

OYSTER CRACKERS

BOX OF WHEATIES

ANIMAL CRACKERS (VINTAGE)

SPECIAL K

TRISCUITS

JOHN MCCANN'S STEEL-CUT IRISH OATMEAL

WHEAT THINS

SACK OF WHITE FLOUR

OPEN JAR OF MARASCHINO CHERRIES; NO EXPIRATION DATE

BOX OF RAISINS

2 CANS OF CHICKEN BROTH

CAN OF CAMPBELL'S TOMATO SOUP

JAR OF MARINATED ARTICHOKE HEARTS

JAR OF PEANUTS

CAN OF PETITS POIS

CAN OF BAKED BEANS

EXTRA-LARGE BOTTLE OF KETCHUP

8 LITER BOTTLES TONIC WATER

BOX OF LIPTON ONION SOUP

PACKAGE CHEESECLOTH

BAR OF BAKING CHOCOLATE

BOX REGULAR SUGAR

RED WINE VINEGAR

BOX BROWN SUGAR

COOKING SHERRY

PACKAGE OF PAPER PLATES

WHITE VINEGAR

EXTRA BOXES OF BAGGIES, FOIL

ROLL OF SARAN WRAP

FANCY BALSAMIC VINEGAR

FOOD DYE FOR EASTER EGGS

SEASON BRISLING SARDINES IN OIL

BOTTLE OF VANILLA EXTRACT, EMPTY

I JUST SHOT DINNER:
A QUAIL RECIPE.

Whenever we have friends visit us down South, we take them shooting. Even if they don't shoot, it's just nice to walk outside on a fine morning. If all goes according to plan, we'll have dinner for six.

Cooking the quail is easier than you think, and delicious besides. If you don't have access to your own game, you can use this recipe on birds you order at your butcher or on the Web from D'Artagnan. They will be plucked and all bones gone except for the wings and legs.

SERVES 6.

8 quail
8 cloves of garlic, peeled
Juice of 1 lemon
*3 tablespoons fresh rosemary
(just stripped from its branchlets)*
½ teaspoon salt
Freshly ground black pepper
⅔ cup virgin olive oil

Rinse and dry each bird. Prepare a marinade by throwing the garlic, lemon juice, rosemary, salt, 10 or so grinds of pepper, and olive oil in a Cuisinart and pulsing the ingredients to a wet paste, being sure to finely grind up the garlic and rosemary.

Thoroughly coat each quail, inside and out, with the marinade, cover, and place in fridge.

About 45 minutes before you want to sit down to dinner, light the grill. (You're using real charcoal and a chimney instead of lighter fluid, aren't you?) Once the fire is ready, grill for 5-plus minutes a side, turning occasionally, until the skin is crisp. Encourage guests to pick the birds up and eat them with their fingers.

*Suggested appetizer: homemade gazpacho from the Cuisinart.
Suggested wine: Côtes du Rhône.*

SHEPHERD'S PIE.

SERVES 6-8.

6 medium potatoes
2–3 tablespoons butter
Salt and freshly ground pepper to taste
5 cups chopped cooked lamb (leftover lamb is fine)
3 large cloves of garlic, peeled and minced or put through a garlic press
1 large onion, finely chopped
1 tablespoon crumbled dried rosemary
2 cups gravy (freshly made from your butcher, or any
canned gravy from the supermarket)

Preheat the oven to 325°F.

Peel the potatoes and cut them into quarters. Put them in a deep pot, cover with cold water, and boil for 15 to 20 minutes or until tender. Drain well and put back in the pot. Add butter, salt, and pepper. Mash potatoes by hand until smooth. Set aside.

Thoroughly mix the chopped lamb, garlic, onion, rosemary, gravy, and more salt and pepper in a bowl, then spread the mixture evenly in a 15x10-inch baking dish. Spread the mashed potatoes evenly on top of the lamb mixture, then make a crisscross design in the potatoes with a fork. Bake for 45 to 50 minutes, or until the meat is bubbling hot and the potatoes are browned.

Inspired by Marion Cunningham

LIPTON'S MEATLOAF.

SERVES 8.

1 envelope Lipton Recipe Secrets onion soup mix
2 pounds ground beef (or ground turkey), or one pound of each
¾ cup plain dry bread crumbs
2 eggs
¾ cup water
⅓ cup ketchup

Mix all the ingredients together in a large bowl. Shape the mixture into a loaf and place in a 13x9-inch Corning glass baking dish and microwave at full power for 12 minutes.

Note: Leftovers make great cold meatloaf sandwiches for the next couple of days!

CODFISH CAKES.

1½ pounds fresh skinless codfish fillets
Salt and freshly ground black pepper
5 medium potatoes
1 cup chopped onion
2 large eggs, well beaten

2½ tablespoons Dijon mustard
1 tablespoon Worcestershire sauce
¾ cup finely chopped fresh Italian parsley
½ cup finely chopped onion
1 to 2 cups all-purpose flour
½ to ¾ cup canola oil

Preheat the oven to 400° F. Season the codfish fillets on both sides with salt and pepper and place them in a baking dish. Place that dish in a slightly larger pan filled with about 1 inch of water. Cover all with foil and cook for about 25 minutes. Remove and cool. Drain excess water from pan.

Peel the potatoes, cut them into cubes, put them in a deep pot, and cover with cold water. Add the chopped onion and season with more salt and pepper. Cook until tender.

Drain the potatoes and put back in the pot. Using a potato masher, mash the potatoes until smooth. Set aside.

Flake the codfish with a fork and set it aside.

Mix the eggs, mustard, Worcestershire sauce, parsley, and finely chopped onion in a large bowl. Add the codfish and mashed potatoes, and blend well. Season with salt and pepper as desired, then cover with plastic wrap and chill.

When the mixture is thoroughly cool, form it into small balls using a spoon. Roll each ball in the flour and flatten into a patty shape. Shake off any excess flour.

Heat the oil in a large frying pan over medium heat. Fry the codfish cakes about 3 minutes on each side, or until desired brownness.

When cooked, place the codfish cakes on a cookie sheet lined with paper towels to drain the excess oil.

Inspired by Pierre Franey and Bryan Miller

OLD BAY.

If you've ever been to a traditional beachside shrimp or crab boil in Maryland, you know what it means to have your palate sparked by good old Old Bay seasoning. Sixty years in the making (and counting), it's a curiously stupendous combination of salt and pepper, along with a secret combination of potent spices that we're not allowed to know (and, frankly, don't need to) that delightfully cake the crustaceans in question. The point is that the mere taste of it sends us seaside, and whenever we're longing for the docks we put it on our eggs and into our bloodies in the morning, in lieu of the next crab boil. Here's to another seventy zesty years.

MAISIE'S
APPLE PUDDING.

SERVES 6-8.

Preparation time: 2 hours, 5 minutes

What you need:

1 tub of Cool Whip
1 jar of Musselman's
(or any other organic) applesauce
1 box vanilla Jell-O pudding
Cinnamon sugar (to taste)

To make:
Mix all ingredients well in a bowl, then refrigerate for 2 hours.
* Serve with Nilla Wafers.

BROWNIES.

6 ounces unsweetened chocolate
¾ cup butter (1½ sticks), plus more for preparing pan
4 eggs
2 tablespoons vanilla
½ teaspoon salt
2¾ cups sugar
1½ cups all-purpose flour, plus more for pan

Preheat the oven to 375°F.
  Butter and lightly flour a 9x13-inch baking pan.
Carefully melt the chocolate and butter over low heat,
stirring often and watching that the mixture does not
burn. Remove from the heat when fully melted, and let
cool. Toss the eggs, vanilla, salt, and sugar in a mixing
bowl, and beat well for about 10 minutes. Gradually stir
in the chocolate mixture and then the flour, mixing until
only just blended. Spread evenly in the pan and bake for
25 minutes. Remove from the oven, let cool for a few
hours, then cut into squares.

Makes about two dozen 2x2-inch brownies.
Inspired by Marion Cunningham

Jelly Shots or Sauternes Jelly à l'Orange.

BY CHRISTOPHE PRÉAU

5 full gelatin leaves (found at gourmet market)
750 milliliters of Sauternes wine (a bottle of Bordeaux sweet wine)
¾ cup of superfine sugar
2 oranges
⅛ cup of orange syrup (Monin) or orange juice,
not mandatory for recipe but better if used

Chill 5 dessert glasses in the refrigerator. Soak the gelatin leaves one at a time in a bowl of cold water until soft. Pour the Sauternes into a saucepan and add the sugar. Grate the skin of half an orange, and stir the gratings into the saucepan. Bring almost to the boil, simmer for 5 seconds, then remove from the heat and pour through a strainer into a bowl.

Pour the softened gelatin and soaking liquid through your hands and gently squeeze the water out; discard the soaking liquid. Drop the gelatin leaves into the hot wine and stir until dissolved. Pour in the ⅛ cup of orange syrup or orange juice. Let it cool down, stirring occasionally. (You can hurry the cooling by placing the bowl into a larger bowl filled with water and ice cubes.) Meanwhile, extract the orange segments from the oranges, discarding pits and any pith.

Remove the chilled glasses from the fridge and, using half of the wine jelly, pour equal amounts of it into each glass. Refrigerate for 1 to 2 hours. When the jelly has set, pat the orange segments dry with a paper towel and arrange two or three on top of the jelly in each glass, then pour half the amount of the remaining wine jelly in equal amounts on top until the orange segments are almost covered (but don't cover them entirely or they'll float on top). Chill again, then cover them with the remaining wine, and chill again until ready to serve. This may seem complicated for Prep cooks, but in the end—it's just spiked Jell-O.

Note: You can prepare this recipe 2 or 3 days ahead of when you need it, covering the glasses with Saran wrap and refrigerating them.

THE LEMON: A TRIBUTE.

All hail the mighty lemon! That great ambassador between Savory and Sweet, the double agent in your kitchen that is as decorative as it is delicious (and no calories!). You should never be without a dozen of them—a big bowlful on the table is brighter than a vase of daffodils. For a pleasantly perky surprise, squeeze half a lemon into: a pot of chicken soup, a batch of chili, a saucepan of marinara sauce, a plate of cold crab salad, a fish taco, or a platter of fresh fruit salad. They will all be invariably improved. The same cannot be said for, say, squeezing an orange. Or even a lime. How is this possible? Hmm.

Limoncello, liquid sun.

Limoncello, the glorious Italian lemon liqueur, couldn't be easier to make—as long as you have the time. As in months. It gets its power from steeping fresh lemon peels in high-proof vodka for weeks and weeks on end. The longer you wait, the better it is, sort of like a drinkable savings bond. We found this recipe in Mummy's utility drawer. What was it doing there?

A quart of 100-proof vodka (premium brands not necessary). The zest of a dozen lemons. Combine in a large jar, and store for a month in a dark cabinet. Then combine 2 cups of water and 1½ cups of sugar, bring to a boil, cool, and add to the vodka mix. Put it all back in the dark cabinet for another month. When it has settled, stewed, and reached perfection, strain the mixture, put it in bottles, and store in the freezer until there are guests you need to impress. Serve in small frozen glasses, boast of having made it at home, and be prepared for praise and revelry.

9.

SUITS, 1977. TINA BARNEY. *Courtesy of Janet Borden Gallery.*

HAPPY HOURS, Part 1.

WHAT WE DO.

It was so like Hollingsworth . . . There was a man rich enough to do what he pleased—had he been capable of being pleased—yet barred from all conceivable achievement by his own impervious dulness [sic].
—Edith Wharton, *The Touchstone*

WEEKEND AS GERUND.

Don't look for us in the city on the weekends. We are not there. We're religious about going to the country every Friday through Sunday. Even if the country is a teensy cottage or bungalow (or condo) on a tiny lot with a tree and a geranium plant very close to the highway, less than an hour away—if it's not in the city, it is the country! Our countries. (Actually, many of them are solidly suburban.) Urban preppies thus are engaged in an activity we call "weekending."

When we are young and struggling to get a handle on our finances (some of us actually do have to repay college loans and pay bills), we might stay in the city, since working late nights at our jobs forces us to go out on weekend nights and meet friends for brunch. But we will weekend at our parents' house. Or we'll weekend with a friend who is going out of town. We might shoot clay pigeons. Or we'll go skiing. Or to the beach (we love it off-season). In the summer, while *summering*, we'll rent a place of our own or with some friends and move the action there (see p. 51).

When we're older, more established, and have the means, a house out of town is our big first purchase (see chapter 2), unless we use our family's country house. We are less concerned with the car we use to get there. We might rent a car, or buy a used one, or take a train to our "country," and keep a "station car" parked there.

Weekending can be a lazy time, after all the running around we do during the week. Married preppies conduct their social lives during the weeknights. We go to parties, to openings, to the theater and to concerts, or just out to dinner with friends. Weekends are reserved for just us. We recharge our batteries. We play our necessary sports then. We cook. We go antiquing. We sit around. We nap. We watch TV. We read. We play Scrabble. We watch our Netflix. We take a picnic on our bikes. We drink bloodies. We do nothing.

When we have children, the country is beyond important. Even a small country house is bigger than most city apartments. The children have a playroom of their own. They can spread out. They can build a snowman. They can play on the swing set. The dog can be outdoors without nagging someone to walk him. And it's valuable family time.

We invite friends to weekend with us. When our children are young, we invite friends with other young children and then spend the busy city week recovering from all the noise and cleaning up we had to do on Sunday. We swear we won't have that family again, but you know what? We do.

Weekending reaches a fevered pitch during the summer months. You know this is true because the city clears out in the staid residential neighborhoods, where even tourists find nothing to lure them. If you have no house, no friends, and no prospects for weekending, you can say that you "just love the city in the summer; it's so quiet, and you can get a reservation anywhere." We've all been there and said it ourselves. But not so deep down, we'd rather be weekending.

ENTERTAINING OUR WAY.

We are good at coming up with ideas for parties. Designing table settings and centerpieces. Figuring out who sits where. And with whom. Getting the best flowers. For the least amount of money. We are better than average at coming up with a good alibi for a surprise party. We can invent kicky themes, and some of us are organized.

So we entertain. We like to socialize in big groups and small groups, but mostly big groups. We love ritual. If we threw a good party the last Friday in October, with just the merest push or hint, we will make it an annual event. Why do something small when you can make it big and memorable?

And then there will be pictures and an album, and the memories will multiply, and we'll have new inside jokes about what happened, and we'll do it again next year. Our dream? Permanence, stability, legend.

THE COUNTRY CLUB.

Ah, summer. When thoughts turn to leaving work early on Friday (or skipping it altogether), driving with the top down, sailing with the headwind, and cigars on the club lawn. Oops, scratch that last one. We keep hoping that the Head of the House Committee, aka RuleZilla, will be otherwise indisposed when we light up, but no such luck. We're *still* getting used to this. Isn't the point of a club to relax and have fun? Didn't we have enough rules at Choate to last us the rest of our lives? Doesn't RZ have better things to do, like preventing Murphy Anderson from breast-feeding her baby in the ladies' locker room? Ah, summer.

"Quick, before RuleZilla notices!"

"Too late. Let's move to the steam room."

"Cuban cigars don't count. They're neutral, like Guantánamo."

"Oh, give us a BREAK—we're outside!"

WIN. Senior managing partner at Covington & Burling. Hasn't done a day's work in years beyond forwarding dirty jokes on the Internet. Princeton man with a glorious orange-and-black tattoo of a tiger in a straw boater on his right buttock. Married to a long-suffering Mount Holyoke alumna.

SKIP. Art director at Ogilvy. A Duke graduate who lived in Europe for years postgraduation. Longtime bachelor with rumored boy- and girl-friends. His collection of vintage clip-ons numbers in the hundreds. Keeps four extra pairs in the glove compartment of his MGA convertible.

KYLE. Yalie who gave his life to Lehman Brothers. Now searching for new opportunities through alumni Web site, squash games at Yale Club, and vacations at Lyford. Debating new start-ups. Leads a somewhat "separate life" from his Connecticut College-educated wife.

NO CELL PHONES WHATSOEVER.

NO STROLLERS OR PLAYPENS
AT THE CLUB.

NO BREAST-FEEDING.

NO SHORT SHORTS ON
THE GOLF COURSE.

NO RAISED VOICES.

NO SPANDEX BICYCLE WEAR.

ALL WHITE ON TENNIS COURT. NO
CUTOFFS, EVEN IF THEY'RE WHITE.
MEN MUST WEAR COLLARED SHIRTS
ON TERRACE, TENNIS COURTS,
AND GOLF COURSE.

NO JEANS.

NO RADIOS.

JUNIORS MUST GIVE UP THE
COURT IMMEDIATELY.

MEMBERS' DOUBLES RECEIVE
PRIORITY OVER MEMBERS' SINGLES.

SWIMMERS ARE REQUESTED TO
SHOWER BEFORE USING THE POOL.

SMOKING IS PROHIBITED IN ALL
AREAS OF THE CLUBHOUSE AND
OUTDOOR DINING AREAS.

AUDIBLE BEEPERS ARE
PROHIBITED IN ALL PUBLIC AREAS.

MEMBERS ARE ASKED NOT TO
REPRIMAND EMPLOYEES, NOR TO
DISCUSS EMPLOYEE GRIEVANCES.

FOOD AND BEVERAGES MAY NOT
BE BROUGHT TO THE CLUB.

DOGS ARE NOT ALLOWED ON
THE PREMISES.

THESE RULES MUST NOT BE
SHARED WITH NONMEMBERS.

WE NEITHER SEEK NOR
WELCOME PUBLICITY.

*"Even when I liked you
I didn't like you."*

TOMMY. *Newest member of the club; not yet aware of no-cigar rule. RISD-trained architect, specializing in summer cottages costing more than $2 million. Engaged for first time to young associate in his office, whose mummy is a Phipps. He goes mute, however, on the subject of his mummy.*

JEREMY. *Golf club genetically attached to his hands, and not just in the summer. Married to Boo, who features in every other uttered sentence. Reporter, covering mergers for* The Wall Street Journal *but really wants to write for the* Times. *About golf.*

RULEZILLA. *Former admissions head at Winsor. Embittered by the collapse of her second marriage; her husband ran off with the pool boy. When she's not telling everyone what to do, she knits with a ferocity to rival Madame Defarge.*

CITY CLUBS.

ATLANTA

Atlanta Athletic Club. 1930 Bobby Jones
Drive, Johns Creek, 30097
(770) 448-2166
Burns Club Atlanta. 988 Alloway Place
Southeast, 30316 (404) 627-2941
Capital City Club. 7 Harris St., 30303
(404) 523-8221
Commerce Club. 34 Broad Street Northwest,
30303 (404) 525-1661
Piedmont Driving Club. 1215 Piedmont Ave.
N.E., 30309 (404) 875-2565

BOSTON

St. Botolph Club. 199 Commonwealth Ave.,
02116 (617) 536-7570
Somerset Club. 42 Beacon St., 02108
(617) 227-1731
Union Club. 8 Park St., 02108
(617) 227-0589

CHICAGO

Chicago Club. 81 E. Van Buren St., 60605
(312) 427-1825
Racquet Club of Chicago. 1365 North
Dearborn St., 60610
(312) 787-3201
Standard Club. 320 South Plymouth Court,
60604 (312) 427-9100
Union League Club. 65 West Jackson Blvd.,
60604 (312) 427-7800
University Club. 76 East Monroe St., 60603
(312) 726-2840

DALLAS

Dallas Petroleum Club. 2200 Ross Ave., 75201
(214) 871-1500

DISTRICT OF COLUMBIA

Cosmos Club. 2121 Massachusetts Ave. NW,
20008 (202) 387-7783
Metropolitan Club. 1700 H Street NW,
20006 (202) 835-2500

LOS ANGELES

The Jonathan Club. 545 South Figueroa St.,
90071 (213) 624-0881

NEW ORLEANS

Boston Club. 824 Canal St., 70112
(504) 523-3443
Pickwick Club. 115 Saint Charles Ave., 70130
(504) 524-5341

NEW YORK

The Brook. 111 East 54th St.,
10022 (212) 753-7020
Century Association. 7 West 43rd St., 10036
(212) 944-0090
Knickerbocker Club. 807 5th Ave./2 East
62nd St., 10065 (212) 644-4460
The Links Club. 36 East 62nd St., 10065
(212) 832-0625
Racquet and Tennis Club. 370 Park Ave.,
10022 (212) 753-9700
Union Club. 101 East 69th St., 10021
(212) 734-5400
Union League Club. 38 East 37th St., 10016
(212) 685-3800
University Club. 1 West 54th St., 10019
(212) 247-2100

WOMEN'S CLUBS:
Colony Club. 564 Park Ave./51 East 62nd St.,
10065 (212) 838-3540
Cosmopolitan Club. 122 East 66th St.,
10065 (212) 734-5950

PHILADELPHIA

Racquet Club of Philadelphia. 215 South
16th St., 19102 (215) 735-1525

SAN FRANCISCO

Bohemian Club. 624 Taylor St., 94102
(415) 885-2440
Pacific-Union Club. 1000 California St.,
94108 (415) 775-1234

SEATTLE

The Rainier Club. 820 Fourth Ave.,
98104 (206) 296-6902
Washington Athletic Club. 1325 Sixth Ave.,
98101 (206) 622-7900

WILMINGTON

University & Whist Club. 805 North Broom St.,
19806 (302) 658-5125

DIRTY POOL.

Arriving at the club. Let's check to see what we need. Sunglasses? Check. Bikini wax? Check. Lilly bathing suit? Check. Tote with beach towel and magazine? Affirmative. Got to finish that article in *Bazaar* about the papaya diet. Arnold Palmer from snack bar? Check. Boyfriend? Whoops! I knew I was missing something. Who is Duncan talking to? Tory Titmouse? TTFW. That's not nice. I didn't realize Duncan liked girls with cellulite.

Ponytail suitable for tanning and swimming (we never wear caps). (Duh.)

The ultimate club drink: half lemonade, half iced tea. It's called an Arnold Palmer. Go through one an hour. Carl at the snack bar makes the best Arnold Palmers in the whole world.

Took big towel from Mummy's linen closet. She's probably looking for it.

Vineyard Vines tote. Limited edition and very discreet.

Flip-flops—inexpensive but don't look it.

SPORTS WE PLAY.

We are sporty. (Doesn't CeCe call herself "Sporty Spice"? She's a hoot.) We don't live to work, and we don't work to live. We live to have fun and win the club tournament. (It's our competitive streak.)

We don't play football, but we might play touch football during Thanksgiving weekend, when all the family gets together. We don't play baseball. We don't play basketball, but we shoot hoops when we are at school or visit our kids at school. We used to play soccer, lacrosse, field hockey, ice hockey, and rugby but gave them up when we became, um, responsible adults. We play "hide the flag" at the Kennedy's whenever we're asked.

We prefer sports that are, indeed, clubby. Golf clubby (see p. 170), yacht clubby, tennis clubby, squash clubby, court tennis clubby, bridge clubby, swim clubby, country clubby. Let's not forget polo. Prince Charles hasn't. As for sports in which we engage by ourselves, we ski, of course, and fish (see p. 176). And run. And bike. And hike, the latter two often with friends.

We love sports over which we can achieve some mastery. You don't have to be supergood to be a fun addition to a round of golf or a doubles match, though it certainly helps. Good social skills, charm, and a new harvest of jokes will add to your appeal as an invited guest if you yourself are not a member of the club. Loud swearing when your ball goes way out of bounds or a constant hum of "sorry"s will not put you at the top of the list the next time your friends need an extra person to fill in.

Racquet sports are truly prep, as are equipment and special uniforms. You'll find many preppies fetishize their gear: will only play with Calloway clubs, only hit with Penn balls, only wear Puma shoes or Fred Perry shorts—in other words, something to blame if the points don't go their way.

Lounging around the club, getting involved in club politics, and entertaining friends at your clubs are all preppy pastimes, and help you spend your club quotas.

Daily or triweekly devotions at yoga or spin class, Pilates, or just weightlifting are not overtly prep or non-prep, just as brushing one's teeth is neither prep nor non-prep. It just is what it is. Obviously, our own men allege they have no vanity. Whatever you say, Tucker.

SPORTS WE DON'T PLAY.

Football (after college). Jai Alai. Handball. Synchronized Swimming. Curling. Anything involving hurling "little people." Unicycling. Dog Racing. Dog Fighting. Cockfighting. NASCAR. Ultimate Frisbee. Ultimate Anything. Boxing. Competitive Ballroom Dancing. Speed Walking (an Olympic sport). Bowling. Competitive Hula-Hooping. Pairs Figure Skating. Ice Dancing. Women's Basketball (after college). Baseball (after college). Competitive Cheerleading. Competitive Eating. And never: Folk Dancing.

Which doesn't mean, incidentally, that we wouldn't watch them on TV when we are in extremis (insomnia/bedridden/drunk/pregnant/room spinning/bored out of our minds). We also have been known to watch Home Shopping, infomercials, the Game Show Network, televised poker, obscure beauty pageants, Herbalife seminars, aerobics shows, and, if all else fails, CSPAN.

Any other sport—especially those involving water or racquets—we'll do or try, at least once.

THE BIG GAME.

HOW DRINKING ENRICHES SPECTATING.

AN OBVIOUS GUIDE TO THE OBVIOUS.

Alcohol is like truth serum, in its way. It could be said that drinking enhances one's emotions as it disinhibits one's natural tendencies to edit oneself.

Therefore, if you are a Red Sox fan (and if you are reading this book and a baseball lover, you probably are), the beer you drink at a game amplifies your feeling of passion for your team.

If you go to football games, you already know that some of your favorite memories consist of your unbelievable tailgate picnics, replete with thermoses of bloodies and huge bottles of single-malt scotch.

Why is beer (and now wine and mixed drinks) sold at stadiums and tournaments? Because spectators become more involved when they drink. Because there is nothing like sitting in the sun watching other people exert themselves while you are drinking something cold out of a plastic cup.

You can drink champagne at Wimbledon (or while watching the matches on your television). You can drink mint juleps while in Kentucky watching the Derby (or, again, at home in front of the TV). Of course, it can take longer than the entirety of the race to mix a julep, so plan accordingly.

Rule of thumb: Beer is the go-to spectating beverage. However, there are lots of preppies (women in particular) who are not beer lovers. So when watching a morning match, try bloodies or the twenty-first-century answer to screwdrivers, the mimosa. In the afternoon, G&Ts are crisp and tasty, and bartenders can't mess them up. If you are in England or Jamaica, drink Pimm's. If you are on the wagon, remember that you alone will remember the critical moments of play in the game or match, and you alone will feel good the next day.

A Preppy Stands in It.

Most preppies are active types who use their free time to bounce around from sport to sport, from lunch to cocktails, from small talk to more small talk. Standing silently in cold water for hours alone, watching and waiting for a fish to bite, and perchance, to catch it, only to release it back into the river whence it came . . . no talking . . . no drinking . . . no sitting . . . It doesn't sound like a preppy's dream come true.

Nick Cox is that rare fisherman who is both passionate—"One year I fished 200 days; I was really possessed"—about the sport and objectively analytical about its appeal. Based year-round in Ketchum, Idaho, he fishes, he guides, he writes, and he considers all it takes to be possessed by fly fishing. "There is a definite mystique around it," he agrees one morning. "After people saw the movie *A River Runs Through It*, they stormed through here and bought gear and didn't know how to fish . . . and you can't do anything without spending [at least] two grand."

But just a second, Nick. Preppies love nature and love traveling to remote locations, and even more than that, we love expensive equipment. Handmade rod? Want it. Handmade *bamboo* rod? Need it. Sounds like the perfect vacation for us.

However, as Nick explains, fly fishing is not for dabblers. "You just can't try it. You can test it out by renting gear and hiring a guide to cut the learning curve, but you can't cast [instantly], and casting is the name of the game. You have to practice casting, and not while you're fishing." Professional fly fishermen have reached the consensus that it takes about thirty hours of casting (broken up into half-hour sessions)—perhaps while standing on one's lawn—to learn to cast. Um, that doesn't sound so glamorous. "It looks stupid, but it pays dividends." Besides how dumb it looks, Cox warns that "it's men with sticks. Like cavemen.

Men just want to hit that stick . . . hard—even with a fly rod, and that's a bad thing to do."

So now we've established that patience—a virtue to most, a distant goal for the average prepster—is what is needed to succeed and savor the experience. There are four well-known stages to becoming a real fisherman. "Stage one: You want to catch a fish—any fish will do. Stage two: The more fish you catch, the better. Stage three: You want big fish, then bigger fish. Stage four: It's no longer about the fish." It's just thrilling to be out there. For those of us who've never experienced this thrill, when you are focused and intent, "there's a tremendous adrenaline rush as you get to the river, especially if you see the fish rising. The anticipation itself is compelling."

As Nick describes it, the pleasures of fly fishing sound Zen-like: "A form of meditation that can take four hours . . . you cannot experience it with anyone else. It's a contemplation thing. In nature. In the water."

The other side of fly fishing is that no matter who you are, no matter where you went to school or how many times you were nominated for a Nobel or a Pulitzer, or "if you are a captain of the universe with $50 billion, fishing is a circumstance over which you have no control." Sounds frustrating. Plus, cell phones are discouraged, to say the least. And you really have to let the guy who got there first have his spot to himself. "If you cut in front, you're a jerk." Head upstream. One last thing: The waders, vest, hat, rod, reel, and flies are cool. We all agree. But if you're seen on the banks of the river keeping your fish out of the water too long in a catch-and-release area, or lying about the numbers and sizes of fish you caught, "you're a jerk," says Cox, using a favorite (though, one suspects, unofficial) term. And if you're a beginner you don't want (or need) top-of-the-line equipment. To real fishermen, it'll just give you away.

FISHING AND SHOOTING CLUBS.

Fishing.

At Home or Near Home.

ALASKA
Bristol Bay Lodge in the
Wood-Tikchik Park.
Trout, King Salmon, Arctic Char

BAHAMAS
Mangrove Cay Club on Andros. *Bonefish*

BRITISH COLUMBIA
The Lower Dean River Lodge.
Steelhead, Salmon

CANADA
A few good camps open to the public:
Cold Spring Camp on the Matapédia.
Atlantic Salmon
Wilson's Camp on the Miramichi.
Atlantic Salmon

IDAHO
Henry's Fork Lodge on the Henry's Fork
offers ten rivers to be fished. *Trout*

MONTANA
Big Hole Lodge on the Wise River. *Trout*

Abroad.

ARGENTINA
Arroyo Verde on the Traful.
Trout and Landlocked Salmon
Private Estancia on the Caleufu. *Trout*
Private Estancia Tecka on the Corcovado
and Tecka rivers. *Trout*
San Huberto on the Malleo. *Trout*

CHILE
Nomads of the Sea (a boat that takes you to
virgin rivers). *Trout*

MONGOLIA
Sweetwater lodges on Eg and Ur rivers.
Taimen, Lenok Trout

NEW ZEALAND
Tongariro Lodge on the Tongariro River.
Trout

RUSSIA
Lodges on Kharlovka,
East Litza and Rynda rivers. *Atlantic Salmon*

SCOTLAND
Tulchan Lodge on the Spey. *Atlantic Salmon*

Wing shooting.

At Home.

ALABAMA
Enon Plantation. *Quail, Duck*

GEORGIA
Woodhaven Plantation. *Quail*

MARYLAND
Quaker Neck Gun Club.
Duck, Geese, Dove

NEW YORK
Mashomack Preserve Club *
(also clays, skeet)
Pawling Mountain *
Pheasant, Hungarian Partridge, Chukar
Tamarack Preserve *
(also clays, skeet)

PENNSYLVANIA
Blooming Grove Hunting and Fishing Club.*
Trout; Chicken, Grouse, Pheasant
Rolling Rock Club.*
(Dick Cheney's favorite club)
Duck, Pheasant, Partridge

SOUTH CAROLINA
Bray's Island.*
Quail, Duck, Pheasant, Turkey
Cherokee Plantation.*
Quail, Partridge, Pheasant

TEXAS
King Ranch. *Quail, Duck, Dove*

Abroad.

ARGENTINA
Estancia Santa Ana Córdoba. *Dove*

SCOTLAND
Tulchan Estate on the Spey.
Pheasant, Grouse, Duck

SOUTHERN AFRICA
Gamebirds Train Shoots on
Rovos Rail and Lodge Based Fly out shoots
(Zambia, Botswana, South Africa)
*Guinea Fowl, Francolin, Dove, Ducks,
Geese, Sandgrouse*

—Jesse Saunders
Eaglebrook (x), Avon Old Farms, Roanoke

* *private club*

OUR BOOK CLUB.

We start a book club because we feel intellectually thwarted by the endless devotion to our children: making their lunches; buying them miniature cashmere sweaters, which they keep losing; packing for camp; and the relentless torment of carpooling. We remember how our intelligence was once piqued long ago in that class we took. Was it at Deerfield or at Pomona? How could we have forgotten? What was that class? The role of gender in the works of Manet and Dickens? Who taught it?

Anyway, it doesn't matter anymore. What matters is that you and Tricia and Weesa, Luce, Bead, Steen, Bimmie, Mimo, and probably someone else we can't remember right now have our mornings free (after Gyrotonics and yoga, that is) and could use the brain stimulation. Who wants to host the first one? Should it be Thursday at eleven? And then break for lunch? Perfect. Once a month? Perfect. The first Thursday of the month? Or the second? Excellent. That'll give us time to read the damn books. What should we serve? Tea sandwiches and coffee and wine and cookies? We have to have a salad? Oh, just skip the sandwiches and the cookies and the salad. Bimmie, you're so bad! Okay, everyone just serve what you want to serve. Luce and Mimo never eat, anyway.

But what should we read? Something cozy and familiar? Or something new and harder? Didn't we always promise ourselves we would read Camus or Proust? Whatever.

"She actually thinks no one can tell which nostril is fake."

"Is she BLIND? Someone needs to get her to a decent specialist. Or do you think it's too late?"

LUCE. Former NBC news producer, now studying landscape architecture. Wharton graduate and trustee. Normally reads The Wall Street Journal *only.*

WEESA. A walking advertisement for Tory Burch but actually a mother of four children under the age of twelve and stepmother of four more (teenagers). How does she do it? Vino, vino, vino.

JET. (opposite, cross-legged) Named for Daddy's favorite toy. Prodigious reader. "Where does he come from?" Mummy (Mimo) just announced she's dyslexic.

What kind of wine will be served?

We join a book club because we need to find meaning and sisterhood and community. That's why we're rereading that book by what's-his-name? McGowan? The guy? That prize? We join it because now we only read *Vogue* and *US* and look at the cartoons in *The New Yorker* and feel like our minds are turning to oatmeal. Because it would be fun to carry a big book like *Infinite Jest* when we're getting our pedicures. (And then we can still read *People* and *Hello!* and *OK!*) We join book clubs because we crave discipline and routine. And Cal's hardly ever home anymore, anyway.

You know, we're never going to get through a single book, with the Dohertys' divorce and Lila's affair . . . Why don't we make this a magazine club?

"I thought it was amazing that just when you thought his ex-wife's lover was a man all along—"

"STOP! Don't tell me the ending! I haven't even started it!"

"I know. Genius. What, this? It's okay, I'm in my ninth month."

BEAD. *Always reads the books, because her husband is always away . . . and she has no kids. Graduated from Harvard at nineteen.*

"I could see the ending a mile away."

TRICIA. *Recently remarried (third time) interior designer. Rumored to have been long-ago mistress of Agnelli, which would explain the house in Capri.*

BIMMIE. *Never reads the book for book club but still talks too much. Claims to be "working on a project," but it's been four years. In coffee cup: vodka.*

STEEN. *Working mother. Dartmouth graduate and senior editor at* Time. *Knows John Irving personally. In her ninth month. Really.*

THE TRUE PREP
MASTER READING LIST.

In addition to the books taught in school'd at Hotchkiss, here is a list of books you will enjoy . . . some fiction, some nonfiction, some about schools, some about suburbs, some about WASPs, some about Jews, some about divorce, and some about money. Yes, many are memoirs. Some are set in the past, and some are set in the present. As with everything else, the older, the preppier.

Slim Aarons	*Once Upon a Time*
Joan Aiken	*The Wolves of Willoughby Chase*
Nelson W. Aldrich	*Old Money: The Mythology of America's Upper Class; Tommy Hitchcock: An American Hero; George, Being George: George Plimpton's Life as Told, Admired, Deplored, etc., etc.*
Louis S. Auchincloss	*The Rector of Justin; East Side Story*
Anne Bernays	*Growing Up Rich*
Stephen Birmingham	*"Our Crowd"*
Art Brewer and C. R. Stecyk III	*Bunker Spreckels: Surfing's Divine Prince of Decadence*
David Brooks	*Bobos in Paradise*
Christopher Buckley	*Losing Mum and Pup*
William F. Buckley Jr.	*God and Man at Yale*
Josiah Bunting III	*All Loves Excelling*
Frances Hodgson Burnett	*A Little Princess*
John Cheever	*The Wapshot Scandal; The Stories of John Cheever*
Ron Chernow	*The House of Morgan: An American Banking Dynasty and the Rise of Modern Finance*
Julia Child	*Mastering the Art of French Cooking*, volumes 1 and 2
William D. Cohan	*House of Cards: A Tale of Hubris and Wretched Excess on Wall Street*
Stephen Colbert	*I Am America (and So Can You!)*
James Collins	*Beginner's Greek*
Laurie Colwin	*The Lone Pilgrim*
Evan Connell Jr.	*Mr. Bridge; Mrs. Bridge*
Charlotte Curtis	*The Rich, and Other Atrocities*
Roald Dahl	*Fantastic Mr. Fox; Kiss Kiss*
Charles Dickens	*Great Expectations; Oliver Twist; Bleak House*
Joan Didion	*Slouching Towards Bethlehem; The White Album*
Dominick Dunne	*The Two Mrs. Grenvilles: A Novel*
Dave Eggers	*A Heartbreaking Work of Staggering Genius*
Jeffrey Eugenides	*Middlesex*
F. Scott Fitzgerald	*All of his work*
Jane Fonda	*My Life So Far*
Tad Friend	*Cheerful Money: Me, My Family, and the Last Days of WASP Splendor*
Paul Fussell	*Class*
Barbara Goldsmith	*Little Gloria, Happy At Last*
Katharine Graham	*Personal History*
Beth Gutcheon	*The New Girls*
John Hawkes	*The Blood Oranges*
Brooke Hayward	*Haywire*
Ernest Hemingway	*A Moveable Feast*
John Irving	*The World According to Garp*

Walter Isaacson and Evan Thomas	*The Wise Men: Six Friends and the World They Made*
Henry James	*Daisy Miller; The Portrait of a Lady*
Nora Johnson	*The World of Henry Orient*
Abigail Jones and Marissa Miley	*Restless Virgins: Love, Sex, and Survival in Prep School*
E. L. Konigsburg	*From the Mixed-up Files of Mrs. Basil E. Frankweiler*
Jean Hanff Korelitz	*Admission*
Alison Lurie	*The War Between the Tates*
Patricia Marx and Roz Chast	*Meet My Staff*
William Maxwell	*The Folded Leaf*
Mary McCarthy	*The Group*
James Merrill	*Selected Poems*
Susan Minot	*Evening*
Nancy Mitford	*Love in a Cold Climate*
Rick Moody	*The Ice Storm*
Ogden Nash	*The Best of Ogden Nash*
Barack Obama	*Dreams from My Father*
John O'Hara	*Appointment at Samarra; Butterfield 8*
George Plimpton	*As Told at The Explorers Club: More Than Fifty Gripping Tales of Adventure* (Explorers Club Classic)
Anne Roiphe	*1185 Park Avenue*
Philip Roth	*Goodbye, Columbus*
J. D. Salinger	*Nine Stories*
Christine Schutt	*All Souls*
John Sedgwick	*In My Blood: Six Generations of Madness and Desire in an American Family*
Erich Segal	*Love Story*
Thomas Shomo	*To Manner Born, To Manners Bred*
Cornelia Otis Skinner	*Our Hearts Were Young and Gay*
Richard Stengel	*You're Too Kind: A Brief History of Flattery*
Sarah Payne Stuart	*My First Cousin Once Removed: Money, Madness, and the Family of Robert Lowell*
J. Courtney Sullivan	*Commencement*
Booth Tarkington	*Alice Adams; The Magnificent Ambersons*
Andrew Tobias	*The Best Little Boy in the World Grows Up*
Calvin Tompkins	*Living Well Is the Best Revenge*
John Kennedy Toole	*A Confederacy of Dunces*
John Updike	*The Maple Stories; Couples*
Gore Vidal	*Burr*
Wendy Wasserstein	*Elements of Style: A Novel*
Paul Watkins	*Stand Before Your God*
Evelyn Waugh	*Brideshead Revisited*
Edith Wharton	Everything but *Ethan Frome*
Edmund White	*A Boy's Own Story*
Oscar Wilde	*The Importance of Being Earnest*
Sean Wilsey	*Oh the Glory of It All*
Tom Wolfe	*Radical Chic & Mau-Mauing the Flak Catchers; The Kandy-Kolored Tangerine-Flake Streamline Baby; I Am Charlotte Simmons: A Novel*
Geoffrey Wolff	*The Duke of Deception; The Final Club*
Tobias Wolff	*Old School*
Richard Yates	*A Good School; Revolutionary Road*

REUNIONS.

Let's just say that college was the best four or five years of your life. You graduated with a new nickname, new friends, a new set of interests, a new waistline, a new plan for your future . . . In short, you were remade by your school. It happens all the time.

You and your pals can't wait till your first reunion. If you went to Princeton, of course, that would be a year after graduation . . . and every year thereafter.

At most other colleges, that means you return to campus on your fifth, tenth, fifteenth, quinquennial—every five years—anniversary, should you choose to or need to, or because preppies love to attend reunions.

Of course, you could always get your group together somewhere else, at a more convenient time and location. While it wouldn't be an official reunion, you could have a much better time, and you won't feel bullied into buying memorabilia you will never wear or put on your car. Some people get married for just this reason.

REUNION SPOILER ALERT

Unless you put in real time working with your friends scattered here and afar to produce the perfect reunion, we urge you to lower your expectations. You may be more disappointed with who didn't show up than with who did. You may feel you didn't get to reconnect with the very classmate who inspired you to return to campus. You may feel old and not enjoy not being carded this time around. If you are female, you may not feel as lithe and desirable as you once were. (If you are pregnant, though, you won't care at all.) If you are male, you will worry about your hair.

Having said all that, you can still have a terrific time at your reunion. You have tacit permission to act silly, to regress, to drink too much at your fraternity's open house, and to annoy your spouse. Having tagged alongside you at one reunion and having had a thoroughly un-wonderful time, your spouse may also decide to sit this one out, in which case you will have nothing to apologize for.

If you are wondering whether you are ready to appear at your reunion, consider these important questions:

- Have you accomplished anything since graduation? Anything at all? (Marriage, engagement, divorce, children, job, more degrees, dramatic weight loss, and a great suntan all count.)
- Do you have a good-looking partner? Do you have a not-great-looking but accomplished or successful partner?
- Do you have some "unfinished business" with a classmate that must be resolved at last?
- Have you become a movie or TV star since you last walked through the quad?
- Did you get the world's most subtle face-lift? Brow lift? Liposuction?
- Is your life better than it was at your previous reunion five years ago (or in the case of Princeton, last year)?

If you responded yes to at least four of the six sets of questions, run—don't walk—to your alma mater. You need to go, nay, you need to be seen. You will look younger and cooler than most alumni, and you don't have to stay all weekend.

Alumni Notes.

Go on. Open your alumni/ae magazine to your class notes. Ooh! So many classmates; this will be fun to read.

Or will it? Even though you only graduated ten years ago, none of these people sounds familiar. Who are they? The geniuses you never met? The people who kept asking you to "keep it down" so they could study? On Friday nights?

Where are the classmates who are your friends? The people who might have been better known to the local police or to the dean who gave out extensions rather than to the Rhodes and Fulbright committees . . . hmmm. Not here.

The problem with life is you think you're doing okay until you find out that you had a slew of classmates you never knew who are way more successful than you on every level. They run a department at the hospital and have three exceptional children. They help the poor in the Third World and are married to an Olympic silver medalist (and they have three exceptional children). They eat organic food and wake up refreshed every morning and have never been hungover in their lives. (And they have those three exceptional . . .) Or suddenly you have tons of classmates (not to mention the people the year behind you) who have given buildings to your alma mater in gratitude. Our career counselor never told us to run a fund of funds; if only they had, we'd be giving buildings, too.

If you are like us, you might wonder if these wunderkinds even attended your college. Alumni ringers? Perhaps. Find your yearbook. Look to see if these people are real. You had great times and you have great memories, but at no time did you go to class with or live near Einstein Jr. Who are these people? Did the alumni office dream them up to make you feel like a loser? To inspire you to do better? To rub it (whatever "it" is) in?

Is it even cool for a preppy to send in his or her class notes? Not really. It is much cooler for the news department of your college to find you and ask you if they can write about you. Or to include you in a big article on MacArthur Fellows. Or National Book Award short-listers. Or to reprint your photograph at Sundance with Robert Redford.

Failing that, assuming you are a normal, middle-class, somewhat well-adjusted person with nice clothes, a European automobile, and maybe a few children or a few dogs or a few degrees . . . what is there to say or brag about? Is it enough to say you flew to Chicago to attend a classmate's (second) wedding? Dare you mention that you didn't remember where you were when you woke up?

For those of us who are fallible, human, and a bit flawed (we're preppies, and we're okay with that), the arrival of our alumni quarterly can be traumatic. It's a diary of hair loss. It's a reminder of the books not read. It's a passage of time. You were just a recent alum; now you are an old-timer. It's the rude awakening that you never made the Young Presidents' Organization.

But hey! Life is good! We are superior vacationers. We may not be sybarites, but we know how to enjoy ourselves. We can sort of carry a tune. We are fast readers. We still have our memories, our diplomas, our teeth, and the keys to our family's beach house.

PREP PORNOGRAPHY.

When it comes to online pornography, prep-pies are extremely creative and can avail themselves of more than one kind.

There is the obvious. Due to their emotional and sexual arrested development (going away to an all-boys' school can do that to you), boys will be boys and enjoy conventional online pornography. This comes to them at no cost, unlike buying the dirty magazines of Daddy's day.

There is also real-estate pornography, where we can stare and lust after listings in all our favorite places and neighborhoods, and take virtual tours of guest cottages, boathouses, and state-of-the-art kitchens. Ooh! Exciting! Don't forget 1stdibs, where vintage looks so good, you wonder why you told Grandmother you

didn't want any of her Wedgwood collection or her old Buccellati bracelet. (Libby, sometimes I wonder what's wrong with you.)

If you do it enough, and can't stop, it does become pornography in a way. If you keep returning to sites (even your ex's Facebook page) at the expense of leading a normal life and engaging in normal activities, like gossiping, drinking, and hanging out, anything becomes a problem. Couples have split up over one spouse's addiction to eBay. Going to www.theknot.com incessantly is not healthy if you are not in the throes of planning a wedding.

The word is moderation, in all things: drinking, giltgroupe.com, net-a-porter.com, and Awfulplasticsurgery.com. You can do it, Sterling.

SHOPPING AS RECREATION.

For those preppies who prefer their exercise to be on foot, balancing bulky objects in both hands to work various muscle groups, shopping or window-shopping is often the activity of choice. It can start as a leisurely little walk and grow to be a vigorous workout. A notion can develop into a serious reconnaissance mission, especially if whatever you're searching for is sold out in your size.

You could stroll through a farmers' market (and eat free samples as you go), walk down North Michigan Avenue, up Madison Avenue, or along Robertson

Boulevard. What are people wearing? What's the zeitgeist in this city today? (You may not really care, but it's impressive to say.) Stop for coffee—Pause for a bite. Think about the book you're not writing, the closet you are not organizing, the calls you are not returning. Take your dog along. (Aside from food stores, dogs are remarkably welcome in most other shops.)

By the end of your adventure you will have somehow acquired things you urgently needed at 1 pm that you no longer want at 4 pm. (Deposit them in your gift closet. They will suit someone you know.)

TARTAN AND TWEED.

Where would preppies be without Ralph Lauren? (And for that matter, where would Ralph Lauren be without us?) We need one another for what is a most symbiotic relationship.

Inspired by the traditional tailoring of British and Ivy League menswear, Ralph Lauren and his Polo labels have been taking over the world with their Prep-Meets-Fashion merger. Some of the most exceptionally handsome and well-dressed people who don't even speak English are outfitted from head to toe by the empire.

Each store is an elegant or retro environment that we love—whether it's a vintage villa, an Adirondack lodge, a colonial beach cottage, a ski chalet, a western ranch, or the library straight out of a stately home of England. There, the customers feel they are absorbing an ambience, and they are. Lauren allows us to dream a bit,

to take his seductive journey through the meticulous interiors. His stores are like a theme park for decorators and decorating enthusiasts. His RL, a restaurant adjacent to his grand store on North Michigan Avenue in Chicago, takes the Polo-ness to a new level. The U.S. Olympic team has worn Polo since 2008. The U.S. Open—America's Grand Slam tennis tournament—always wears Polo (since 2004), as does Wimbledon (since 2005).

By 1980, the Polo brand was established as a sportswear line, starting with silk ties, and was famous for polo shirts in a dizzying range of colors. It did not get much of a mention in a certain madras-bound book because, well, it was a new company, and we were more comfortable wearing the brands our parents had worn. (We can be sticks-in-the-mud sometimes, if you must know.)

THE PREPPY MIX TAPE.

The golden age of preppy music must be the 1980s, when *The Official Preppy Handbook* was published. We learned then that dressing just the way we always do was considered so bold, so outré, that we gained admission into all those places everyone yearned for. No shrieking out the doormen's names for us. We walked right past the velvet stanchions. With our love of nostalgia, we lean towards '60s R&B, classic rock, disco, and anything that reminds us of our junior year abroad. Make room for irony. (Not really.)

This tape is a work in progress. Feel free to add your own songs.
DRINK. DANCE. REPEAT.

Rock Lobster	The B-52's	*They Just Can't Stop It*	The Spinners
Girls Talk	Dave Edmunds	*(Games People Play)*	
Brown Sugar	The Rolling Stones	*Disco Inferno*	The Trammps
Jumpin' Jack Flash	The Rolling Stones	*Jump*	Van Halen
My Girl	The Four Tops	*I Want a New Drug*	Huey Lewis and
Build Me Up Buttercup	The Foundations		the News
(Sittin' on)	Otis Redding Jr.	*Mansard Roof*	Vampire Weekend
The Dock of the Bay		*Borderline*	Madonna
Psycho Killer	Talking Heads	*Smooth Operator*	Sade
Don't You Want Me	The Human League	*Got to Be Real*	Cheryl Lynn
I Will Survive	Gloria Gaynor	*No More Tears*	Donna Summer
Is She Really Going	Joe Jackson	*(Enough Is Enough)*	& Barbra Streisand
Out with Him?		*Boogie Oogie Oogie*	A Taste of Honey
Alison	Elvis Costello	*Gloria*	Laura Brannigan
Rock the Casbah	The Clash	*Tonight She Comes*	The Cars
Bad Girls	Donna Summer	*Stayin' Alive*	Bee Gees
Superstition	Stevie Wonder	*Love to Love You Baby*	Donna Summer
I Love the Nightlife	Alicia Bridges	*Welcome to the Working Week*	Elvis Costello
Love Rollercoaster	The Ohio Players	*Good Times*	Chic
Black Coffee in Bed	Squeeze	*You Sexy Thing*	Hot Chocolate
Call Me	Blondie	*If I Can't Have You*	Yvonne Elliman
I Touch Myself	The Divinyls	*Don't Stop 'Til You Get Enough*	Michael Jackson
My Sharona	The Knack	*The Love You Save*	The Jackson 5
Take Me to the River	Talking Heads	*Local Girls*	Graham Parker
Stop! In the Name of Love	The Supremes	*What Do All the People Know?*	The Monroes
Don't Leave Me This Way	Thelma Houston	*Forever Young*	Alphaville
Love Shack	The B-52's	*Love Will Tear Us Apart*	Joy Division
Heart of Glass	Blondie	*Tainted Love*	Soft Cell
Rock the Boat	The Hues Corporation	*Cars*	Gary Numan
Oxford Comma	Vampire Weekend	*1979*	Smashing Pumpkins
Rich Girl	Hall & Oates	*Smells Like Teen Spirit*	Nirvana
Hungry Like a Wolf	Duran Duran	*Bizarre Love Triangle*	New Order
This Will Be	Natalie Cole	*How Soon Is Now?*	The Smiths
Pick Up the Pieces	Average White Band	*Everthing Counts*	Depeche Mode
Shining Star	Earth, Wind & Fire	*Pump It Up*	Elvis Costello
Lady Marmalade	LaBelle	*Pop Muzik*	M
Brick House	The Commodores	*The Perfect Kiss*	New Order
Everybody Everybody	Black Box	*This Love*	Maroon Five

DANCING CLASS.

HOW TO CUT THE RUG.

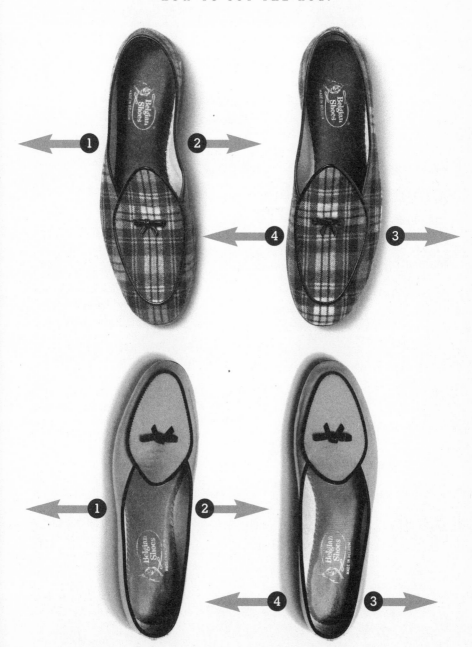

Till There Was You.

Love and/or lust don't always show up when you think they will. Sometimes it really is a matter of convenience. Say hello to Anderson Flatto and Julia Kelly. We know that they will end up together tonight—maybe even through the holiday season—but they don't know it quite yet. Although they both dressed for the best of possibilities, no one ever meets at Reid Hallowell's parties; most bring dates (and occasionally lose dates) here. But hey,

it's getting late, and you know a lot of the same people . . . which is important, since you will both report on what happens after you leave Mr. and Mrs. Hallowell's house to everyone you know in common. You were both raised within the same world. Your parents know one another, even if they are not really friends. Anderson is accountable. You can check on him. You know him. And despite pretending otherwise, Andy, you've known Julia since that after-school ice-skating program in elementary school.

3

4

Destination weddings.

In one sense, a destination wedding is incredibly prep. It suggests you love your friends so much that you want them on your honeymoon . . . a kind of continuation of Spring Weekend at DU mixed with summer camp and a family reunion.

On the other hand, insisting that your friends spend their vacation time and money to travel to your wedding, get a new outfit for your occasion (especially if you asked them to be in the wedding party), and buy you appropriate wedding gifts is a bit much, isn't it?

If you or your parents are able to foot the travel bill, forget what we just said. Invite your friends to Hawaii; we won't object. If you ask friends to travel to your wedding, you will be expected to organize and host other events besides the mere wedding. You should host the "rehearsal dinner" the night before, arrange for some kind of sporting activity for "the boys" early on the wedding day (so that someone is terribly sunburnt by the ceremony itself), as well as the brunch the following morning.

For many couples, a destination wedding is cheaper than the traditional service and big black-tie reception they would have to have at home. Instead of 225 guests, including your parents' friends that you don't even know, you have about thirty of your closest. Instead of serving surf and turf, you can get away with an informal seaside buffet, serving just surf.

We recommend that you not choose a wedding factory for your big day. Lots of places advertise to the bridal market, but it is less romantic if you are rushed because the banquet manager has another restless bridal party circling outside the ballroom. Places that advertise as special, unique, once-in-a-lifetime, and sprinkle the word "memories" like too much salt from the salt shaker are not special. We're thinking now of Atlantis in Nassau, the Ahwahnee in Yosemite, and Sandals in Jamaica.

Carley Roney, editor in chief of theknot .com, the Internet wedding site (see p. 184), points out that 20 percent of all weddings are "destination weddings" in the first place. For example, you and most of your friends live in and around Minneapolis but are going to Ardmore, Pennsylvania, to the bride's parents' house for the ceremony. Hometown is a destination, too. And half of those weddings are what we think of as real destination weddings: Everyone has to travel somewhere else to be part of the fun.

Most popular now? The Nantucket wedding, with a clambake dinner for all the out-of-town guests the night before, the ski wedding in Aspen, and the beach wedding in Cabo San Lucas, Mexico.

Who does this? Roney says it's tremendous among couples in their thirties, the kind who "want everyone's undivided attention. It's a 48-hour party 'with me and my best friends.' Ordinarily, a wedding lasts an average of four hours. A destination wedding makes it as long as is humanly possible."

ON LOVE.

It was often said of the first President George Bush that he "reminded every woman of her first husband." This was hyperbole: President Bush did not remind every woman of her First Husband, just every preppy woman. Bush was preppiness incarnate. He reminded every preppy woman of her first husband because he was a good mixer, from a good background, a decent sportsman, a bit of a goofball, and totally unreflective. The preppy First Husband may be accomplished and intelligent, but—like Bush—his ideas will be 100 percent received, he will be a philistine, and he will have the psychological depth of an inchworm. Likewise, the preppy First Wife will be presentable and fun, and will have absolutely no interior life, unless you count interior decorating—she will know her way around Scully & Scully, she will have majored in art history at Rollins, she will be "social," and she will have serious unresolved issues with her mother, of which she is entirely unconscious.

The photos on the following six pages are of a second wedding. The preppy Second Marriage is a fascinating phenomenon because it reveals something quite astonishing: that the preppy, male and female, can change, can even "grow." Indeed, the preppy's second spouse, whether male or female, is almost invariably a psychotherapist. All right, that is a slight exaggeration. But most notably, the second spouse will have the capacity for thought and feeling and love that the first spouse almost entirely lacked.

Yes, even a preppy can learn the value of thought and feeling and love. After fifteen or twenty years of marriage to someone who cries only when he thinks about having joined the wrong club at Harvard, or who finds all the psychic nourishment she needs in the ladies' intermediate tennis clinic, even a preppy may feel unfulfilled. As a youth, the preppy usually assumes that, having been accepted both at the bank training program and as a junior member of the club, he or she can expect no more trouble in life, and this illusion usually persists through the first few years of Marriage One. It is a shock to discover thereafter that life brings its horrors—death, madness, illness, infidelity, debt, the bastardization of Abercrombie & Fitch—to a preppy family as much as any other. What often happens is that a crisis or two causes one member of the preppy couple to mature, to understand a bit better the tragic nature of our existence, while the other remains the same goofball. Then comes the failed couples' therapy, and the decision of one member of the couple to continue seeing Dr. Pasternak individually.

Wisdom—to say nothing of a tragic worldview—ill suits the preppy, and, as always in a case of lost innocence, one almost feels sorry for the preppy who has gained it. The wise preppy, his or her expression tinged with sorrow, seems out of place in gay green plumage at the yacht-club dance. Yet there are compensations: After the divorce and the period of being alone, the preppy meets and falls in love with someone who *understands*—sometimes a psychotherapist (in which case the preppy may be overcompensating for what the first marriage lacked), sometimes another divorced preppy who possesses a surprisingly sensitive soul and who has been through it all. Both preppies, if that is the case, experience a kind of love that they never knew existed, and they marry.

How much happier an event—albeit in a subdued way—is the second wedding as compared to the first, no matter how much fun the first may have seemed. The bride's mother is totally out of the picture. There have been no agonizing hassles with the food-and- beverage manager. The guests are all true friends, none of the irritating, pointless people who had to be invited the first time around are there. Only two or three people, real friends, remain from the cast of two dozen that formed the original wedding party.

Most important, the bride and groom are really in love, and they really love each other. They are happy. They have made their choice of the heart relatively—relatively— free from the psychic and social forces that have controlled them most of their lives. Their souls are joined together like two ropes tied with a full carrick bend rather than, as in the first marriage, with a granny knot. Yes, you can have true love and your whale belt, too.

—James Collins
Phillips Exeter Academy, Harvard, Columbia Business School

TRULY, MADLY, DEEPLY PREPPY.

THE SECOND WEDDING.

VOWS:

**SERENA ÐERBY WELLMORE SANTO
RÉAL WHITMARSH**

&

FREDERICK PEABODY BLAKE

"Serena is both a true romantic and a true ec-centric," her longtime friend Houghton Wood Livermore observed on the evening before her Loomis Chaffee School roommate's second—or was it third?—wedding. "Years ago in our dorm, all the girls were discussing God. I can't imagine why. And one by one, each declared whether they believed or didn't, and there was Derby announcing, 'I believe in love.' I will never forget it." True, her attempts at finding love have taken her hither and yon. After Georgetown there was a time in northern California and then in Washington State, where she bought a llama farm. (Daughter Olympia—not pictured—is from those days.) Falling in love with the polo star Felipe Santo Réal was the next stage, and Derby, now going by her first name, Serena, fol-lowed him to Argentina with Olympia, and they married. Eventually they had another daughter, Anabella, now eleven.

Meanwhile, Frederick Blake was following a more conventional, prescribed course. After Gro-ton and Yale, he worked for General Foods in the pudding division, married his girlfriend from Mt. Holyoke, moved to Darien, Connecticut, and had a daughter, Esmé (photographed here with her husband, Fairfield, and their sons, Stamford and Wilton).

He left puddings and transferred his talents to the early word processors at IBM. While he moved up the ladder at Big Blue, life was pre-dictably on track, like an excerpt from John Cheever or Richard Yates. His wife, Gillian, fell under the spell of Guru Rajneesh and was on her way to Mysore, India, by way of the Orient Ex-press. There she met Countess Maria Ornagy-Szezhni von Klepthammer. Gillian Blake has lived with the Countess in the Dolomites since 1984.

FAIRFIELD, ESMÉ, BROOKS, AND ANABELLA SANTO RÉAL:
SHE LEARNED HOW TO POUR WHEN SHE LIVED IN ARGENTINA.

While Serena was enjoying life in Argentina, Frederick's nose was to the grindstone. "I'd meet girls, you know, through my friends and their wives but no one who stuck," he said from his office at Barton, Blake and Forrester Wealth Management. "But I was never lonely. I was busy working, fulfilled with Esmé, and sailing. My life felt whole."

How did the free bird meet the buttoned-down banker? "I saw him across the room at a wedding," the bride, then known as Derby Whitmarsh, said. "It was just this past October. It's been like a cork flying off a bottle of vintage champagne!"

Houghton Livermore was nonplussed, having seen her old friend through many love affairs. "I would never have thought that at his age Frederick would want to be surrounded by so many kids, but what the hell? One more won't hurt." Is there a baby under her fabulous ecru Vera Wang suit? No one will say for sure, but the ring Frederick designed for Derby has four oversized brown diamonds gathered in a cluster by the jeweler Maja duBrul. Four? "It's my lucky number," coos the bride, who may or may not be pregnant with her fourth child, and may or may not be on her fourth marriage.

FREDERICK AND SERENA DERBY WELLMORE SANTO RÉAL WHITMARSH BLAKE:
HAPPILY, SURPRISINGLY, LEGALLY WED.

COLIN, FREDERICK'S FOSTER SON; AUNT FAITH, SERENA'S SURROGATE MOM;
AND MAID OF HONOR, HOUGHTON, JUST AFTER THE CEREMONY. "DERBY
ONLY CALLED ME LAST TUESDAY, I'M STILL IN SHOCK."

OVER HERE! AUNT FAITH IS READY FOR HER THIRD HUSBAND.

STILL LIFE WITH BOUQUET, CRISTAL, GLOVES, PHONE, LIP BALM,
STRING CHEESE, VALIUM, AND VBH BAG.

THE BEST BABYSITTER MONEY CAN BUY: SPONGEBOB.
WILTON CUMMINGS, TYLER BURKE, ANABELLA AND VIOLET WHITMARSH.

10

HAPPY HOURS, Part II.

WHAT WE WATCH AND WHERE WE GO.

"I was just thinking," she said slowly, "what different things Rome stands for to each generation of travellers. To our grandmothers, Roman fever; to our mothers, sentimental dangers . . . to our daughters, no more dangers than the middle of Main Street."
—Edith Wharton, *Roman Fever*

OBSERVATIONS AND EXCURSIONS.

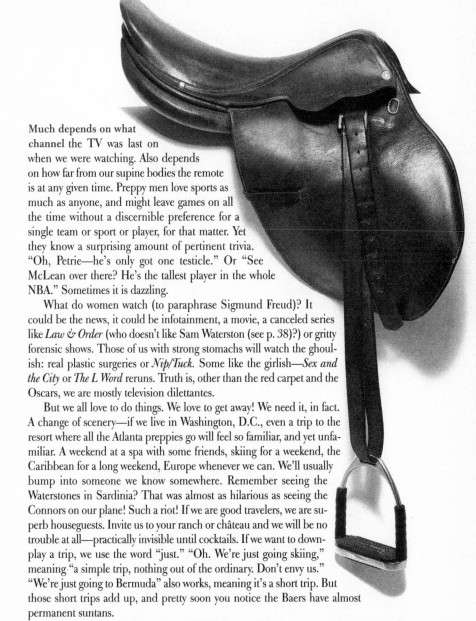

Much depends on what channel the TV was last on when we were watching. Also depends on how far from our supine bodies the remote is at any given time. Preppy men love sports as much as anyone, and might leave games on all the time without a discernible preference for a single team or sport or player, for that matter. Yet they know a surprising amount of pertinent trivia. "Oh, Petrie—he's only got one testicle." Or "See McLean over there? He's the tallest player in the whole NBA." Sometimes it is dazzling.

What do women watch (to paraphrase Sigmund Freud)? It could be the news, it could be infotainment, a movie, a canceled series like *Law & Order* (who doesn't like Sam Waterston (see p. 38)?) or gritty forensic shows. Those of us with strong stomachs will watch the ghoulish: real plastic surgeries or *Nip/Tuck*. Some like the girlish—*Sex and the City* or *The L Word* reruns. Truth is, other than the red carpet and the Oscars, we are mostly television dilettantes.

But we all love to do things. We love to get away! We need it, in fact. A change of scenery—if we live in Washington, D.C., even a trip to the resort where all the Atlanta preppies go will feel so familiar, and yet unfamiliar. A weekend at a spa with some friends, skiing for a weekend, the Caribbean for a long weekend, Europe whenever we can. We'll usually bump into someone we know somewhere. Remember seeing the Waterstones in Sardinia? That was almost as hilarious as seeing the Connors on our plane! Such a riot! If we are good travelers, we are superb houseguests. Invite us to your ranch or château and we will be no trouble at all—practically invisible until cocktails. If we want to downplay a trip, we use the word "just." "Oh. We're just going skiing," meaning "a simple trip, nothing out of the ordinary. Don't envy us." "We're just going to Bermuda" also works, meaning it's a short trip. But those short trips add up, and pretty soon you notice the Baers have almost permanent suntans.

Yet some of us are distance snobs. We'll go to Asia the way you go to Beaver Creek: frequently. Do we go because we love it, or because we want to tell people we just came back from India? Long-distance travel is not unlike Harvard in this way, and as with that ancient institution of higher learning, we have to leave it to say we enjoy it to people who will be duly impressed.

SATURDAYS IN FAUQUIER COUNTY.

Don't complain to us about hunting. We've heard the arguments about it being barbaric, blah, blah, and that they've even outlawed it in England (which doesn't mean it has stopped in England, btw), and we know you think foxes are sweet furry things like Rupert your pet ferret, but when you look to a field on a wintry morning and hear the horn, the thrill is like no other. Galloping, jumping the lovely low stone walls, a little frost on the ground, a little sherry in our bellies . . . It's heaven. Aside from the Unionville Hunt with Mr. Stewart's Cheshire foxhounds, there's nowhere we'd rather be than Fauquier County, Virginia.

There the season lasts from early fall through late winter, and hunts take place three days a week, the most formidable being Saturday mornings, which have the largest "field." The Middleburg and the Piedmont Hunts—officially Piedmont Fox Hounds—("Originally established as a private pack in 1840. Recognized 1899. Hunt attire: scarlet, old gold collar; Evening: scarlet, old gold collar and waistcoat") are almost the very best in this country, but nothing tops the Orange County Hunt, which was "established in 1900, recognized in 1902. Hunt attire: scarlet for staff only; no scarlet in the field, no hunt collars, buttons only. Evening: scarlet, white facings."

Parvenus who attempt membership are studied carefully: The ultimate sin is being overmounted (too much horse for the rider) or too carefully dressed.

Afterwards, we go to The Rail Stop, our favorite watering hole in The Plains, a village five miles away from Middleburg.

Preppy Stars of the Rerun Galaxy.

Scary but true. Sixties TV character **Thurston Howell III,** (1) a somewhat two-dimensional preppy with a patrician accent, a supporting player on *Gilligan's Island*, was ranked—for real—on Forbes.com every year since 2006 (see p. 241). There he is, between Tony Stark (Iron Man) and Bruce Wayne (Batman). He is the CEO of Howell Industries, a Harvard man, and a billionaire set in the amber permanence of reruns.

Howell, portrayed by Ohio-born actor Jim Backus ("Mr. Magoo"), was important in the suspend-all-reality world of '60s sitcoms because he and his wife, Eunice (known to all as "Lovey"), took a tourist cruise around Hawaii with a mismatched group of kooks. (Funny they didn't just buy a boat or the state, for example.) And, better for the plotlines, Thurston Howell brought thousands and thousands of dollars and many changes of ascots to wear for the three hours he expected to be gone. Good preppy thinking. The money, though not useful tender on a deserted island, still bought power and influence among the shipwrecked, and the Howells enjoyed that power. While the professor and the skipper and the first mate did real work, the Howells showed us how to be elegant and well dressed even during a natural catastrophe. One had to admire Lovey's willingness to trim the grass with her delicate manicure scissors. She was just trying to help.

We love lists. So let's look at other preppies who somehow made it through the homogenizing filter of television. We hereby present the rest of True Prep's Fictional Top Five (in chronological order):

Miss Jane Hathaway (2) Possessor of a plummy lockjaw, a boyish haircut, and a Vassar degree, Jane Hathaway somehow became the secretary to the head of a Beverly Hills bank. Played by actress Nancy Kulp (see p. 29), Miss Jane had to facilitate matters at the Clampetts' every day, if not more often. As an eastern snob, Miss Jane was another fish out of water in a show about fish out of water. Rich but uncouth Southerners who refer to their swimming pool as a "see-ment pond" are droll enough in 90210, but regarding Miss Hathaway, with no curves on her bony physique, and severe except for a nutty crush on hunky but stupid Jethro Bodine (she was slumming)—you get the feeling she was written into the show after a spectacular audition.

Murphy Brown (3) What can you say about a character whose backstory is that she is just returning from rehab at the Betty Ford clinic (see p. 148)? Played by real-life prep Candice Bergen (Westlake School, University of Pennsylvania [x]), Brown was a have-it-all career girl in the '90s: with beauty, a great job, lots of friends, wealth, and as much club soda as she could drink. In later seasons, she became pregnant, and without a relationship had the child on her own (VP Dan Quayle did not approve). Colleen Dewhurst played her mother, Avery Brown. Marian Seldes portrayed her aunt, Brooke Brown.

The Crane Brothers: Dr. Frasier and Dr. Niles (4, 5) Two psychiatrists who live in Seattle would not seem like preppies off the bat (you know we rarely go to medical school), but if you saw and heard the Cranes you would change your point of view. Two effete and well-spoken fellows—their late mother was also a psychiatrist; their father, who lives with the divorced Frasier, was a police detective. Both boys were said to be named after their mother's lab rats. At Bryce Academy, his fictional prep school, Frasier Winslow Crane (Kelsey Grammer) was known as "The Bryce Academy Crier." From there it was to Harvard where he earned his BA, Harvard Medical School (M.D., Ph.D.), and a postdoctoral stint at Corpus Christi College at Oxford. Niles, on the other hand, attended Yale (BA) (as did his real-life self, David Hyde Pierce—see p. 32), Yale Medical School (M.D., Ph.D.), and did his postdoctoral work at Cambridge University. Even more astonishing, there are Web sites that are filled with this arcana.

TO THE PRODUCERS OF *GOSSIP GIRL*: IF YOU'RE SERIOUS, WE'RE HERE TO HELP.

Oh, *Gossip Girl*, what can we do with you? We watch you filming; among the hordes of teen girls, we stare, arms crossed, thinking only, "Really?" Your show, meant to depict our lives as seniors in the elite private schools in Manhattan, is a travesty. We decided that instead of just bashing your faux preppiness, we would offer our help to your production staff, to bring a little pink and green authenticity to TV. We can get credit for it.

To Whom It May Concern:

After much viewing of your television show, we would like to offer some constructive criticism to make *Gossip Girl*, well, more genuine. It seems that no true preps work on your show. You just need a little guidance, and that's where we come in.

BLAIR WALDORF: Our preppy wannabe. Blair, wearing a strand of pearls and a headband does not make you a preppy. You also tote your maid Dorota around like a purse. Let Dorota live her life . . . in the kitchen, where she's supposed to be.

SERENA VAN DER WOODSEN: God gave you a three-part last name for a reason! And we will not let you throw away a great name for nothing. So take off your faux-bohemian thigh-high boots and sequined dresses and put on a tweed skirt and simple cable-knit sweater. And I am concerned about the martini glass that seems to be glued to your hand; you are partying every night of the week. You have SATs to study for, and you must talk to your grandfather about helping you score a place at Yale. Now go clean up.

NATE ARCHIBALD: We like you–ish. You have few plot lines, but you have a good family name on your shoulders. Your dad got indicted, and you slept with an older woman. You go to Columbia. How about studying?

Let us conclude with the worst case of preppy fraud, CHUCK BASS. Chuckie, the only people who take stretch limousines to school are pedophiles offering young children candy and a puppy to get inside. A regular Lincoln Town Car would be quite acceptable. And the ascot you have been seen sporting has got to wait for another 40–50 years, if at all. (Do you want to be George Hamilton when you grow up?) Your commitment issues with Blair are boring. Didn't you know that your parents pick out the girl you are going to marry when you are an infant? Then, Chuckles, you snubbed Skull and Bones on your visit to Yale. Is it not one of the most important unspoken rules of Prepdom that if a secret society at Yale asks you to join, it is impolite to say no? This is an actionable offense.

Gang, one last piece of advice: cut out the PDA. The sex on your show is gross. We would never actually allow a camera crew to cross that line. So please, all of you, keep the corduroys on, the cameras out of the bedroom, and think of England.

Love,

Boco

a real seventeen-year-old-uniform-wearing Manhattan private-school student

---

The Problem with Reality TV.

Where to begin? Once upon a time we weren't allowed to chew gum in public, wear shoes that were not laced, read comic books, or discuss politics at a social event. If all the mummies and daddies who laid down the law then could have imagined reality television, with all its vulgarity, materialism, sniping, backstabbing, catfights, first dates in hot tubs, sex, and foul language, they would certainly not be pleased. What has the world come to, they might ask, as do nice people who are still amongst the living.

To suggest that reality TV is unprep doesn't go deeply enough into its deviltry.

We value our privacy. So people who agree to live surrounded by cameramen and soundmen and lights and need the attention to feel validated are constitutionally not prep. Even if you attended private school and college, and have many traceable nice ancestors, and play the right sports, your commission within reality TV disqualifies you immediately. No true preppy—whether she had a storied last name or not—would allow herself to be so exposed and to live at the mercy of TV producers and editors. That means all you "housewives." By the way, if you were an actual socialite, you would never refer to yourself that way.

But we're sounding cranky and hypocritical, after all Logan, we have killed quite a few hours watching MTV, Bravo, Lifetime, Oxygen, TLC, and whatever channel *Hoarders* is on (reminds us of our distant cousin Maldwin).

Of course, watching reality shows is a bit like defiantly sticking a piece of Juicy Fruit up around your top molars when you're walking outside. We know it's disgusting, but it can be irresistible. Still, we believe that one day, no matter what machine we watch, we will be able to see a well-written sitcom about a nice family in Connecticut who forgot to buy a beach pass until the town hall ran out of them. Hope springs eternal.

TOTES FOR TRAVEL.

ELLA VICKERS

THE MONOGRAM SHOP

After Coachella, Sophie is at Dallas-Fort Worth Airport with her T. Anthony bag for the beginning of her fishing trip to Patagonia with Andréas. This is their third anniversary. Could there be a ring in his zippered vest?

BROOKS BROTHERS

RALPH LAUREN

HERVÉ CHAPELIER

TORY BURCH

VINEYARD VINES

L.L.BEAN

Away we go!

If we have an opportunity to travel, we seize it. We have had passports since we were babies. The hand of our nurse, Hilaria, is larger in our first passport pictures than our little heads. Having been bred for it, we fly and sail and drive and take trains and ferries. We once rode a donkey up the cliffs of Santorini with a guide's hands on our, um, flanks. Believe us now?

Europe is somehow still the most important destination, but not all countries are equal in the prep travel lineup. England, France, Italy, and Switzerland are 1, 2, 3, and 4, respectively. But it's preppier to go somewhere far for a quick trip. You are no longer a sightseer; you *have* to visit friends, or go to a wedding, or get married, or go to see Wimbledon or the French Open or to an antiques show, or to the couture shows or to the Cannes Film Festival. (Do not go to Cannes unless you or your partner have a movie screening there. Otherwise, you're just a tourist.)

We don't want to be thought of as tourists. They go in groups and have to wear name tags or put stickers on their bags. They have to eat in big touristy restaurants and not discover little corners of their own. Plus, we've already been to the Tower of London, the Eiffel Tower, and the Leaning Tower of Pisa. We're towered out, in fact.

Preppies have taken on the world. We go to India and Bhutan. We go on safari in Africa. We go to the Galápagos to play with turtles and blue-footed boobies. We go to Bora-Bora and New Zealand. We take the train across Namibia. We go to Tokyo on business. We go to Sydney for surfing. We go to South America for hiking and fishing. We go to Spain to eat at I Bulli, before it closes. We will travel for an incredible exhibit, at the Moderna Museum in Stockholm, or the Rijksmuseum in Amsterdam, or an opera at Glyndebourne or at La Scala. The Edinburgh Festival. Two days of theater in the West End. Skiing in Austria. To meet the Dalai Lama in Vienna. We go to Turkey to buy rugs. Anything that sounds special and exclusive and . . . special. And really, really exclusive.

If we are young preps in our twenties, we will go to music festivals—South by Southwest in Austin. Coachella in Indio, California. Burning Man. The New Orleans Jazz Fest. Ultra in Miami. Sacred Music in Fez. Bonnaroo in Tennessee. That music festival in West Africa. These adventures combine our very favorite things: friends, travel, music, drinking, photographs, and souvenirs.

WHERE WE **DON'T** GO.

When a preppy heads to a career in medicine, very often it's to surgery—specifically, orthopedic surgery. Your patients need you, but they aren't sick. Your work is fun and manual, like shop class or woodworking, with higher stakes. Admit it: It's a little bit macho, figuring out how many knees you can replace or how many spines you can fuse in a year. One of the other aspects of being an orthopedic surgeon is your annual medical convention in . . . Las Vegas. This is our introduction to Las Vegas.

According to every travel site you can find, the two most popular travel destinations for Americans are, in fact, Las Vegas and Orlando, Florida (Disney World and Universal Studios theme park). We find this fascinating because without our medical conventions (a two-day stay in Las Vegas, maximum), preppies might never experience the Strip. And Orlando! A once-in-a-lifetime (two, if you have children from two different marriages) experience. There are no two destinations of less interest to preppies. But before you feel too guilty and too un-American, remember that you do travel widely in America . . . to New York and Vermont, Colorado, and Washington, D.C., and you've been to New Orleans and that lake in Wisconsin. You've been to Toronto/Halifax (oh, wait, that's not America). You've been to Palm Beach and Hobe Sound but not to Orlando or Las Vegas.

Las Vegas would love you to visit. In addition to being a city with legalized prostitution, it has decided that it is a family destination with such family-friendly features as twenty-four-hour everything, slot machines everywhere (including the baggage-claim area of the airport, to give you a taste even before you're officially there), and smoking is permitted indoors. In addition to providing the thrills of overseas travel (To Paris! To New York! To Venice! To the pyramids of Egypt!), Las Vegas is the new Broadway, where you and the kids can catch up on those musicals you missed last time you were in New York. Las Vegas has lured the world's great chefs to open outposts, so no longer do you need to go to Paris to be fed by Guy Savoy and Joël Robuchon, or to New York for Daniel Boulud and Jean-Georges Vongerichten.

The other theme-park destination is Orlando. You only go there because your children have begged you to, and because there are so many commercials for it on TV (duh). A word of caution: Wait until your youngest is five years old; otherwise, he or she will have no memories of the magical trip (while you will have many memories of your migraines, the shockingly overpriced souvenirs, and the real Americans with whom you stood on lines for hour after hour).

WHY SAILING?

People sail for sport or pleasure but rarely anymore for commerce. The end of sail-borne trade could have meant the end of sailing itself, but sailing, of course, survived. Yet, today there are those who say that sailing is dying, that it is no longer relevant. On the contrary, not since Columbus set off for the Orient has sailing been more relevant as a response to the maladies of an era. In a time of complexity, here is simplicity. In an era of individualism, here is community. In an age of artificiality, here is nature. In a life of automation, here is responsibility. And in a climate of financial and environmental crisis, here is an activity dedicated to efficiently harnessing the world's cleanest, freest, and most renewable energy source: the wind.

From the time I was a small child—and not coming from a sailing family—I stared out endlessly at boats in the harbor. I was as ignorant about my passion as I was hooked. But my skills have developed, and it has defined my life in the most personal and even in a professional way. I have made lifelong friends of whom I have no clue what they do "on land." Living on board is like having fifty summer homes. You are a nomad who drops in on other people's lives—you might even add some excitement without their ever having to don Top-Siders. Sailing affects the way I think, the way I process what's happening in the world, and it is a place to retreat to at times. It's a skill, a survival skill, and has the most pleasant moments with the thrill of a sail or a sky that has just cleared. It is nature at its finest. —CHARLIE DANA, GUNNERY(X), NORTHWOOD(X), CHESHIRE, UNIVERSITY OF DENVER

A few "musts" for any respectable yachtie:

- Center console RIB as tender
- Tervis tumblers (plastic insulated glasses with yacht club or pvt signal)
- Yachting pillows (think . . . "Captain's Word Is Law")
- Propane grill (hideous, but they all have them)
- Phone directories for Dark Harbor (Islesboro) and Northeast Harbor (Southwest Harbor, Seal Harbor, Cranberry Islands)
- Enough Mount Gay to circumnavigate the globe
- Leatherette on settees, navy Sunbrella piped in white cushions on deck
- Helly Hanson "foulies"
- Croakies for those expensive Kaenon sunglasses
- Sperry Sea Boots
- Towels with boat name: *Ariel*
- Carved model of previous boat, *Bikini*, prominently displayed for all to see how you have "upgraded"
- America's Cup Jubilee 2001 Participant
- Polarfleece blanket with *Ariel*
- Folding bicycle
- Nantucket Reds
- Almost anything that will fit in an embroidery machine to stitch your boat's name —C.D.

THE FRIENDSHIP 40

DAS BEAN.

The debate over the relative merits of L.L.Bean's Maine Hunting Boot vs. the L.L.Bean Boot vs. the L.L.Bean Duck Boot is one we could spend hours reading on the Web. Non-preppy hunters, non-hunting preppies, and preppy hunters have devoted themselves to arguing and proselytizing on this very topic. In fact, it may be one of our favorite hobbies: passionate debates about all things (especially those the size of a breadbox) that preppies care about. Pull up a chair.

There are discussions about which sole makes less noise while walking on twigs (so prey won't hear you stalking them). Discussions of how comfortable the rubber base feels after a long day on one's feet. And of course, the pricing.

L. L. Bean—the man—a hunting enthusiast from Freeport, Maine, designed boots with rubber waterproof bottoms and breathable leather uppers in 1912. He somehow procured a list of all hunting permit holders and sent them a little mail-order piece advertising the boots. He sold 100 pairs, 90 of which were returned for a full refund. He fixed the problem and was back in business. The hunting boots, as they were originally called, have always been among the store's best sellers. In 1980, they cost $42.50. Now they range from $69 to $164. Today there are twenty styles for men and seventeen for women, and a new style, with waxed cotton uppers, designed for Bean's more fashiony Signature line.

Which we've photographed here. Vive la différence.

1 1.
WE DON'T DO THAT.

WHY ETIQUETTE COUNTS.

She had said the proper thing as mechanically as she would have put on the appropriate gown or written the correct form of dinner invitation.
—Edith Wharton, *The Touchstone*

On Greetings.

It is important to make real eye contact when meeting someone for the first time. A good, firm handshake cements your initial impression and lets the other person know that you are really there. This applies to women as well. If germs are your weakness, please do not resort to a fist bump or **rub antibacterial lotion on your hands just after shaking them with a stranger.** Bear with the handshake, and head to a bathroom as soon as is socially feasible.

If you are greeting a friend and you are moved to do so, a kiss is also perfectly fine. This means, in most cases, a peck on the cheek or near their cheek in their general vicinity. Try not to aim at their ear. More and more, the cosmopolitan world is used to the two-cheek kiss, which is also fine, particularly if you are saying hello to a European friend. Sometimes people will suggest, "Let's do both cheeks, the European way." We suppose that is fine, but it seems like a lot of bother to make this announcement. If you've just returned from your Junior Semester Abroad or an assignment at the bank of more than three months in Europe, go right ahead. It is your privilege and signals you have become even more sophisticated.

If you are a man under the age of sixty, do not kiss women on the hand unless they ask you to kiss a boo-boo on their finger. Men over the age of sixty may kiss a woman's hand, but be prepared to defend this action. If you meet the Pope, you may kiss his ring.

Some friends will say hello by kissing on the mouth. This happens particularly when the people in question used to be romantically involved. Your tongue must remain firmly within your own mouth, and your lips should remain closed.

Kissing, romantically.

Even as we age and marry or remarry, preppies like to kiss. Preppies can even be sensual kissers; no oxymoron there. Alas, despite pleading females, prep men still call it "making out," "swapping spit," or whatever term they heard when their experience of kissing began. It's as if they were hit on the back of the head at that moment, and instead of becoming stuck in the cross-eyed position as legend had it, they stayed adolescent. Thus (and we apologize in advance) "sucking face," "tongue sushi," and so on never quite die. You fellows risk losing a date to the vulgar terminology you first thought cool in eighth grade.

We endorse kissing, if for no other reason than it helps the emotionally stunted among us to express emotions. It is also a wonderfully efficient way to divine interpersonal chemistry. But do not forget the rush of endorphins, dopamine, and oxytocin which result from a warm exchange of smooches. There is an expectation that a satisfying kissing experience will result in a future kissing experience, and certainly a chance to get to know each other better. Be of sound mind when you begin the flirtation of kissing. While you are at it, public slobbering is gauche and unamusing and unattractive. If you are moved to express your love in public, choose a darkened doorway or a relatively quiet street, in order not to create a disturbance. Words work, too.

Introductions.

Never skimp on introductions. This is key. You may introduce two people who will never see each other again, but it is flat-out rude to stand with an acquaintance (new or old) and not introduce him or her to your friend who joins you at a drinks party. And while you're at it, please give us a tidbit that will help us remember the new person.

Did you go to school together? (Were you friends at Exeter?) Or did you go to school together? (Did you attend Exeter at the same time but not really know one another there?) Or, perhaps, did you go to school together? (Were you at the University of Virginia in the same dorm?) Maybe you went to school together? (A finance class at Amos Tuck?) Or maybe you go to school together. (Do your children both attend Wheeler School?) All of this specific color will help distinguish one shiny face from another when yet a fourth person enters your cluster.

Depending on the situation—life is not all about parties all the time, alas—you may or may not need a full name to make these introductions. "Anne, this is Blake. Blake, meet Anne. I know Anne from school; we crewed together. Blake is my neighbor in the country. I had no idea she knew the Armstrongs! What a small world!"

When one of the strangers in a group is well known, one must acknowledge that by using the full name. "Governor Weld, this is Cap, I mean, Casper Higginbottom, who also works with me on the Annual Fund."

One of the pleasures of being an inveterate introducer is that you soon discover that, yes, Caldwell, it is a small world. As preppies (and non-preppies alike) discover, the older we get, the more the people we know know the other people we know. You know? We realized this before the invention of Facebook.

In a perfect world, we love to connect to and for one another. We love to know that your future squash partner was the guy we introduced you to at the Kleins. We are proud that your daughter got an internship at Foreign Affairs because we both sat next to the Ambassador. We are tickled that you dated Baxter Thorndike because you met him at the book party. We think these connections help pave our way to—if not heaven, at least a long weekend on Nantucket.

Thank-you Notes for All Occasions.

Preppies, so rarely accused of overdoing it, can sometimes be guilty of underdoing it. When is a hostess gift called for?

If you're invited to a dinner party, you are not obliged to give the Stones, your hosts, a gift, unless: a) They brought you a gift when they came for dinner chez vous, b) They feed you all the time, c) You have been remiss in managing this friendship and feel a little something is in order, or d) You always keep scented candles in your gift closet, and this is as good a time as any to give one away.

You most certainly do not bestow presents in order to have them bestowed back to you. That's primitive thinking. Sometimes, though, a gift is just too much, and can have the undesired effect of an excessive payback. In this case a charming handwritten note will suffice.

A charming handwritten note will always suffice in any case. If you and the Johnstons are very close and cozy, and you have what we'd call an "informal relationship," you may occasionally send an e-mail thank-you note instead, but don't make a practice of it.

Dear B&B,
  Fab time last night! Can't wait to do Thai with you soon!
                                    Love, A & E

If you've been invited to a big event, say, a wedding, a debut, a black-tie Christmas party, a bar mitzvah, a formal christening, or anything ceremonial, you may—wait for it—call your host the next day to chat with him or her or them. This is called the Postmortem. You are allowed, in this personal conversation, eventually, after the inevitable praise ("And the blue satin set off Laura's eyes so beautifully"), to gently make more honest (i.e., critical) comments about the event ("And who does Kipper think he is with that earring? Keith Richards? And why was Ames not wearing her big stone? Trouble in paradise?"). This does not excuse your obligation to write a more formal hand-written thank-you to your hosts.

The Thank-you Note.

In the right hands, the simple thank-you note is a work of art. Your penmanship doesn't count, as long as it is legible. We don't need to mention it, but obviously an ink pen is used, never a pencil. A fountain pen is nice, but it is an unnecessary affectation.

A thank-you note may not be generic. You must thank your benefactor for his gift but never without identifying that gift.

Thank you so much for the fantastic oar! I don't know how Bly and I ever lived without it! We can't wait to take it out with us this summer at the lake. And the green stripe will look terrific with our canoe! It was great to see you at our [fill in the blank] OR We were so sorry you missed our [fill in the blank], and/but we hope to see you again soon.
                                    Lots of love, Hooper.

Dear Corny,
Your tea party yesterday was divine. I've never had such sublime cucumber sandwiches, and I've eaten cucumber sandwiches for at least twenty years! I can't wait until we see each other for a long catch-up!
                                    Xoxoxo Page

As real PDA (prep display of affection) is frowned upon, and outward manifestations of genuine affection are as rare as a five-leaf clover, adult preppies, dipping into their childlike wells of enthusiasm, proffer lots and lots of love and hugs and kisses as their sign-offs, male and female alike. In this way they are compensating for a life of not so much love and hugs and kisses.

Hi Genevieve,
I found your library book behind the dog bed in the mudroom. Come and pick it up whenever.
                                    Xxxxxooooo love, Biv

You may read the personal into all this extravagant love, but there's a small chance, a teeny possibility that Biv became distracted while writing that last note, and forgot to whom he was writing or why, and just enjoyed the making of the x's and o's. But that's us: Affectionate on paper, distracted in person.

Letters of Recommendation.

When the Chans ask you for a letter of recommendation to the board of the co-op apartment they wish to buy. When Joe Washington asks you to sing his praises to the admissions committee at the club. When Pookie Powell needs an in at Princeton. When the Goldbergs want that single non-sibling girl's space in the nursery-school class. These are all occasions when you could be asked to write a letter on behalf of someone else. Similarly, there may come a day when you will need a good word from Adrian Chan, Joe Washington, Pookie Powell, or Amy Goldberg, so this is not a time to cavil. Unless you have a damned good reason for not being able to write the letter,* just prep up and write the letter. For example:

TO WHOM IT MAY CONCERN:

I have known Adrian and Eleanor Chan for twelve years, having met them when their Claire and my Alfred attended St. Timothy's. Since that time both families have enjoyed many happy occasions together. Indeed, Christmas isn't Christmas without Eleanor Chan's warm but quiet hospitality.

Having bought at the top of the market in a limestone prewar building in 2007, I fully understand Adrian's wish to rent until now. You could say that in addition to his good financial sense, he is a prudent man, the kind any of us would love to have as a neighbor. The Chans are a low-key, discreet family, not at all interested in entertaining. Not only would he make a fine addition to your building (I also know the Alberts in 4E), but I am certain that you could benefit from Adrian's joining the board. I have the highest regard for the Chan family: Adrian, Eleanor, Claire, John, and their silent French bulldog, La Neige.

Please do not hesitate to call on me if I can be of further assistance to you.

(Note, no xxx's or ooo's.)

Yours sincerely,
Adam Taylor Frimbo

*Acceptable reasons include: You truly can't stand Eleanor Chan. (No one likes her, but they love Adrian.) Joe Washington denied you a ride home once when you couldn't find your car following a prolonged Happy Hour after work. Your son flunked out of Princeton (duh). Despite your asking him to cut it out, Andrew Goldberg continues to slap your behind.

SMYTHSON.

What is the well-dressed desk wearing this season? This and every season, it is outfitted in timeless classics. Smythson of Bond Street, Mrs. John L. Strong, Tiffany, or your local engravers have been in the business of selling writing papers, leather-bound notebooks, and small leather goods for traveling for decades. Scattered about, here are some adorable accessories provided by Verdura—the enamel desk clock, the silver bamboo pen, and the sterling-silver sea urchin pencil sharpener. What else could you ever need?

Your trove of personalized cards, papers, and envelopes will run out one day, and then you get to restock. Unless you've moved, gotten married or divorced, or changed your name, the Smythson deep blue stationery can always be your signature. Or your signature's signature. Hold onto your die!

Unlike their generally Luddite ancestors, the new generation of preps seems to have embraced the Internet, making it their very own cyber country club. Long ago, in the annals of reinvention, Jerry Rubin of the Chicago Seven (Google him if you are thirty-five or younger) cut his hair, bought some nicely tailored suits, and taught New Yorkers how to "network." Before the Web, preppies formed social networking groups, like the Junior International Society, a regular calendar of parties thrown by Marc de Gontaut Biron, a Euro-aristo who would gather his Rolodex (remember those? see p. 119) of well-bred pals to meet at nightclubs like Au Bar in New York City. But with the Internet, who needs to get dressed up (or even dressed) and actually socialize in person, when you can make all the connections you need without ever leaving your laptop?

The first Web site to kickstart the online social scene was Friendster, which became an open site in August 2006. In the beginning, preppies flocked to Friendster, but when other sites like MySpace started hogging new members, Friendster quickly faded away. Today it's reported that over 90 percent of Friendster's traffic comes from Asia. And that doesn't mean that true preps on vacation on a Thai island are logging in and updating their profiles.

Friendster's swift demise can be blamed on one site: Facebook—which went from a Harvard site in 2004 to a buzz bin where porn stars promote their latest dirty videos and online flirting is the norm—is democratic, if not pure anarchy. Anyone can join, and fake celebrity profiles are as ubiquitous as photos posted of boarding-school kids huddled around a keg, red plastic cups and Parliament Lights in hand. Preps are loyal Facebookers and make sure only to accept friend requests like "Your third kid is so cute. Always loved the name Cricket!!!" but then there are the naughty preppies . . . Marriages and engagements have been broken up by errant scandalous photos of a "work weekend" being posted and tagged on FB. For the still-in-school set, be warned: Big Mummy is watching. That photo of you inhaling is just one Google search away from being sent home, where the only face time you'll get, Missy, is in group therapy.

Some preppies found Facebook a little too much of a free-for-all, and invitation-only sites started to pop up all over the Web. For example, to join asmallworld.net (where members post announcements like "Seeking motorcycle and hot girl to tour Italy and stay in five-star hotels"), one must be invited by a member with "invitation rights"—meaning they have proven to be an invaluable member of this "small world." Even though members are warned to only accept connection requests from people they actually know in the "real world," some people boast hundreds of "connections," proving it's actually not a small world after all. Because preppies love to be surrounded by other preppies, asmallworld.net's list of recommended restaurants ranks a highly regarded serious foodie temple like Le Bernardin equal to the East Side watering hole J. G. Melon, which serves mostly hamburgers and club sandwiches.

Taking a cue from asmallworld.net, APrivateClub.com is very members-only. Listing which private schools and Ivy League colleges you attended and who you know is the key to entry. The Web site boasts, "APrivateClub members are leaders in social and cultural organizations. All members are between the ages of 21 to 40 years old and many were born and raised in Manhattan." The site requires a formal written application and an in-person interview. Think of it as the cyber version of applying for membership at The Bathing Corporation in Southampton, minus the ocean, your parents' charge account, and the over-forty crowd with permanent windburn.

—Peter Davis

The vanquished congratulates the victor.

September 4, 1925.

Gerald Patterson of Australia (left) being congratulated by René Lacoste, whom Patterson defeated in the opening match of the singles, score 6–3, 6–4, 6–2. Forest Hills, Queens, New York. (Note the stadium was not entirely sold out.)

COURTLY MANNERS.

Great sportsmanship is not secondary to being a fine athlete. It is neck and neck as important as one's prowess. You don't have to sacrifice one to have the other. Both make you a champion with whom preppies want to play and spend time.

Let's look at Andy Roddick, a talented tennis player who's been ranked in the top ten of men's singles players for the last ten years and has the fastest recorded serve in the sport. It was during the 2005 Rome Masters tournament, played on clay, that Roddick was in the quarterfinals match against Fernando Verdasco of Spain. With a triple match point and the victory within reach, the umpire called a double fault against Verdasco. Roddick walked up to the umpire and told him he thought Verdasco's ball had landed *in*, not outside, the court. He didn't have to do that. Verdasco rebounded and won the match. Andy Roddick will always be remembered for this honorable move. (And, little children, you see what happened because of his good sportsmanship? Andy Roddick ended up marrying the model on the cover of the *Sports Illustrated* swimsuit issue. That's called "karma.")

Tennis is full of good sports: Pancho Gonzalez, Arthur Ashe, Virginia Wade, Billie Jean King, Stefan Edberg, and Roger Federer all come to mind. These are not people who pump their fists in the air and scream "AWRIGHT!" when they win a crucial point or match. These are real-life heroes who congratulate their opponents, and when they lose, they lose with valor. Although Rafael Nadal sometimes wears terrible tennis clothes, he has good manners, and he is real. When Nadal loses, he praises his victor.

We've all seen Roger Federer cry from time to time. He has cried publicly in joy and in pain. There is nothing wrong or unprep about it. Competing alone in a stadium while the world watches is high pressure, high stakes, incredibly stressful. No one is asking a great athlete to suppress his or her real feelings. However, when John McEnroe (whose reputation has been revived as a great commentator) screams at an umpire or at the crowd, or when Jimmy Connors throws his racquet, or when Andy Murray gloats in victory, or when Novak Djokovic sulks between points, it is very bad—for them, and for tennis.

Preppies no longer own tennis. The sport regains popularity with the people depending on the allure of its champions. Even when the players show grace on the court, the fans can leave a lot to be desired. Screaming, trying to jinx players mid-serve, cheering—this is all new and often rude. It is nice to applaud a win. It is not nice to applaud a loss.

CELL PHONE ETIQUETTE.

It is not entirely your fault if you've grown up in an etiquette wasteland. These days when you offer a sincere "thank you," you are apt to hear "no prob" or "sure" or worse, "no worries." Who was worried? Waiters or—here it is—waitpersons like to ask you if "you're still working on that" salad/meal/drink, when they seem more than anything eager to clear your plates and glasses.

In general, today people push and shove and complain, are insanely impatient, and make too much noise, and we haven't even mentioned the Cell Phone. Yet.

Where to begin? The cell phone, which has brought so much independence to so many middle schoolers, has created a kind of noise pollution that has broken down civilized society.

Waiting at the post office. Sitting in a waiting room. While the proctor is explaining the rules before the SATs. At the shoe department of Saks. At jury duty. In Starbucks. As the lights dim at the theater. In (small and enclosed) elevators, where only Verizon works, anyway. At your son's cello recital. And always on the street. And when we can't see the little gizmo attached to your head—you are walking with an earpiece and appear to be talking loudly to yourself—we think you are mental. They've been around a long time, but we still think it.

Why is it that nice people forget how publicly—not to mention loudly—they are broadcasting private content? Yes, you're afraid you are in a no-reception gulag, but must we remind you how we overheard about Jock's mysterious six-hour disappearance, which coincided with an unexplained hotel charge while waiting for Caroline in the foyer of ballet school? (There are places you can talk without seven other mothers listening in.) If little Greggy has Fifth Disease, do you want to hear it at the hair salon where you have to shout to his doctor over the roar of the hair dryers? And if there are no seats on the 9 pm flight to Geneva on Thursday and your reservations at the Palace Hotel in Gstaad (which you struggled to get) start on Friday, well, is it necessary for everyone around you in the restaurant to hear that? Perhaps you think someone at the surrounding tables will feel sorry for you and give you his plane reservations?

One unintended consequence of public cell phone abuse is that it makes everyone around you feel invisible. We cannot shut off our hearing (perhaps those with hearing aids can and do), so we find ourselves in the uncomfortable position of eavesdropping. We weren't going to mention it, but we were at the Four Seasons that night that Jock was AWOL and that woman was carrying a briefcase—an old Mark Cross one, if memory serves. (It's too bad they went out of business, isn't it?) And it might have been a business meeting after all, but since you brought it up, we'll have to call Kate and see if she knows anything; her husband, Carlson, works with Jock. Soon the whole firm will know about the $565 bill, and why couldn't Jock drive home late when it was not snowing that hard? And doesn't the firm keep a pied-à-terre in the city for just these circumstances?

We digress.

You are cleared for takeoff, and just as you are about to turn off your BlackBerry, your phone comes to life, throbbing with "Single Ladies (Put a Ring on It)" and a picture of Louisa, who just seconded you for the garden club. You reflexively say hello, oblivious to the inappropriateness of this conversation. Even if your phone is set to vibrate (which on most instruments is a highly audible and annoying buzz), you have to resist temptation. Be strong, Phillipa! Be patient, Ned, and listen to your voice mail later.

Please choose a ringtone that at least won't offend the Dean of Admissions if you are caught during an interview. (This should be your basic barometer for life.) When in doubt, keep the basic tone that came on your phone.

Taxi drivers—when they are in mid-conversation—are kind enough to pick up passengers. No matter what language they speak, cabbies in the United States are not held to looser standards than noncommercial drivers. Maybe they can be on one long phone call all day where they come from (Quince's theory) but not here. (The same applies to you if you are driving a group to your fifth reunion.)

And finally, everyone who is in possession of a mobile phone has committed faux pas with them. Everyone! What of the pocket dialer who inadvertently places a call to Bronson while describing Bronson's new date to a friend? What of the text or e-mail that was the result of a drunken mistaken "SEND"? Needless to say, once sent, nothing can be unsent. It lives on in cyberspace forever and ever, and your inebriated joke can become a perpetual social liability.

TEXTING DON'TS.

Texting is quick. It can convey information in a neutral way. You can send a helpful "Running late" text that will be understood and appreciated. You can send a text that says, "Bobby's here. He looks amazing. Come over ASAP!!!!!!!!" But what of the couple at a restaurant dinner who are sitting in silence as they text, scroll, and write? Is this what has happened to the art of conversation? People who are addicted to their thingies cannot quite convince us that they wouldn't prefer reading a text to anything else in the world. We are made to feel as if we are always in competition with it. Indeed, texting (and its dirty cousin, "sexting") are eroding our capacities for charm, wit, good listening, and spelling. And that means U. (Do not dare LOL!)

AVOID THE TEMPTATION, TRICIA!

DO NOT ANSWER YOUR CELL PHONE IF:

- The call is from an 800 number.

- You are in a doctor's waiting room.

- You are at a job interview.

- The caller is in the room with you.

- You just took a call from this person.

- You just took a call from this person, and now this person is in the room with you.

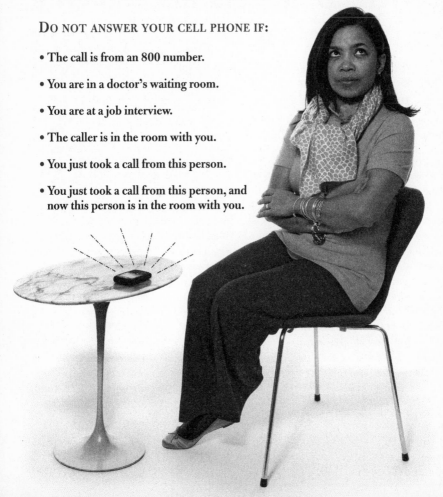

On Privacy, Shame, and a Lost Cause.

We like to hide our heads in the sand and pretend nothing's changed since Scott met Zelda at that dance. But now we are in the throes of several twenty-first-century phenomena that are hard to escape. One of the worst is oversharing.

Those things that used to be taboo—and rightly so—are now enticements to grab fame at any cost. This insatiable desire for attention comes at the price of devaluing accomplishment, merit, and civility. It arrived in the thin arms of Paris Hilton, we think. Notoriety and achievement have been thrown into the Cuisinart of the media and blended together until what? Until Amy Winehouse blogs about Al Gore? Until Courtney Love announces she's in love with Nelson Mandela? (She hasn't yet, has she?) Nowadays, one can be famous for the discovery of a sex tape, the spending of shareholders' money on prohibitively expensive office furnishings, or an affair with a sports star. Stop the presses. This flies in the face of all things prep.

Add to that the paradigm of the cheating politician confessing and apologizing to his constituents (and oh, yeah, his family), and no one can keep a secret any longer. Not all of everyone's mistakes are our beeswax. Sometimes they should be left between husband and wife.

Visit the blogosphere, and what do you find? Anger and resentment. People airing their dirty laundry and IMs, sexts, and tweets looking for attention. This bully pulpit is wearying. A kind of opinionated clutter, as well, not to mention a great waste of time.

Not to sound like prudes, but preppies are averse to all this openness. You can't have a private life if your life isn't private. You can't be discreet if you have a press agent. (And press agent is not a career that attracts an abundance of preppies.)

The shame, really, is that shame and embarrassment, our judgment's natural security guards, seem to be on a long coffee break. Luckily, preppies are still hugely capable of embarrassment; all we have to do is think of our stern old headmaster or headmistress, and we're practically a puddle. We never fail to remember the times we were caught passing that note in French class, or the time people laughed at you in *A Midsummer Night's Dream* because your fly was open, or the way we dressed ourselves for our Junior Dance. With mortification like that lingering in our memories, we tend to be better behaved than you would think. People would do well to imitate our appreciation of shame. It keeps us on the up-and-up.

And now, for something completely different: Fun.

You might be surprised that with all our lamenting about sharing, oversharing, mortification, and guilt we could say that we miss fun, but we do. Real fun is creative—Fulco di Verdura (see p. 94) thought up all kinds of costume parties with his friends, and they had fun. Truman Capote's black-and-white ball honoring Katharine Graham was fun. Dressing up wasn't the only fun to be had, but once upon a time, preppies could enjoy themselves in a more unaffected way. They could throw themselves into the fun of a house party without worrying about how the market would close on Friday afternoon. Or they could go to the theater with friends without their cell phone on silent and one eye glued to it because their two-year-old had the croup and they had to be able to leave at a moment's notice. There was a sense of abandon and adventure. Now everyone is too serious, or has an early morning or a report to read before bed. We have become boring. We need to make more fun. And we should be able to laugh our heads off and enjoy ourselves without overdoing the booze, the chemicals, or the scandals.

Isabel Montgomery Butler

Wall | **Info** | **Photos** | **Travel** ✈

View Photos of Isabel (32)

Suggest Friends for Isabel

Send Isabel a Message

Poke Isabel

Is it summer yet?

Information

Relationship Status:
Single

Birthday:
May 16, 1987

Current City:
New York, NY

Hometown:
Dallas, TX

Mutual Friends

Basic Information

Current City:	New York, NY
Birthday:	May 16, 1987
Hometown:	Dallas, TX
Relationship Status:	Single
Political Views:	Wah-Hoo-Wah

Likes and Interests

Activities:	Swimming, pretending to look for acceptable employment, trying to convince people that my intelligence wasn't hindered even though I attended school in Texas until the age of 14
Interests:	Vodka tonics- extra lime
Favorite Movies:	American Psycho, Igby Goes Down, Fight Club, Pillow Talk
Favorite Books:	People, Us Weekly, Town & Country, ELLE, Vogue, do the NY Mag blogs count?
Favorite Quotations:	"That was a crazy game of poker."

Contact Information

Email:	isabelmbutler@gmail.com

Education and Work

College:	Dartmouth '09 Art History, Business
High School:	St. Paul's School '05
Position:	Gallerina
Time Period:	August 2009 – Present
Description:	The brochure is on the table.

Photos of Isabel 32 photos

View Comments

1 2 3 Next

No Texting at the Table, Please!

G2G2JC
Got to Go to J. Crew.

G2GPS
Got to Go Play Squash.

LPP
Least Preppy Person.

MMATC
Meet Me at the Club.

ILYLAAS
I Love You Like an
Argyle Sweater.

G2GBTTP
Got to Go Before Teacher
Takes Phone.

MMAVV
Meet Me at Vineyard Vines.

IHTU
I Hate the Uniform.

MPP
Most Preppy Person.

TTISNP
This Teacher Is *So* Not Prep.

ISYL
I'm Stealing Your Loafers.

TMT
Too Many Torys.

NTP
Not True Prep.

NEP
Not Enough Plaid.

Stepparents, Half Siblings, and What to Call Them.

Will. Allison. Woody. Pop. Stepmonster.

You will probably prefer to use your parent's new partner's first name in the declarative rather than call him or her a variation of Mummy or Daddy. The fact is, this person is a replacement spouse, but not a replacement parent. That's patently obvious, every time you see him or her hold your parent's hand (which never happened when your real parents were married).

Yes, it matters when they entered your life, and whether your missing biological parent is around and acting, well, parental. If your stepfather joined your family when you were a young child, supports you, coaches your soccer team, and lives full-time with you and your mummy, and you consider him the father figure in your life, then call him what you like. In a made-for-TV tearjerker, that moment when you call him "dad"—shyly—would cause the background music to swell and everyone to feel pretty darn good about the high divorce rate in this country.

If your parents are the marrying kind, and between the two of them there are halfs, steps, and foster children, it might be best to use numbers to keep everyone straight.

As everyone—including Daddy—knows, it is really gross when Daddy begins a relationship with someone close to your age. It is nothing less than disgusting when Mummy does the same. You have the upper hand here. Be strong! Tell your parents you won't accept a substitute parent who was a junior when you were a freshman, who dated someone you dated, or who had lower SAT scores than you. This is just basic.

Literature is full of stepparents who promise love and loyalty to the first set of kids and welsh on that promise after the wedding ("Hansel and Gretel," *The Parent Trap*, Sean Wilsey's memoir [see p. 181]). In the spirit of *The Parent Trap* (Hayley Mills's version) feel justified in putting your parent's intended through a few tests. It's for your parent's own good, even if he or she doesn't understand at first.

Some of us are able to have friendly, reciprocal relationships with our quasi-siblings. It usually takes some effort and generosity of spirit, but it is possible. As for the new placeholder in your parent's life—start them out on probation.

Will you ever adjust to this new person? Will you ever tolerate her? Could you love her? If she makes Daddy happy, that's a decent beginning, but she has to make you happy, too. She has to be sensitive to your needs now. She can't keep touching Daddy in front of you. She might have to buy your love, but she must pay attention to where you like to shop and what you like to do.

Will the two sides of this new, oddly matched blended family ever feel like one big, happy feel-good movie? Keep your expectations low and focus on your own life (as if you haven't), and perhaps in time you won't even notice that you are living in some version of Capulet-Montague peace. Hold onto those frequent-flyer miles.

12.

T.T.F.N.

One can remain alive long past the usual date of disintegration if
one is unafraid of change, insatiable in intellectual curiosity,
interested in big things, and happy in small ways.
—Edith Wharton, *A Backward Glance*

Looking Good vs.
Feeling Good.

For people who grew up gatoring, had tête-à-têtes with porcelain (and you know we're not just talking about you, Cooper), and like to be known by their childhood nicknames, we age with surprising dignity. It's incredible, really, when you think about it. How could a population so unself-conscious that they summer as fifty-year-olds—with their parents—do anything with dignity?

It's because in some ways, we don't change. You may be looking at the near side of seventy, but don't you still fit into your wedding suit? And Laurinda, you are still wearing your hair in the same style of, well—your whole life: bangs pulled back in a tortoiseshell barrette, straight hair to your chin. You both look, well, kind of radiantly boyish, and well scrubbed. And since we're all still active, we stay trim and firm. We may have added a little poundage over the years but not enough to make us jiggle.

And by staying the same, we don't just mean the same looks. We mean the *same*. We keep our friends, our hobbies, even go to the office (it's a nice place to read the paper and hang with old friends) until we are no longer upright, if we are aging prepsters, as Christopher Buckley prematurely calls himself (see p. 16). We stay put, even if we are travelers and ad-venturers. We are content with our lives; so why change them? That contentment helps us weather things over which we have no control.

Cognitive therapy (huh?) teaches us that if we put on a smile, we will feel better—one fakes it until one makes it. So we smile and wave to our friends, and we catch up and drink and even dance a bit . . . When it gets cool out, Penn still drapes his blazer around our shoulders with a casual hug, pieces still fall into place. We know we can charge a chef's salad and an iced tea at the club (at this point, we don't even have to sign for it; the waiters know our account number as well as we do).

Good luck does not favor the preppy. We have overindulged and are susceptible to the same vicissitudes of the modern toxic world. But by the time we hit our second half, it turns out we know people.

We know people who know the head of the hospital board. We know the DA. We know the very best lawyer for that. We know the cardiologist who helped the President. We know the head pro. We know the maître d'. We know Aunt Chapin's orthopedic surgeon, and he is *the* knee man.

So we might as well look good.

CHOOSING YOUR DOCTORS.

Welcome to the Real World, Payne. As you have perhaps surmised by now, you have to be organized and figure out who can help you if ever things were to go awry. (This is the unpredictable twenty-first century we're living in.)

The obvious first steps are to consult Daddy and Mummy or, better still, to rely on them entirely. Maybe it's time to remember this harsh reality: Mummy and Daddy can't help. Or Mummy is in a home, and Daddy hasn't been right for years. Your brother Timmy has a public-access cable TV show about mosaics, and your sister is living somewhere in Costa Rica without a phone. What we're saying, Pookie, is that you have to grow up. Okay, pour yourself another drink.

You need to be prepared to make some decisions on your own. Which means you need to hire smart people you can trust to make these decisions for you.

Let's start with your medical team; over forty it's more than one doctor.

Your primary physician needs to be selected with these questions in mind: Did he or she graduate from a top medical school? (Aha! It matters.) Is he or she young enough to be curious and energetic but not so young as to be arrogant? Will he or she be around for me for the long haul? Could I bear getting difficult news relayed from this person? Is she an athlete? (A team player is a nice quality in a medical doctor.) Do you like their hospital of affiliation? Is that where your friends go when they're sick? Think about your own physical vulnerabilities: If it's your liver, your heart, your metabolism, your internist could be a specialist in that area.

Don't look at this chapter of your life as getting older, look at it as assembling a top-notch medical group. Your eye doctor, dentist, orthopedic surgeon, urologist, physical therapist, and hairdresser should all radiate competence and reassurance when you see them. After enough years of being their patient you may consider breaking the doctor-patient wall and inviting him to your box at the game, inviting her to one of your cocktail parties, or offering to write a letter of recommendation for him or her at your children's school, your club, or their co-op board. Bottom line: You need your doctor to offer you his or her cell number. You won't over-use it, but it's a nice feeling to have it.

Official tie of the American College of Physicians.

Lawyers, a Necessity.

As we are surrounded by lawyers at our clubs, at our resorts, at home, at our restaurants, and even in our law firms, we don't need much in the way of guidance here. But (as givers) we always want to be of assistance.

Specifically, have you thought about your will? It's an unpleasant task at best, forcing you to confront your . . . you know. Even thinking about it, you'll want to pour yourself a stiff drink and get into bed and pull up the covers. When you come to, you will realize that someone has to do it for you. Hire a lawyer. Do not—under any circumstances—reread Dickens's *Bleak House* (see p. 180) now. Save it for later.

Good lawyers (we never say "attorneys") charge at least $300 per hour, but more typically in the $500 to $700 range. Consider what your time is worth: $50 an hour? Less? Could you be more affronted by having to spend a fortune to dispense with your fortune? And while they've got you on the phone, they want to talk about golf, the movies, or their son's award from the Latin master of his school. (Are you being charged for all this? You would tolerate and even possibly enjoy their chatter if you bumped into them while getting your morning lattes after your weekend jog, but over the phone you sense that the meter is running.)

And while we're at it, the practice of calling our house, our Milton Avery print, our sailboat, our antique silver gravy boats, the set of of twenty-four mother-of-pearl–handled fish forks and knives, our grapefruit spoons, our prized chandelier, and our grandmother's charm bracelets "assets" sounds icky. Remember that Jane always admired your emerald earrings. If you can bear it, use your will to bestow them to her after, you know.

It is likely your family has worked with one firm in particular which has lawyers engaged in all specialties. It is even likely that by now you have met Daddy and Mummy's trust and estate lawyer, since they probably wrote up their wills a while ago (before they sold Microsoft at $179). If you find all this too morbid, ask your brother or sister to be the point person. If you don't trust your brother, Tudor, who's joined that group in Coeur d'Alene, Idaho, or your sister, Cabot, will try to divert your share of the inheritance to her tree hugger in Oregon, then, Phillipa, it's up to you.

from **The New York Times,** *March 13, 2000.*

GERTRUDE SANFORD LEGENDRE, 97
SOCIALITE TURNED HUNTER AND PRISONER OF WAR

BY ENID NEMY

Gertrude Sanford Legendre, an unlikely debutante of the 1920s who forsook society to become a big-game hunter and then to work during World War II for the Office of Strategic Services, predecessor of the Central Intelligence Agency, died on Wednesday at Medway, her historic plantation near Charleston, S.C. She was 97 and also had a home on Fishers Island, off Long Island.

Gertrude Sanford was in her teens when she took a hunting trip to the Grand Tetons of Wyoming and shot her first elk. For years, she pursued big game in Africa, India, Iran and Indochina, and contributed rare specimens to museums.

In her later years, she established the Medway Environmental Trust for educational purposes and to ensure that Medway would forever be managed as a nature preserve.

Mrs. Legendre began her wartime career as a secretary with the O.S.S. in Washington. In 1944, the agency transferred her to Paris and gave her a WAC uniform and paperwork identifying her as a second lieutenant.

She became the first American woman captured in France when, on a visit to the front northeast of Paris, she found herself pinned down by German sniper fire. Held as a prisoner of war for six months, she escaped and went by train to Switzerland. The train stopped short of the border; as she dashed to the frontier, a German guard ordered her to halt or be shot. She continued, and reached the border.

After the war, Mrs. Legendre helped a German prison guard who had been kind to her emigrate to the United States. She established the Medway Plan to provide medical help to countries devastated by the war.

Mrs. Legendre was born in 1902 in Aiken, S.C., the youngest of three children of John and Ethel Sanford. She, her brother, Stephen Sanford, an internationally recognized polo player known as Laddie, and her sister, Sara Jane Sanford, were said to have been the inspiration for Philip Barry's 1929 play "Holiday," made into a classic movie starring Katharine Hepburn and Cary Grant. She wrote two autobiographies, "The Sands Ceased to Run" (1947) and "The Time of My Life" (1987).

Mrs. Legendre was reared in Amsterdam, N.Y., and in a Manhattan town house on East 72nd Street now occupied by the Lycée Français. She was educated at the Foxcroft School in Middleburg, Va., and made her debut after her graduation in 1920. She and Sidney J. Legendre married in 1929. He died in 1948.

Mrs. Legendre is survived by two daughters, Bokara Legendre of Manhattan and Mill Valley, Calif., and Landine Manigault of Stonington, Conn.; four grandchildren, and three great-grandchildren.

Known as one of the grand dames of Charleston, Mrs. Legendre gave a New Year's Eve costume party that was a tradition for half a century. At one of the last of those parties, she offered a toast: "I look ahead. I always have. I don't contemplate life, I live it. And I'm having the time of my life."

Good mourning.

"I'm not crying, I'm checking my mascara. I used that lash primer with the fibers, and I think one fell into my eye. Martha will not believe it was standing room only at India's memorial service. It's not that we didn't all love her, though we didn't, really . . . love her. There must be 200 people here! More than at the Easter Ball. I wonder what Lyon would say about that. 'India Powell. Looks like an owl,' he always sang. God, she was not so 'charmingly original.' She wore funny hats, that's all. And red lipstick even to just go out for the paper.

"I wonder if there are 300 people here. Oh, wait, I can see the Maxwells in my compact mirror. He looks embalmed already, and is Fiona crying? I read somewhere—probably in *Vogue*—that each new loss brings up old pains. Maybe it was on *Oprah*. Anyway. Fiona is probably thinking of her mummy. Or her brother Duke. That was awful, falling off that diving board. How did India make a difference? By reading to the blind? Don't they use books on tape now? Everyone does. Marian uses them on her treadmill. I'd use it at the gym, but my trainer would be hurt. But maybe if I told her once that I was in the middle of this book and I couldn't put it down, she'd shut up about her gorgeous four-year-old she's still nursing. It's worth a shot.

"I wonder how many people will go to the reception at the Powells'. I'd be amazed if the Symingtons went. Oh, no. More? I promised Lucinda I'd pick up the cupcakes for her. No funeral should be more than one hour. Honor Cadbury? She was friends with India?"

The Do-It-Yourself
True Prep Eulogy.

What is more stressful than trying to write a tribute to a relative or friend when you are grieving and unable to focus? (Focus was never your strong suit, anyway.) Here, to make your job easier, is a fill-in-the-blanks eulogy, intended to be a template, or at least a way to collect your thoughts about your beloved _____.

Thank you all for coming today. (Allow time for seat shifting and murmurs.) How to best describe _____? He/She was such a unique _____. He/She was the total _____. We each have our different memories of him/her. Whether he/she was on the _____, at his/her _____, or just _____ at the _____ club, he/she was always _____. We first met at _____. It was (*season, year*) _____, and _____ was wearing a classic _____, without socks/with her pearls. I'll never forget looking at _____ the first time and hearing _____. What a singular laugh he/she had! It sounded like a crow. (Speaker now tries to emulate, as do several mourners.)

_____ lived for his/her _____. Every summer he/she loved to _____, sometimes alone at _____, sometimes with friends at _____. He/She once _____!!! (Pause for chuckles.) Then in the Fall, it was always _____ time, which _____ also adored. How I can still hear his/her voice now, saying _____! Let's _____! Because _____ loved life. And he/she was so modest, he/she never boasted about winning the _____ in (*year*)_____. Do you know what he/she said to the runner-up/Silver Medalist? _____. Only _____ could be that generous as a winner.

I thought I'd tell you about the origins of _____'s nickname. Many of you called our _____, "_____." But in-deed, that was not his/her actual given name. He/She was said to be born on/under (*a lunar circumstance*) _____ that affected his/her mother as she went into labor. OR, as a baby, _____ looked like _____. OR as a child, _____ loved to eat _____. That plus the fact that he/she was named for his/her father/mother—as was family tradition—meant that a nickname was the only way possible to distinguish between them. And now, his/her daughter/son carries his/her name so well. We are all proud of him/her.

Which brings us to _____'s home life. At (*name of house*) _____, you always felt welcome, whether you were expected or not. (*Name of housekeeper, pointed out by speaker, weeping in the second row*) _____ would always set a place for you at the table and offer you your favorite drink. Or in Woody's case, a pitcher of _____s. (General laughter.) _____ was always looking for his car keys/reading glasses/pills. Being there was like being in your own house, with your own family. As a parent, _____ was so proud of his/her children. They'd sometimes go for a drive, just _____ and _____, and hit some balls/shoot at cans/look at houses/buy liquor across the border to save taxes, only to return to tell the most amazing stories about getting lost in (*strange neighborhood*) _____, where they observed (*some kind of behavior or ritual they'd never seen before*) _____. It was like listening to Margaret Mead talking about Samoa! Buying a GPS would never do for _____. It wasn't the money, it was the adventure he/she would have missed. Well, that and the money.

A few weeks ago, when I last saw _____, he/she was talking about something he/she learned at (*alma mater*) _____. How he/she was inspired by his/her English teacher/coach/dean. How he/she had his/her eyes opened to the whole world thanks to this man/woman. When the library reading room/junior lounge/humanities building/weight room was dedicated to _____ last year, I never heard him/her so happy, so proud, so fulfilled.

_____, we will miss you. We will miss your warmth, your grace, your awful sense of direction, your competitiveness, your sense of humor, and your laugh. I will miss you. The world of (*community*) _____ will miss you.

And now, the (*alma mater marching band*) _____ will play _____'s favorite hymn, followed by their fight song.

Coming Home: Should You Be Interred at Your Alma Mater?

Some people can never get enough of their old school. You know the type. They return for every possible event: homecomings, reunions (at Princeton, though, this is an annual ritual; see p. 182), and even concerts and lectures. They collar students and point out that the (not so) new Middle Eastern Studies building used to be the music building, or some other factoid almost as fascinating. Their spouses can't bear to show up. They know about the music building.

Now some schools are offering campus burials to these loyal alumni. And a surprising number are choosing this option as their final resting place.

Many old prep schools, colleges, and universities built cemeteries because people used to die so young. The University of North Carolina at Chapel Hill has a cemetery that is 6.98 acres. It has survived the Civil War (many Confederate soldiers are buried there) and lots of vandalism. In 2005 an area called Memorial Grove was created for the spreading of ashes, along with a wall where the names of those former Carolinans are inscribed.

Princeton University's cemetery is home to Aaron Burr, and his father and father-in-law, who were the second and third presidents of that most prep university. Author Harriet Beecher Stowe is buried in the Andover cemetery, but obviously, she was not an alumna.

The University of Notre Dame, home of the "Fighting Irish" (and not a hotbed of preppiness, though they do exist in Fort Wayne, Indiana), has an enormous death program for its community in its lush and well-maintained Cedar Grove Cemetery. Called "Come Home," it offers a "dignified Christian burial," not only in-ground for Notre Damers who fulfill several criteria (full-time faculty and staff as well as former faculty and staff, if they meet age and service thresholds) but also many opportunities to be buried above ground in crypts or have one's cremated remains stored in niches. Alumni and surviving spouses are welcome, and may purchase up to four places—even a combination of niches and crypts—if they like, in the two (and here's the plural) mausolea. To make it easier for graduates to choose, the cemetery offers Open Houses every Friday and Saturday during football season.

The glorious campus that was designed by Thomas Jefferson, the University of Virginia in Charlottesville, has a cemetery, which in its earliest days experienced so many grave robbers that families had to fake-bury their dead by day—using bundles of rocks or logs covered in shrouds—only to return in the dark of night to actually bury the bodies. By the end of the Civil War, 1,907 Confederate soldiers were buried there, including two generals.

The story we'd like to tell you is that of Beta, the university's first mascot. A black-and-white mutt who turned up one morning at the front porch of the Beta house, the dog loved beer and hamburgers. He became such a beloved campus presence that when a car ran him over, on April 6, 1939, 1,000 people attended his funeral. The dean of

IN MEMORY OF "BETA" BELOVED FRIEND AND MASCOT OF...

the college gave the eulogy. When a new dog turned up on campus in the 1940s, he somehow became the new mascot. Seal, as he was named, traveled with the football team, and once elicited swooning from Virginia's fans when they watched him pee on Penn's side at Franklin Field in Philadelphia. When Seal died on December 11, 1953, 1,500 showed up to pay their respects at his funeral. Both Beta and Seal are buried at the UVA cemetery, and are the only non-humans to be so.

When the last plots were sold in 1966, there was still sufficient demand to create more berths for more human bodies. In 1987, the Board of Visitors approved new walls, each containing 180 vaults. The first one is sold out, but the second, completed in 2003, still has niches available in its columbarium, "a sepulchral vault or other structure with recesses in the walls to receive the ashes of the dead."

Social scientists are still mulling over this trend. For our rootless, transient society, returning to one's alma mater is returning to "the closest thing they've had to a real community in their lives," says one. On a more practical note, some campuses regard the burgeoning burial business to be a new way of raising money.

Considering the renewed popularity of inviting one's prep school's or college's marching band to perform their school's fight song during funerals even outside the walls of academe, perhaps this is just the thing. But since preppies have so much of their own community (and that's not counting places like Squirrel Hill), will this be our future? Most important, this will help our grandchildren be admitted.

Airedale or Heirdog: What to Do If You Predecease Your Pet.

If you are beginning to see the white light and you have dachshunds, we recommend you get in touch immediately with madcap anthropologist/dachshund fanatic Iris Love (see p. 29), who inherited Brooke Astor's two, Boysie and Girlsie.

Otherwise, let's put our heads together. Leaving your pooch(es) a $12 million trust fund, as Leona Helmsley did, is not only selfish, it becomes her headline for all eternity: "Queen of Mean Loves Trouble" (her Maltese). You don't want an heirdog, but you do want to ensure that your darling pets have a good life after you are . . . you know.

Do your dogs love someone else (obviously, not as much as you, but) almost as much as they love you? Is there any reason not to talk to this person about your pets and suss out whether he or she would want the responsibility for taking care of your dog at home? If said person happens to be a personal employee, you must establish a fund through which he or she can support the animal and/or upgrade their home so Henry has a room or space of his own. And if it's a friend, you should offer this friend something for taking such loving care of Henry.

Just be grateful you don't have an African Grey (parrot), which has an average life span of about sixty years.

My Little Dog—a heartbeat at my feet.
—Edith Wharton

Unacceptable Euphemisms for "Dead."

Asleep, be taken, bought the farm, called to a higher place, crossed over, danced the last dance, departed, diagnostic misadventure of high magnitude, entered the slumber room, expended, expired, extinction of the person, faded quickly, failed to fulfill his/her wellness potential, gathered to his people, going into the fertilizer business, going to the big place in the sky, gone, gone to a better place, gone to meet their Maker, gone to be with the Lord, gone to sleep, got his wings, heaven-bound, in a better place, in heaven/hell, in a kinder gentler place, in repose, joined the choir invisible, kicked the bucket, late, left us, lay down with one's fathers, living-impaired, lost, metabolic processes are now history, negative patient-care outcome, no longer with us, no more, off the twig, paid Charon's fare, passed away/on/over, popped off, promoted to Sub-Terranean Truffle Inspector, returned to the ground, rode off into the sunset, shuffled off the mortal coil, six feet under, sprouted wings, stiff, succumbed, sustained a therapeutic misadventure, taken from us, taking a dirt nap, that good night, took his/her last breath, T.U. (Toes Up), wandering the Elysian Fields, went to the big blue baseball field/shopping mall in the sky, whacked, with the ancestors, and worm food.

Acceptable Euphemisms for "Dead."

Dead.

November 19, 1980
Brooke Shields purrs, "Nothing comes between me and my Calvins," which prompts CBS to ban the Dwight-Englewood graduate's racy Calvin Klein commercials.

November 22, 1980
Melina Mercouri attends Harvard/Yale game in Cambridge, Massachusetts, "for some reason." (Technically, the stadium is in the Allston neighborhood of Boston.)

January 4, 1981
The Official Preppy Handbook hits #1 on the *New York Times* trade paperback bestseller list and stays on the list for sixty-five weeks.

January 22, 1981
Judge Robert Kendall issues a decision supporting practices at the Bohemian Club—California's elite male club famous for its summer outings at its "encampment" on 2,400 acres in Monte Rio, California, where valets serve, but bathrooms are the Great Outdoors. Members included Walter Cronkite, Robert Kennedy, David Rockefeller, William Hearst, American presidents Eisenhower, Reagan, Ford, Taft, Hoover, the Roosevelts, and Nixon. Current members are Rummy, Kissinger, George Shultz, Colin Powell, the Bushes, David Rockefeller Jr., and Christopher Buckley (his daddy was a member). The club did not allow any women (including employees), noting that club members at the Grove "urinate in the open without even the use of rudimentary toilet facilities" and that the presence of females would alter club members' behavior.

September 14, 1981
Michelle Robinson (Obama) starts classes at Princeton.

October 17, 1981
The California Department of Fair Employment and Housing countered the Kendall ruling by ordering the Bohemian Club to begin recruiting and hiring women as employees.

February 1, 1982
Lisa Henson, daughter of muppeteer Jim, becomes the first female president of the Harvard Lampoon.

October 16, 1982
Williams College ends maid service.

December 13, 1982
Martha Stewart, a relatively unknown caterer from Westport, Connecticut, publishes her first book, *Entertaining*, with Clarkson Potter.

January 1983
The first copy of a new catalogue, called J.Crew, is in the mail.

May 30, 1983
John F. Kennedy Jr. graduates from Brown University, quite possibly the first time he is photographed with a shirt on.

September 26, 1983
Day of Preppy Infamy—United States loses its first ever defense of the America's Cup to Australia after 132 years. American skipper Dennis Conner is shamed.

February 25, 1984
Amherst College administration announces that fraternities will be abolished at the college.

April 23, 1984
Choate Rosemary Hall upperclassman Derek Oatis attempts to smuggle $300,000 worth of cocaine, bought with students' money, upon

return from trip to Venezuela and is arrested at Kennedy Airport. Fourteen students are expelled.

November 1984
Christie Brinkley's *Playboy* cover appears, solves decorating problems at Portsmouth Abbey's dorms.

June 28, 1985
Post-college preppy life is explained in *St. Elmo's Fire,* released today.

September 1985
Lawrenceville School, founded in 1810 as Maidenhead Academy, refounded as Lawrenceville School in 1883, votes to admit girls. John Gore, director of alumni relations, explains that it took until September 1987 to get women on campus because they had to build housing, locker rooms, and restrooms, update facilities, and so on.

November 12, 1985
Dodge Morgan sails *Friendship 40* designer Ted Fontaine's boat, *American Harbour,* from Bermuda to Bermuda, breaking the single-handed nonstop circumnavigation record. His journey takes 150 days, one hour, and six minutes, finishing on April 11, 1986.

April 21, 1986
Ralph Lauren opens his new "flagship" store in the landmark Rhinelander mansion on Madison Avenue and 72nd Street in Manhattan. Built by architects Kimball &

old Jennifer Levin at Dorrian's Red Hand, an Upper East Side bar that caters to the children of the well-heeled. Later that night, the two walk into Central Park together. Jennifer's body was found the next day; she had been strangled. Thereafter it was known as "The Preppy Murder" (thanks a lot). Despite good looks and a promising start, Chambers continues to serve time in prison for a seemingly endless series of crimes, both on the outside and the inside.

November 21, 1986
The California Supreme Court strikes down the ban over hiring women at the Bohemian Club and, denying a further review in 1987, forces the Club to begin hiring female workers during the summer encampment at the Grove in Monte Rio. This ruling became quoted as a legal precedent and was discussed during the 1995–1996 floor debate surrounding California Senate Bill SB 2110, a proposed bill concerning whether tax-exempt organizations (including fraternal clubs) should be exempt from the Unruh Civil Rights Act.

February 4, 1987
Disgraced America's Cup skipper "Dirty Dennis" Conner and the crew of *Stars & Stripes* win back the America's Cup in Fremantle, Australia, in a demonstration of prep defiance.

Thompson in 1898, the French Renaissance Revival building cost Lauren somewhere between $14 and $35 million to renovate. He leases the building; however, he owns the antiques.

August 26, 1986
Robert Chambers, a 200-pound 6'4" tall wastrel who attended St. David's, Choate, Browning, York Prep, a year of Boston University, and Hazelden, meets eighteen-year-

June 1987
In Palm Beach, the Breakers Hotel begins to repeal its jackets-and-ties-after-five rule in their lobby as it becomes harder to force guests to dress for dinner.

July 11, 1987
Martha Stewart writes *Weddings.*

October 19, 1987
"Black Monday." Stock Market Crashes, trust funds/inheritances take a major hit.

May 29, 1989
Nantucket Nectar founders Tom First and Tom Scott graduate from Brown University. That summer they begin a delivery service in Nantucket Harbor: "everything from newspapers to laundry." By 1990, they began selling "Peach Nectar," something

May 1, 1990
John F. Kennedy Jr. fails the New York Bar exam for the second time.

July 1990
Daughter of Park Avenue Vera Wang goes into trade. (Fortunately, it's a bridal salon at the hotel Carlyle.)

they accidentally made while trying to mix the perfect after-work cocktail.

July 27, 1989
The New York Athletic Club announces that it is voluntarily ending its two-year legal battle to keep women out. Forevermore, men must wear bathing suits in the swimming pool.

September 12, 1989
Deerfield Academy, founded in 1797, alma mater of former Manhattan DA Robert Morgenthau, author John McPhee, poet John Ashbery, Time Warner CEO Jeffrey Bewkes, actor Matthew Fox, and King Abdullah of Jordan, readmits girls for the first time since 1943, when headmaster Frank Boyden canceled coeducation.

November 1, 1989
John F. Kennedy Jr. fails the New York Bar exam for the first time.

January 1, 1990
Senator Claiborne Pell, a preppy till the end, dies.

February 1990
Banana Republic begins to transform itself from a safari clothier to a young, urban preppy emporium, filled with all the colors from grey to putty.

March 26, 1990
Tom Schulman, Montgomery Bell Academy (Nashville) '68, wins the Best Original Screenplay Oscar for *Dead Poets Society* (also nominated for Best Picture 1989).

July 24, 1990
After failing the New York Bar exam twice, JFK Jr. takes the exam for the third time.

July 26, 1990
JFK Jr. takes the Connecticut Bar exam "just in case," as it is reported to be easier than New York's test.

September 1990
Alexandra Miller, youngest of the three socialite daughters of Robert (Duty-Free Shoppers) Miller, begins classes at Brown.

November 2, 1990
It is confirmed that JFK Jr. passes the Connecticut Bar exam.

November 3, 1990
It is confirmed that JFK Jr. passes the New York Bar exam.

January 1991
T. Anthony begins manufacturing leather CD cases, and monograms them at no extra charge.

March 6, 1991
Bret Easton Ellis publishes *American Psycho*. It becomes an instant prep cult classic.

March 29–30, 1991
Senator Ted Kennedy and his nephew, William Kennedy Smith, embark on a boys' night out at Au Bar, Palm Beach, which ends, as things do—increasingly—in a courtroom. A twenty-nine-year-old woman Smith met at the bar claims she was raped by the younger Kennedy. Despite tes-

timony from three other women who claimed to have been sexually assaulted by him, Smith is eventually acquitted of the crime.

Bessette under a veil of secrecy. By the time Mr. and Mrs. John F. Kennedy Jr. arrive at their reception at the Greyfield Inn, millions of women's dreams are shattered.

January 1993
The Lilly Pulitzer company is revived by Scott Beaumont and James Bradbeer Jr., two Pennsylvania businessmen. Lilly Pulitzer is now sold in 75 signature stores and 178 doors (253 locations total). (Lilly's sisters were Mary Maude [called Memsey] and Florence Fitch [Flossie].)

June 1993
Eighteen-year-old Shoshanna Lonstein graduates from Nightingale-Bamford School; her thirty-nine-year-old boyfriend, Jerry Seinfeld, celebrates with her.

September 4, 1993
Martha Stewart Living, the domestic goddess' own syndicated TV show, is scheduled to launch today. The topics in the episode include potato latkes, succulents in a stone wall, and decorating napkins.

December 8, 1994
Kerry Washington stars in "ABC Afterschool Special" *Magical Make-Over* in her senior year at the Spence School.

January 1995
The Frick Museum begins to quietly rent out its space for private parties (the program officially starts in 2006).

August 2, 1996
Gwyneth Paltrow (Spence '90) does not require coaching in piano playing or archery for her work in the film *Emma,* which opens today.

September 21, 1996
At the First African Baptist Church on Cumberland Island, off Georgia, JFK Jr. — prepdom's sexiest male—marries Carolyn

April 13, 1997
Tiger Woods wins his first Masters and receives his kelly-green blazer just like those once worn by waiters in the Florentine Room at The Breakers.

December 1997
Due to pesky airbag regulations, the last Land Rover Defender, beloved summer vehicle of Nantucket/MV, is sold in the United States. (They are still available overseas.)

February 1998
The seven remaining Mark Cross leather goods stores close, after a four-year attempt by Sara Lee Corp. to rescue the brand. Founded in 1846 in Boston, it was run from 1934 to 1956 by Gerald Murphy, the grandson of its owner, whose life inspired Fitzgerald's *Tender Is the Night*.

September 1998
The Hill School, founded in 1851 in Pottstown, Pennsylvania, and alma mater of James Baker (Secretary of State, Secretary of Treasury, and presidential Chief of Staff), Harry Hamlin (actor), James Cromwell (actor), Robert Horchow (the Horchow catalogue), Norman Pearlstine (former EIC, Time Inc.), Oliver Stone (rogue film director), and the sons of Donald Trump, admits females.

July 16, 1999
John F. Kennedy Jr. is killed in plane crash off Martha's Vineyard; an incredulous world mourns.

October 19, 1999
Martha Stewart Omnimedia goes public at the New York Stock Exchange. Ms. Stewart becomes a paper billionaire that day.

June 2000
Midnight Farm begins selling hand-painted clogs—which originated in Sweden and were worn by hippies in the '60s—and are now bought by sixty-year-old hippies on Martha's Vineyard.

July 15, 2000
Filmmaker Alex Jones and a cameraman sneak into the Bohemian Grove with a hidden camera.

June 7, 2001
First regular-season Major League Lacrosse game is played, as Baltimore defeats Long Island 16–13.

November 23, 2001
Smith & Hawken opens its forty-fifth store, in Deer Park, Illinois.

November 29, 2001
Lifelong Brooks Brothers customer, Italian businessman Claudio Del Vecchio, acquires Brooks Brothers from Marks & Spencer, pledging to rescue it after years of British neglect.

October 3, 2002
Martha Stewart resigns from the board of directors of the New York Stock Exchange.

December 30, 2002
Mayor Bloomberg signs a law banning indoor smoking in New York City.

February 21, 2003
The Guardian announces that Chelsea Clinton is headed to McKinsey, where she will work with other preppies.

October 28, 2003
Mark Zuckerberg invents Facemash while attending Harvard as a sophomore. The site represented a Harvard University version of Hot or Not, according to *The Harvard Crimson.* That night, Zuckerberg was blogging about a girl who had dumped him and trying to think of something to do to get her off his mind.

January 2004
Zuckerberg begins writing code for a new Web site, which eventually becomes Facebook. In March the site opens to Stanford, Columbia, and Yale, and gradually extends to all Ivies, Boston-area schools, and ultimately all universities, and even nursing homes.

January 2004
Former Hollywood CAA agent Scott Sternberg founds Band of Outsiders, whose "This is not a polo shirt" polo shirt has become a hit with celebrities and preppies alike.

April 2004
Phish, led by Taftie Trey Anastasio, announces they are breaking up.

August 2004
Phish breaks up after weekend concert festival in Coventry, Vermont.

October 8, 2004
Martha Stewart arrives at the federal women's prison in Alderson, West Virginia, at 6:15 am to begin her sentence.

October 23, 2004
Rugby, the new Ralph Lauren line, opens its first store, on Newbury Street in Boston.

March 30, 2003
Mayor Bloomberg's smoking ban takes effect in New York City.

June 4, 2003
Martha Stewart is found guilty of obstruction of justice.

March 4, 2005
Martha Stewart leaves the big house for house arrest at her *really* big house for five more months.

July 13, 2005
Cofounder of Vineyard Vines Ian Murray and his band, The Ian Murray Band, release their single "Rich Wife," from the album *Waiting for the Wind.*

May 2006
Delta Airlines begins offering Stirrings, pre-mixed mixers for Bloodies, Mojitos, Margaritas, and Cosmos on flights over 400 miles.

June 2007
Mad River Glen begins renovations on their original single chairlift. Snowboarders still banned.

January 29, 2008
Vampire Weekend releases its first self-titled album, with lyrics about Cape Cod, the 79th Street crosstown bus, and mansard roofs.

September 2, 2008
Robert Chambers, the "Preppie Killer"—out of jail after being convicted of manslaughter—is sentenced to 19 years in prison after being charged with selling cocaine out of his apartment in Manhattan.

October 1, 2008
Phish announces they are getting back together.

June 13, 2007
President George W. Bush is caught wearing Crocs—with socks! People call for his impeachment.

August 13, 2007
Brooke Astor dies at her weekend estate, Holly Hill, in Briarcliff Manor, New York. She was 105 years old. (See p. 146.)

September 14, 2007
Martha Stewart Living Omnimedia joins forces with vintner E & J Gallo to create the "Martha Stewart Vintage" line of wines.

October 26, 2007
Bill Clinton is heckled by a man claiming that the attacks on September 11 were a fraud and mentioning the Bohemian Club. He responds with, "The Bohemian Club! Did you say Bohemian Club? That's where all those rich Republicans go up and stand naked against redwood trees, right? I've never been to the Bohemian Club, but you oughta go. It'd be good for you. You'd get some fresh air."

December 2007
Great Recession forces preps to leave Wall Street, move out west, and take up jobs as ski bums.

December 2008
Caroline Kennedy thinks about accepting unoffered option to become senator from New York, and then changes her mind.

February 17, 2009
Global economy tanks further. According to washingtonpost.com, "Markets around the world plunged Tuesday as evidence mounted that the global economic crisis is worsening. Japan is suffering its worst downturn in 35 years. The British economy is facing its sharpest decline in almost 30 years. Germany is slumping at its worst pace in nearly 20 years. Meanwhile, the job market in the United States, at the epicenter of the global downturn, is the worst in decades." Preppies, other than those with funds of funds or hedge funds, are no longer "taking time off."

March 6, 2009
Phish plays their first official concert at Hampton Coliseum in Hampton, Virginia after an almost five-year hiatus.

July 9, 2009
Smith & Hawken announces that they are closing all of their stores.

August 25, 2009
Longtime senator and dean of the Democrats Edward M. Kennedy, youngest brother of President John F. Kennedy, dies.

Every day of 2010
Miami University in Ohio receives an average of 100 packages from J.Crew.

January 27, 2010
J. D. Salinger dies. The reclusive author, who wrote the seminal preppy coming-of-age novel *The Catcher in the Rye*, was 91. Jerome David Salinger so loathed publicity that the last photograph he permitted to be taken of himself was in 1953. The novel's protagonist (for which the term "antihero" is often used), Holden Caulfield, narrates the story of three days following his expulsion from Pencey Prep, in a voice both tender and sarcastic. Over a quarter of a million copies of the novel have sold annually since the book was published on July 16, 1951, and it has made every "100 Best American Novel" list since then.

February 14, 2010
The last race is completed at the thirty-third America's Cup which was embroiled in controversy regarding regatta venue, dates, boat design, and race rules. Regatta changes and the unsightly Team Prada boat bring tears to preppies' eyes.

February 21, 2010
Trinity Squash wins 12th consecutive national championship, continuing its 224-game winning streak, the longest winning streak in the history of varsity college sports. Team members are compared to preppy rock stars. Not all is well in squash land, however. "As Chaudhry was leaving the court to join the celebration Trinity's team and fans had started on the floor, he surprisingly shoved Chan back onto the court, marring the historic night and concluding a heated match between the two players that included taunting not normally seen in squash."

April 14, 2010
Forbes.com announces today that Thurston Howell III was named the ninth-richest fake person on its annual Forbes Fictional 15 [Richest] List. Situated between #8, the Tooth Fairy, and #10, Sir Topham Hatt, Mr. Howell is estimated to have a net worth of $2.1 billion.

May 21, 2010
Senior Parent Soirée at Lick-Wilmerding High School, San Francisco, 7–9 pm.

May 22, 2010
Francis W. Parker School, in Chicago, hosts its Parkerpalooza Student Community Music Festival.

May 27–30, 2010
Princeton (annual) Reunions 2010. Welcome back, Tigers!

June 14–July 2, 2010
Quiz Bowl Training Camp, every day from 8:30 am–9:40 am at Hawken School, Lyndhurst, Ohio.

July 12, 2010
Brooks Brothers releases a new line for boys and its first for girls: "Fleece."

September 2, 2010
Full-time First Year students' meal plan begins with dinner at Trinity College.

September 6, 2010
First day of New Student Orientation and Registration at University of Denver. (September 12 is the Last Day to Register Without Late Fee.)

September 9, 2010
New York's Trinity School closed for Rosh Hashanah.

September 12, 2010
Men's Final of the U.S. Open scheduled for today, if all goes according to plan (which it often does not).

ACKNOWLEDGMENTS.

Thank-yous large and small: Kevin Abernathy, Nellie Abernathy, Jonathan Adler, Elliot Aguilar, Ernesto Aguilar, Stephonie Alfond, Walter Anderson, Joana Andrade, Gayle Atkins, Genevieve Bahrenburg, Larkin Bailey, Janet Band, Ida A. Becker, Michael Bermingham, Carolyn Bernstein, Archie Dogson Birnbach, Naomi Birnbach, Blue Ribbon Sushi, Janet Borden, Loraine Boyle, Lucy Boyle, James Bradbeer, Joan Brennan, Thom Browne, Si Bunting III, Meredith Melling Burke, Anders Burrows, Kristin Kohler Burrows, Amy Cahners, Margaret Cardone, E. Jean Carroll, Carol Carson, Sue Carswell, Dr. David B. Case, Amanda Cole, Kenneth Cole, Maria Cuomo Cole, Ann Coley, Kathleen Compton, Caroline Connor, Lara Bird Connor, Dana Conroy, R. David Coolidge, Angela Cosmai, Nick Cox, Meaghan Curcio, Jamie Lee Curtis, Posy Dana, Tom Davis, Whitney DeLear, Greg D'Elia, Elizabeth Dickson, Elliot Dickson, Simon Doonan, Mickey Drexler, Gabi duBrul, Maja duBrul, Dennis Dwyer, Buffy Easton, Diane Englander, Jes Feuer, Lisa Fine, Charles A. Fisher, Celeste Ford, George Fournier, Mari Fujiuchi, Janie Hawkins Furse, Dana Gati, Courtney Gillan, Tony Godsick, Jeffrey Goldstein, Laurie Burrows Grad, Peter Grad, Christopher Guest, Daphne Guinness, Maisie Haft, Rebecca Haft, James Hathaway, Jeffrey Paul Hays, Victoria Hersh, Miki Higasa, Jane Hitchcock, Hannah Howe, Seth Jaffe, Robert Jaffee, Joan Jakobson, Freeborn Garretson Jewett III, Marilyn Johnson, Becky Katz, Anne Keating, Caitlin Kelley, Elizabeth Kent, Lauren Kidd, Emily Kim, Michele Knobel, Edmund Komen, Anni Kuan, Bernice Kwok-Gabel, Trey Laird, David Lauren, Lisa Lavora, Kevin Lee, Adam Leven, Lance Lin, Mahmood Mamdani, Dr. Alan Matarasso, Ted Max, Cali Maxwell, Michael McCarty, J. D. McClatchy, Molly McFall, Elissa McLean, Steve Millington, Jacquie Monda, Catherine Connor Monteiro de Barros, David Mortimer, Gigi Mortimer, Lily Mortimer, Ian Murray, Margaret Murray, Shep Murray, Erica Nelson, John Octave, Cornell Owesney Jr., Ameena Paltoo, Anna Pitts, Betsy Pitts, Plaza Florist, Jenny Pouech, Christophe Préau, Sam Prouty, Carolyn "Kiki" Przybylo, Kevin Ramsey, Sugar Rautbord, David Rawle, Katharine and Billy Rayner, Alan Rich, William Rondino, Carley Roney, Michael Root, Jordan Rosenlicht, Lillian Ross, Nikki Rothberg, Katy Russo, Marina Rust, Emily Satloff, Rikki Saunders, Dana Schiller, Peggy Schleiff, Nancy Schulman, Tiffin Schwarzkopf, Emma Sheanshang, George Sheanshang, Christopher Sheppard, Ivy Baer Sherman, Loreal Sherman, Tommy Shomo, Elena Siebert, Nate Simmons, Cynthia Smith, Suzanne Smith, Valerie Smith, Gregg Solomon, Gerardo Somozo, Sasha Soyfer, Jet Spear, Justin Spring, Diane Tucker Stein, Caroline Stetson, Leslie Stevens, Nancy McTague Stock, Robert Stock, Steven Stolman, Maggie Suniewick, Kendall Swenson, Rachel Talbot, Carminda Tamayo, Martin Tandler, Ann Tisch, Andy Tobias, Gary Totten, Alexander Traub, James Traub, Virginia Tupker, Andrew Underberg, Spencer Vahtra, Emerson Van Cleve, Emory Van Cleve, Jackson Van Cleve, Kathleen De Marco Van Cleve, Ella Vickers, Marissa Vitagliano, Kelly Vitko, Darren Walker, Jesse Wann, Cathy Waterman, Arthur Wayne, Julia Wetherell, Marsha Williams, Willie, Lindsey Worster, Martin Zahtra.

Our appreciation to our contributing writers, who added much-needed points of view to this book: Christopher Buckley, Josiah Bunting III, William D. Cohan, James Collins, Charlie Dana, Peter Davis, Boco Haft, Joseph Kanon, Caroline Rennolds Milbank, Jesse Saunders, James Underberg, and Edmund White. Special thanks to Tina Barney, for her photographs.

Thank you to our ad hoc researchers: Lauren Switzer, Jordan Rosenlicht.

Thank you to what feels like all of Knopf and some of Pantheon and Vintage too: Sonny Mehta, Pat Johnson, Paul Bogaards, Nicholas Latimer, Anke Steinecke, Judith Jones, Andy Hughes, Lisa Montebello, Anne-Lise Spitzer, Victoria Pearson, Bonnie Thompson, Andy Goldwasser, Dr. Schneider, Kathyrn Zuckerman, Sara Eagle, Elizabeth Lewis, Mary Buckley, Carol Carson, Megan Wilson, Russell Perreault, Michiko Clark, Pamela Cortland, Sloane Crosley, Anne Diaz, Lily Evans, Caryn Burtt, Jennifer Jackson, Justine LeCates, Mary McClean, Jenny Pouech, Kapo Ng, and Sean Yule.

And to our agent, Gail Hochman, many xxxxxs and ooooos to you. Si Bunting, your ideas and counsel were essential to this volume's development. And to Jim Abernathy: We don't mean to embarrass you, but without you and your family this book would have been only a pamphlet.

A NOTE ON THE TYPE

The text of this book is set in Bulmer, a transitional serif typeface originally designed by William Martin (1757–1830) c. 1790 for the Shakespeare Press. The fonts were used for printing the Boydell Shakespeare folio edition. This is a contemporary digital revival supervised by Robin Nicholas at Monotype Imaging and based on a 1928 revival by Morris Fuller Benton of the American Type Founders.

William Martin also worked under John Baskerville, and his types show Baskerville's influence. They share a vertical stress and a moderate increase of stroke contrast, and more finely cut serifs. D. B. Updike described Martin's types as "delicate and spirited, thoroughly English."

The headlines are set in variations of Stymie, created in 1931 by Morris Fuller Benton for the American Type Founders. Stymie is a reworking of a slab serif type that was popular in Europe at that time. For the past one hundred fifty years, slab serif types (sometimes called Egyptian or Egyptienne-style faces) have been a popular choice for headline text in newspapers, magazines, and advertising.

COMPOSED BY NORTH MARKET STREET GRAPHICS

PRINTED AND BOUND BY BERRYVILLE GRAPHICS

BOOK DESIGN BY CHIP KIDD

CREDITS.

Binding: **Stubbs & Wootton**

Chapter 1

2   *Left*: **model's own Sophie dress and Tory Burch shoes.** *Right*: **model's own Anavini dress and Little Eric shoes.**

7   **Bag, Stubbs & Wootton. Bookbook by TwelveSouth. Jacket, J.Crew. Orvis Field watch. Dior shoes—Bloomingdale's.**

Chapter 2

46   **Luggage, T. Anthony.**

Chapter 3

60   **Crest from Belgian Shoes.**

66   **Mrs. Radcliffe's clothes, Calvin Klein. Her own Ferragamo flats and Van Cleef & Arpels choker.**

67   **Mr. Kent's own Vineyard Vines tie and belt, and Nantucket Reds.**

71   **Callie's own Kenneth Cole peacoat, long-sleeve sweater, and messenger bag. JBrand jeans and Malo scarf. Parker wears his own Loro Piano jacket, custom shirt from Hamilton Shirts, corduroy jeans from J.Crew, and Gucci shoes.**

76   **Porter: skirt, Vineyard Vines; top, Lilly Pulitzer; sweater, Tory Burch; flats, her own London Soles. Muffy: headband, Tucker Blair; scarf, Lilly Pulitzer; top and skirt, Vineyard Vines. Dryden: dress, RL Sport. Anders: Vineyard Vines blazer, his own Black Dog T-shirt, Ralph Lauren Childrenswear khakis.**

77   **Larkin: dress by Milly, Chanel bag her own. Spencer: shirt and vest, Ralph Lauren Childrenswear.**

78–79   **Model's own J.Crew shirt.**

Chapter 4

80   **Vintage Azzedine Alaia dress, found in closet.**

81   **Parker's own Ray-Ban Aviator sunglasses.**

82   **Parker's own belt.**

83   **Jeremy's khakis are his own, as are his L.L.Bean Blucher moccasins. Elliot's own Brooks Brothers shirt.**

84   **Princess Caroline's gown by Jean Paul Gaultier.**

85   **Patagonia pullover courtesy of Polartec.**

86   **His jacket, shirt, khakis from J.Crew. Loafers from Cole-Haan. Briefcase vintage. His take-out coffee from Pain Quotidien. Her own Polo khaki jacket, Thomas Pink shirt, Theory cropped trousers, Tod's blue suede driving shoes, and vintage gold bracelet. E. Goyard bag courtesy of Barneys New York.**

87   **His own sunglasses, belt, and tennis racquet. Clayton's own Lacoste shirt. Shorts, belt, and desert boots from Crewcuts.**

94   **All jewelry from Verdura. Jewelry wardrobe from T. Anthony.**

95   **Her own Anni Kuan dress. Kate Spade cardigan from Bloomingdale's. Shoes and jewelry from J.Crew. Ring from a friend.**

96   **Virginia's dress, Polo from Bloomingdale's. Margot's coat, Kenneth Cole. Breton's own Vince skirt and T, and her own Prada shoes. Cardigan, Signature by L.L.Bean. Emily's sweater, Signature by L.L.Bean. Shoes by Sperry. Her own Polo button-down.**

97   **Ash's own Levi's jeans. Top and sweater—Signature, L.L.Bean. Shoes by Sperry.**

Trevor's sportcoat, Signature by L.L.Bean. His own Brooks Brothers shirt, tie, and trousers. Forrest's coat, his own Cordings of Piccadilly. Bag by the Monogram Shop of East Hampton.

98   Tory Burch tunic. Kenneth Jay Lane jewelry.

102   Model's own Brooks Brothers trench and briefcase. Burberry mini coat from Bloomingdale's and model's own Steven boots and Theory skirt. Coat by Calvin Klein and model's own Hunter rain shoes. L.L.Bean Signature trench coat. Burberry anorak from Bloomingdale's. Model's own Polo boots.

103   Model's own Cordings of Piccadilly raincoat, Giorgio Armani leather trench from Bloomingdale's, her own shoes from Pour la Victoire. Burberry trench dress from Bloomingdale's, model's own BCBG shoes. Burberry modern plaid coat from Bloomingdale's, Brooks Brothers trench coat worn with model's own L.L.Bean hunting boots.

104   Striped dress by Pink Tartan at Bloomingdale's. Ruffled sweater from Tory Burch. "Trim" shoulder bag from Hermès.

105   Bracelet, Jewelry for a Cause. Dog collar, Tucker Blair.

106   Belts from Vineyard Vines.

107   Belts from Kenneth Jay Lane. Vintage silver buckled belt from Tiffany. "Breakup belt" from Rosenlicht collection.

108   Model's own Sperry Top-Siders, Gucci loafers, Polo boots. Stubbs & Wootton embroidered shoes.

109   Model's own Bass, Tanino Crisci, and Prada loafers. Tommy Hilfiger, Ralph Lauren, J. M. Weston, and Brooks Brothers loafers, courtesy of manufacturers.

110   Manolo Blahnik, Celine, Cole-Haan, and Bass Weejun shoes belong to model. Ralph Lauren and Brooks Brothers courtesy of themselves. Burberry and Ferragamo loafers, courtesy Bloomingdale's.

111   Stubbs & Wootton, courtesy of manufacturer. Model's own Prada shoes. Model's own Superga sneakers and Jack Rogers sandals.

112   Anderson's own Barbour jacket, Henri Lloyd vest, Brooks Brothers shirt, CK Bradley belt, J. McLaughlin trousers, and Sperry Top-Siders.

113   Anderson's own Brooks Brothers coat, L.L.Bean sweater, Brooks Brothers shirt, J. McLaughlin trousers, Wellies by Hunter, and duffel by Re-Sails.

114   Tom Davis wears his own wardrobe from Brooks Brothers.

115   Thom Browne wears his own collection except for his shirt, which is Black Fleece at Brooks Brothers.

Chapter 5

119   Daddy's own Anderson & Sheppard (London) bespoke suit, Brooks Brothers made-to-measure shirt, Brooks Brothers tie.

120   Anderson's own blue Hart Schaffner Marx blazer, Loomis Chaffee School tie, Brooks Brothers shirt and corduroys. Briefcase, Cole Haan.

122   Mummy's own Tory Burch leather jacket, Gap pants, and Hermès bag. South Sea pearls from Assael.

124   Mummy's own Tom Ford sunglasses, Burberry jacket, Gap pants, Cartier watch, earrings, and sapphire ring. Necklace and bracelets courtesy of Cathy Waterman.

125   Mummy's own Malika cashmere twinset, Gap pants, headband from Zitomer, necklace, and earrings. Bracelets from Cathy Waterman.

127   Mummy's own Joie top, Nike yoga top, Gap pants, Assael pearls, and Hermès diamond watch.

PERMISSIONS ACKNOWLEDGMENTS.

Larry Page and Sergey Brin: © James Leynse/Corbis

Matthew and Gunnar Nelson: © Barry King/Sygma/Corbis

Gerald Patterson and Réné Lacoste: © Bettmann/Corbis

Lamb: © Digital Vision Photography/Veer

Sigourney Weaver: © Topham/The Image Works

Yo-Yo Ma: © Eric Richmond/ArenaPal/The Image Works

Michelle Obama: © Chris Fitzgerald/CandidatePhotos/The Image Works

Diana Brooks: © Bette Marshall

Broken racquet: Skip O'Donnell/istockphoto

Charlene Marshall: © Marc Hermann/New York *Daily News*

Charlene and Anthony Marshall: © Marc Hermann/New York *Daily News*

The Wrigley Mansion on Catalina Island: © David R. Frazier Photolibrary, Inc./Alamy

Wally Shawn in *The Princess Bride*: © Photos 12/Alamy

Watch Hill Lighthouse: © National Geographic Image Collection/Alamy

Button quail: © Universal Images Group Limited/Alamy

Oak Bluffs: © Michael Matthews/Alamy

Bunch of keys: © Andrew Paterson/Alamy

The Munsters: © Photos 12/Alamy

Beef Cuts Diagram 1855: Mary Evans Picture Library/Alamy

Brazil: © Pictorial Press Ltd/Alamy

Fantastic Mr. Fox: © Reuters/Fox Searchlight Pictures/Handout (U.S. Entertainment Society)

Mary Cassatt: The Granger Collection, New York

Betty Grable: The Granger Collection, New York

Louis Auchincloss: © Garth Vaughn/AP/Wide World

Princess Caroline in striped dress: Getty Images

Shepherd Paul Murray and Ian Charles Murray: John Madere

COOL THEN, COOL NOW.

Stock-tie blouses for women	Lean tops
Chris Burch's Eagle's Eye clothing	Tory Burch's logo
Shetland sweaters	Cashmere sweaters
Ruining leather shoes in the rain	Rubber rain boots
Bruno Magli slingbacks	Pumps and ballet flats
Colorful striped shirts with white collar and cuffs	White shirts with white collars and cuffs
Hermès scarves	Cotton, linen, and wool scarves
Dynasty and *Dallas*	*30 Rock* and *24* (reruns)
NPR	NPR
Happy Hour	Cocktails anytime
Retail banking training programs	Mysterious finance jobs
Electric typewriters	Laptops and iPads
Cassette tapes	Purloined tunes
Walkmans	iPods
Twelve monthly periods	Four monthly periods
Drinking Tab	Wearing Polarfleece made from Tab bottles
Sushi	Crudo
'80s music	'80s music
MTV	Bonnaroo
Broadcast	Broadband
Martha Stewart weddings	Gay and lesbian weddings
Jobs with benefits	Friends with benefits
Smoking sections	Nonsmoking sections
Concorde	G 6
Range Rovers	Hybrids